UNDERSTANDING

THE

QUR'AN

Ahmad H. Sakr, Ph.D.

Library of Congress Catalog Card Number: 00-134370
ISBN: 0-9676602-2-X

Understanding

The

Qur'an

Ahmad H. Sakr, Ph.D.

Published by:
Foundation for Islamic Knowledge
P.O. Box 665
Lombard, Illinois 60148 (USA)
Telephone: (630) 495-4817
FAX: (630) 627-8894
Tax I.D #36-352-8916

NOTE: Your generous contribution to this **Foundation** will enable us to publish more valuable literature and to render more services to all. The **Foundation** has a tax-exempt status with the IRS. Your donations are tax-deductible.

DEDICATION

This book is dedicated to Allah Ta'ala (Almighty) for all the favors He has bestowed upon me in creating and bringing me to this world. His Love, His Mercy, His Compassion, His Forgiveness, His Graciousness, His Kindness and His Bountifulness are above any humble person like me, to be able to thank Him enough and to praise Him.

O Allah !   I am humbly dedicating this work to You.

O Allah !   Accept my humble work and help me disseminate the information to those who need it.

O Allah !   Make this humble work worthy of You.

O Allah !   Forgive my shortcomings.

O Allah !   Help me   live as a Muslim and   die as a Mu'min (Believer).

O Allah !   Let me be summoned on the Day of Judgment with Prophet Muhammad (pbuh), with the other Prophets, the martyrs and the noble believers. Ameen.

iii

Understanding The Qur'an

TABLE OF CONTENTS

And it is He Who has power over all things. [Qur'an, 5:120]

ACKNOWLEDGEMENTS

The author wishes to thank all those friends who helped in making this book available to the readers. Special thanks go to Dr. Yusuf Kamaluddin (Yao-Keng) Chang and his wife, Audrey, for their tremendous help and moral support during the last few years.

Thanks and appreciation go to the Vakil families (Abu Bakr, Usman, Farouq, Ishaq, and Akhtar) for their support to the author and the Foundation. May Allah bless them and bless their late parents (Umar and Amina).

Moreover, the author wishes to thank all the respected brothers and sisters who have helped previously and are still helping. Among the many are Mr. Asad Khan and his wife, Sister Azma Khan; Dr. and Mrs. Mohammed Shafi; Mr. & Mrs. Javed Habib; Mr. & Mrs. Abdul Wahab; Mr. & Mrs. Saghir Aslam; Dr. & Mrs. Nadim Daouk; Mr. Refat M. Abo Elela; Dr. & Mrs. Zeyd A. Merenkov; Dr. and Mrs. Daudur Rahman; Mr. and Mrs. Shakeel Syed; Dr. and Mrs. Maqbool Ahmad; Mr. Zia Khan and his wife Tina Khan; Dr. and Mrs. Syed A. Zahir; Dr. and Mrs. Muhammad K. Zaman; Dr. and Mrs. Mostapha Arafa; Dr. & Mrs. Samir Arafeh; Dr. M. Munir Chaudry and family; Late Dr. F.R. Khan and his respected wife Sister Farhat Khan, may Allah (swt) bless his soul, and many more.

Special thanks and appreciations go to Sister Fawzia Akalal; Sister Sajeda Sultani and her family members; Sister Houyda Najjar Mertaban and her family members; Brother Mohammed Bilal Khan; and Brother Waseem Najmi and his wife Yasmeen; for their kind help in many areas. Also our thanks and appreciations are extended to sister Azizah Abdul Rahman of Singapore, on behalf of her late parents Aminah Bint Ahmad and Abdul Rahman bin Mohamed. May Allah (swt) be pleased with her and her late parents. Ameen.

vi

Special thanks and appreciation to Sister Shadia Hassan and her children for their help, advice, and contributions for the love of Allah. Our prayers of Maghfirah for her husband Mr. Samir Hassan. May Allah (swt) bless his soul and make his final stay in Paradise. Ameen.

Thanks and appreciations go to Mr. Khaled Obagi for his support to the Foundation on behalf of his late father and mother Aref Obagi and Nabila Al-Beik. Our thanks and appreciations also go to Mr. Ahmad Al-Khatib for his support to the Foundation on behalf of his mother Soraya, and his late father Adel Baheej Al-Khatib. Thanks and appreciations also go to Dr. Osama Haikal on behalf of his late father, Mr. Omar Haikal. May Allah be pleased with them and may Allah keep their relatives in Paradise. Ameen.

Our thanks and affections are to Brother Fathy Haggag and his family for their tremendous support to the author for all the years in California. It is only Allah (swt) Who will reward them

Last but not least, my thanks, appreciation and love are to my wife, Zuhar Barhumi Sakr and our loving children, Sara, Hussein, and his wife Dania, Jihad and Basil as well as to my grandchildren Nada, Abdur Rahman, Ibrahim and Jenna from our daughter Sara, and their father Muhammad Nasser.

We pray to Allah (swt) to open the hearts of other friends to invest with Allah in a Sadaqah Jariyah (endowment fund) on behalf of their loving parents before it is too late. Ameen

SPECIAL PRAYERS

The author prays to Allah (swt[1]) to bless Prophet Muhammad and the family of Prophet Muhammad, (pbuh[2]) in as much as He blessed Prophet Ibrahim and the family of Prophet Ibrahim. The author also prays to Allah (swt) to bless the Khulafaa' Rashidoon (Rightly guided) and the Sahaba (Companions) of the Prophet as well as the Tabi`oon (Followers) and the Followers of the Followers till the Day of Judgment.

The author prays to Allah (swt) to reward all the `Ulama', who carried the Message of Allah and His Prophet, and who transmitted it to the new generations.

The author prays to Allah (swt) to reward his parents: his late father Al-Hajj Hussain Mustafa Sakr and his late mother Al-Hajjah Sara Ramadan Sakr for their sacrifices to their twelve children in general and to this author in specific. The author prays to Allah (swt) to reward the late brother of the author, Mr. Muhammad H. Sakr, for helping the author to get his academic education, and his late brothers Mahmood H. Sakr, and Mustafa H. Sakr for taking care of the author's responsibilities overseas.

Special prayers go to the Shaikh of the author who taught him Islam, and trained him from childhood to practice its teaching: Shaikh Muhammad `Umar Da`ooq. May Allah be pleased with him.

Special Du`a' goes to Al-Shaheed Shaikh Hassan Khalid, the late Grand Mufti of Lebanon, who had also great impact on the author's knowledge of Islam. May Allah bless his soul and make him stay in Paradise.

1[1] swt: Subhanahu Wa Ta'ala (Glory be to Allah, and He is The High).

[2] pbuh: Peace Be Upon Him (The Prophet).

Special prayers and Du`a' go to the many teachers, scholars and `Ulamaa' who were directly tutoring this author at the time of his youth. Through the efforts of Shaikh Muhammad `Umar Da'ooq, the following is a partial list of the teachers who taught this author: Dr. Mustafa Siba`ee; Shaikh Muhammad M. Al-Sawwaf; Dr. Muhammad Al-Zo`by; Shaikh Muhammad `Itani; Shaikh Muhammad M. Da`ooq; Shaikh Al-Fudail Al-Wartalani; Shaikh Muhammad `Abdel Kareem Al-Khattabi; Shaikh Malik Bennabi; Shaikh Faheem Abu`Ubeyh; Shaikh Muhammad Al-Shaal; Dr. Sa`eed Ramadan; Atty. `Abdel Hakeem `Abideen; Dr. Tawfic Houri; Shaikh Abu Salih Itani; Shaikh Hashim Daftardar Al-Madani; and the late Shaikh Abdul Badee` Sakr. May Allah bless them and reward them.

A final prayer is to the reader who took the time to read this book. May Allah (swt) bless them all.

Allahumma Ameen.

That this is indeed a Qur'an most honorable,
In a Book well-guarded...
[Qur'an, 56:77-78]

SUPPLICATIONS

DU`A'

O Allah ! I seek refuge in You from anxiety and grief; I seek refuge in You from incapacity and laziness; and I seek refuge in You from the overcoming burden of debts and the overpowering of people.

O Allah ! I seek refuge in You from poverty except to You, from humiliation except for You, and from fear except from You.

O Allah ! I seek refuge in You from stating a false testimony, or committing immorality, or provoking You; and I seek refuge in You from the malice of the enemies, and from enigmatic disease, and from the despair of hope.

O Allah ! I seek refuge in You from the wicked people, from the worries of the livelihood, and from the ill-nature such as from bad attitude.

O Allah ! You are the Mercy of the mercies, and You are the Lord of the universe.

O Allah
Allahumma Ameen

اللّهُمَّ

اللَّهُمَّ إِنِّي أَعُوذُ بِكَ مِنَ الْهَمِّ وَالْحَزَنِ

وَأَعُوذُ بِكَ مِنَ الْعَجْزِ وَالْكَسَلِ

وَأَعُوذُ بِكَ مِنْ غَلَبَةِ الدَّيْنِ وَقَهْرِ الرِّجَالِ

اللَّهُمَّ إِنِّي أَعُوذُ بِكَ مِنَ الْفَقْرِ إِلَّا إِلَيْكَ

وَمِنَ الذُّلِّ إِلَّا لَكَ وَمِنَ الْخَوْفِ إِلَّا مِنْكَ

وَأَعُوذُ بِكَ أَنْ أَقُولَ زُورًا أَوْ أَغْشَى فُجُورًا

أَوْ أَكُونَ بِكَ مَغْرُورًا وَأَعُوذُ بِكَ

مِنْ شَمَاتَةِ الْأَعْدَاءِ وَعُضَالِ الدَّاءِ

وَخَيْبَةِ الرَّجَاءِ اللَّهُمَّ إِنِّي أَعُوذُ بِكَ

مِنْ شَرِّ الْخَلْقِ وَهَمِّ الرِّزْقِ وَسُوءِ الْخُلُقِ

يَا أَرْحَمَ الرَّاحِمِينَ وَيَا رَبَّ الْعَالَمِينَ

xi

PREFACE

The Qur'an is the only Book Revealed and preserved by Allah (swt). In Surah Al-Hijr (The Rocky Tract), Allah (swt) says the following:

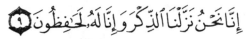

We have , without doubt, sent down the Message; and We will assuredly guard it (from corruption). (15:9)

The Qur'an is also the only Book that has been protected by Allah from corruption, distortion or any change. Allah (swt) says in Surah Al-Waaqi`ah (The Inevitable Event) the following:

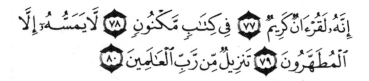

That is indeed a Qur'an most honorable, in a Book well-guarded, which none shall touch but those who are clean: A revelation from the Lord of the Worlds. (56: 77-80)

There is not a single book in the history of mankind that has been memorized by millions of people with love and fervency as much as the Qur'an. Thousands of books have been written about the Qur'an. Thousands of people tried to explain the Qur'an. Hundreds of scholars, Muslims and non-Muslims translated the Qur'an to different languages. None of those translations is perfect, because the translator is a human being, while the author of the Qur'an is Allah (swt) Himself.

The author of this book has felt the impact of the Qur'an on him since childhood. He felt that he should shed light about Qur'an to the English reader. Out of love and respect to Allah (swt), the author tried his best to include certain topics that may allow the reader to read the Qur'an with understanding. Allah (swt) made the Qur'an to be read and to be understood. Accordingly, He made it easy for those who want to read it with honesty and sincerity. Allah (swt) says in Surah Al-Qamar (The Moon) the following:

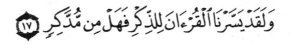

And We have indeed made the Qur'an easy to understand and remember: Then is there any that will receive admonition? (54:17)

Each topic is a book by itself or a series of books to cover the topic. Time and space do not allow anyone to include those items in a small book of this nature. It is recommended to read any book about the Qur'an with the presence of a teacher specialized in the topic being read.

The author recommends that people should seek the help of a group of Muslim Scholars who are specialized in the field of the Qur'an to help them understand some aspects of the Qur'an.

Since the Qur'an contains or comprises many topics that can be discussed the author selected very few of them. Some of the major topics included in this book are the following:

- ❖ Preface
- ❖ General Information
- ❖ Requirements for understanding the Qur'an
- ❖ About the Qur'an from the Qur'an
- ❖ About the Qur'an from Prophet Muhammad
- ❖ Blessings of the Qur'an
- ❖ Benefits of the Qur'an
- ❖ Miracles of the Qur'an
- ❖ Healing Aspects of the Qur'an
- ❖ Subjects of the Qur'an
- ❖ Specific subjects in Qur'an
- ❖ Names of the Qur'an
- ❖ Memorizers of the Qur'an
- ❖ Makkah & Madinah Surahs
- ❖ Luminous Letters of Qur'an
- ❖ Prostration in the Qur'an

- ❖ List of Sadjahs in the Qur'an
- ❖ Reciting the Qur'an
- ❖ Rules of Reciting the Qur'an
- ❖ Reading from the Qur'an
- ❖ Qur'anic Tafseer (Interpretation of the meaning of the Qur'an)
- ❖ Classification of Qur'anic Chapters
- ❖ The Sun and the Moon Letters
- ❖ Prepositions
- ❖ Signs of Stops and Punctuations
- ❖ Translations of Qur'an
- ❖ Reading the Entire Qur'an
- ❖ Inquiries about Qur'an
- ❖ Questions in the Qur'an
- ❖ Worksheet
- ❖ Proposal
- ❖ Quizzes

I. INTRODUCTION

The author has taught a course on Islamic Sharia'h in many places in the world. A textbook on the same subject was published already. One chapter in that textbook is about the Qur'an. The author has also written a series of articles as well as Friday Khutab on the topic of the Qur'an. The following work, "Understanding the Qur'an", is a compilation of all previous works related to the Qur'an but scattered in other volumes. "However, publishing a contemporary book about this topic was necessary."

There is a sizeable group of individuals who believe that they can understand the Qur'an by themselves without the Hadith, the Sunnah, the Sirah, and the understanding of Companions of the Prophet who were his students. This group of people is comprised of both Arabs and non-Arabs. None of them is the student of the Prophet, or a companion of the Prophet. Some people think that they can understand the Qur'an without teachers and without going back to the Prophet himself. Then any person can have some textbook about medicine at home, and can claim himself to be a qulaified medical practitioner. He would have the right to practice medicine! Or someone may read books about architecture. Then claim he can design a building similar to Sears Tower. Or someone would pass a written driving test thinking that he is an expert driver. Assuming that knowledge can be solely acquired through books, then there is no need for schools, colleges and universities. Moreover, there will be no need for teachers, professors, and scholars. In addition, there will be no need for quizzes, tests, exams, and finals. Each person can claim that he knows enough about any subject in every department. He is (so-called) a super hero!!!

Therefore, any person who claims that he does not need the books of Hadith, Sunnah, Sirah, and Tafseer, should reevaluate his understanding because he is gravely off the right track. He should recognize that the only one who understands the Qur'an comprehensively, is the one who received it, namely Prophet Muhammad. Therefore, one has to go to the Hadith, the Sunnah and the Sirah of the Prophet and find out how he explained the Qur'an to his companions. The Prophet received the Qur'an for a period of 23 years. He memorized it, explained it, taught it, lived it, and made sure that his (Sahabah) companions have understood it after memorizing it.

Moreover, whoever thinks that he can understand the Qur'an directly without going back to the Books of Tafseer, is a person elevating his understanding to the knowledge of prophethood. This means that Prophet Muhammad is no more a Prophet. He was a mailman who received the Book without knowing what was in it. An angel came in the dream to Mr. X and delivered that Book to him. The latter should therefore claim himself to be the True Prophet and the True Messenger!! Ma-sha –Allah!

One should remember that Allah (swt) has challenged the early Arab Poets who were experts in Arabic literature to bring a book similar to the Qur'an! They, of course, failed. Then He challenged them to bring ten chapters or even one chapter similar to the Qur'an. Of course, they failed. Finally He challenged them to explain the meaning of the alphabets such as Alif, Lam, Meem. In the Qur'an there are (29) chapters that start with Luminous letters. Some of these letters are a single letter such as Saad, Qaaf and Noon. There are two letters combined together such as Taa-Haa; Yaa Seen; Taa Seen; and Haa Meem. It could be that they are composed of three letters such as Alif Laam Meem; Alif Laam Raa; and Taa Seen Meem. It could be that those letters are composed of four letters such as Alif Laam Meem Saad; and Alif Laam Meem Raa. Finally the luminous letters could be composed of five single but combined letters such as Kaaf, Haa, Yaa, 'Ain, Saad, or Haa Meem 'Ain Seen and Qaaf.

The early Arabs who mastered the Arabic language wrote it more eloquently than contemporary writers and they were surprised and shocked.They could not imagine such letters to mean anything! Those early Arabs, and mainly the poets used to memorize few hundred pages of prose and poems by heart, immediately after they heard them from someone else. Most of them after listening to the Qur'an from the Prophet were modest enough to accept Islam and followed the Prophet. They became his students and his companions. Some of them left their jobs, and associated themselves with the Prophet on a daily basis in order to understand the Qur'an. They were the ones who carried the Message of the Qur'an from the Prophet himself and delivered it in different parts of the world.

Therefore, no one can claim that he understands the Qur'an by himself; otherwise his teacher is Shaitan, the devil, the 'Ifreet, and the demon!! A'oozu Billahi Minash Shaitanir Rajeem.

II. GENERAL INFORMATION

The Sacred Book of Islam is called the Qur'an. It was revealed to Prophet Muhammad (pbuh) through Angel Gabriel (Jibreel) over a period of 23 years. There is only one Qur'an in the whole world, and it is in the Arabic language. The Qur'an has one text, and one language. It has been memorized by millions of Muslims in different parts of the world. The Qur'an is composed of 114 Surah (chapters). It is to be read and recited with rules and regulations. When it is to be touched and/or recited, a Muslim is to be in a state of cleanliness and purity of body, mind and heart.

The authenticity and totality of the Qur'an have been documented and recognized. The Qur'an cannot be translated at all, as the Qur'an is the exact words of Allah (swt). Any translation is considered to be the explanation to the meaning of the Qur'an. No one can give the exact meaning of the Qur'an. Moreover, through the process of translation, the Qur'an loses it spiritual beauty of rhyme, rhythm, and melodic recitation. No person can give its exact meaning or its beauty of Tarteel and Tajweed. No language has enough words or sentences to reflect the exact meaning of the Qur'an.

As far as learning or reading the Qur'an through the process of transliteration is concerned, one has to state here, that it is not easy at all. One will distort the pronunciation of the Arabic words. Examples of that would be:

1. There is no letter for seen or saad (س), (ص)
2. There is no letter for te or taa (ت), (ط)
3. There is no letter for Ha or Haa (ح), (هـ)
4. There is no letter for Alif or 'Ain (ا), (ع)
5. There is no letter for Tha, Tha (Za) (ث), (ظ)
6. There is no letter for Daal, Daad (د), (ض)

Therefore, one has to read the Qur'an in its original language, namely the Arabic language. One has to learn how to pronounce each letter, then he has to learn the rules and regulations of recitation with Tarteel or Tajweed. The Qur'an is so rich and comprehensive in matter. It can easily guide men and women in all walks of their lives. It is the ultimate source of guidance for people in all aspects of their spiritual and material lives.

The names and attributes that are given to the Qur'an in the Qur'an speak for themselves. The Qur'an is described to be: the Recited, the Distinction between good and evil, the Reminder, the Admonition, the Judgement, the Wisdom, the Guidance, the Revelation, the Mercy, the Spirit, the Goodness, the Explainer, Allah's (swt) Favor, the Maintainer, the Guardian, the Light, the Truth, and the Covenant of Allah (swt). The Qur'an is also described to be Bounteous, Glorious, Mighty, Honored, Exalted, Purified, Wonderful, Blessed and Confirming the Truth of Previous Revelations.

The Qur'an has practically proven the truth and effectiveness of all of its names and epithets in the lives of all believers those who practice its teachings sincerely and devoutly. The Qur'an has a universal appeal, regardless of people's color, creed, nationality, and the geographical divisions of the world. The goal of life, as addressed in the Qur'an is to live according to what Allah (swt) created us for, which is to worship Him, and to obey His commandments in this life. These Teachings are, of course, in the interest of people in order to go to Heaven. The winners are going to Heaven and the real losers are going to Hell.

Those who are entirely pre-occupied with their material gains and luxuries, without cultivating their spiritual and moral qualities, are declared by Allah (swt) to be like animals or even worse than animals. The ones who do not believe in Allah (swt) or follow His Commandments are also described in many places of the Qur'an to be dead, deaf, mute and blind. The real living, hearing, speaking, and seeing is caused by the true belief in the heart. So our need for learning, studying, and following the Qur'an should come before our need for breathing, drinking, and eating to survive, because life without such guidance is a miserable life that leads to eternal punishment.

And He (Allah) has power over all things.
(Qur'an, 11:4)

6

III. REQUIREMENTS FOR UNDERSTANDING THE QUR'AN

A. To the Student

There are many factors that are essential for the study and the understanding of the Qur'an. Some of these factors are related to the person who is trying to study the Qur'an and to understand its meaning. The following is a partial list of these requirements:

1. Honesty in finding the Truth without cheating or lying.
2. Sincerity with genuine efforts to find the Truth about the Qur'an.
3. Diligence in seeking the Truth from Allah to His final Prophet and Messenger Muhammad.
4. Humbleness while seeking knowledge.
5. One has to be a student, not a teacher.
6. One has to listen rather than talk.
7. One should refrain from writing unless he is sure, that he is doing it for the love of Allah. He should never look for fame, reputation, or position.
8. One should refrain from printing or publishing anything related to the Qur'an unless some other scholars verify his own writing.
9. Most important of all, no one can understand the Qur'an as much as the Prophet himself.
10. No one can also understand the Qur'an as much as the early companions of the Prophet.
11. One has to understand the language of the Qur'an namely Arabic: rules, regulations, grammar, prose, poetry, rhyme, rhythm, lyric, etc.
12. One has to study: Makhaarij of the letters in Arabic, as well as the rules and regulations of Tarteel and Tajweed.

13. One has to learn the themes of the Qur'an as well as the topics of the Qur'an.
14. One has to study the occasion of every Ayah: when, where, why, and how it was revealed.
15. No one can claim himself to be a super-hero who understands the Qur'an by himself. Such a person then should have Ph.D. in every subject of life such as chemistry, physics, medicine, mathematics, engineering, computer, aerospace, embryology, botany, zoology, history, social sciences, arts, geography, navigation, anatomy, histology, pathology, genetic, accounting, business administration, linguistic, education, etc, and etc. Even if he has all these degrees, he will never ever be able to understand the whole Qur'an, unless he is the True Prophet who received the Qur'an from Allah.

B. To the Teachers

The following is a partial list of recommendations for the scholars who want to teach the Qur'an:

1. They themselves should be educated in the field of the Qur'an and its subjects.
2. The teachers should be among those who read the Qur'an daily with rules and regulations.
3. They should be among those who listen daily to the Recitation of the Qur'an by those famous Recitors of the Qur'an.
4. They should be among those who read about the Qur'an from other scholars, so that when they are teaching the subjects of the Qur'an, they will have comprehensive information.

5. While teaching the Qur'an, they should be in a state of Tahara, and wudoo' at the same time.
6. They should quote the Prophet's sayings and his companions about the meaning of each Ayah and each Surah.
7. They should refrain from pointing out their own opinions to their students.
8. They should refrain from presenting the exceptions: Rather they are to bring the unanimity of scholars of the Ummah of Islam.
9. The teachers have to recognize that they are responsible for any mistake they make intentionally.
10. If they donot know the answer to any question, they should be humble to say: We do not know, We will find out.
11. They should inspire and motivate their students to study the Qur'an, to memorize it, to practice its teachings, and to deliver it to others.
12. They should be a role model to their students. They should never ask their students to do anything that they themselves cannot do.
13. They should be patient with their students; they should take it easy with them: step-by-step toward achieving the goal.

C. Final Remark

The teachers and the students have to work together on a daily basis. The student wills learn from the teachers how to read, recite and understand the Qur'an. The teachers will be able to renew and refresh their memories and their understanding of the Qur'an. Both will learn from one another. We pray for all. Ameen.

IV. ABOUT THE QUR'AN FROM THE QUR'AN

A. General

It is a fact that the Qur'an is a Divinely Revealed Book from Allah (swt) to Prophet Muhammad (pbuh) for all mankind. It was revealed in the Arabic language for a period of twenty-three years in Makkah and Madinah of the Arabian Peninsula. There are some aspects to discuss about the Qur'an, and the most interesting ones are those which have been revealed about the Qur'an itself. It is sometimes strange to find a person discussing and talking about himself, but it is stranger to find a book speaking about itself. This is further a proof that the Qur'an is The Revealed Book. There are a few hundred ayat in the Qur'an about the Qur'an. The following is a short summary:

B. Specifics

1. The Revelation and its Source

a) The Qur'an is a Revealed Book and the revelations are from Allah. In this respect it is mentioned in the Qur'an in Surah Al-An'am (The Cattle) the following:

قُلْ أَىُّ شَىْءٍ أَكْبَرُ شَهَدَةً قُلِ ٱللَّهُ شَهِيدٌ بَيْنِي وَبَيْنَكُمْ وَأُوحِىَ إِلَىَّ هَٰذَا ٱلْقُرْءَانُ لِأُنذِرَكُم بِهِۦ وَمَنۢ بَلَغَ

...this Qur'an has been revealed to me by inspiration, that I may warn you and all whom it reaches. (6:19)

b) Secondly, the Qur'an also states in Surah Ash-Shura (Consultation) that it was revealed from Allah to Prophet Muhammad:

10

وَكَذَٰلِكَ أَوْحَيْنَا إِلَيْكَ قُرْءَانًا عَرَبِيًّا لِّتُنذِرَ أُمَّ ٱلْقُرَىٰ وَمَنْ
حَوْلَهَا وَتُنذِرَ يَوْمَ ٱلْجَمْعِ لَا رَيْبَ فِيهِ

Thus have We sent by inspiration to you an Arabic Qur'an: that you may warn the Mother of Cities and all around her, and warn (them) of the Day of Assembly of which there is no doubt. (42:7)

c) Thirdly, the Qur'an states in Surah An-Naml (The Ants) that Prophet Muhammad has been given the Qur'an from Allah:

وَإِنَّكَ لَتُلَقَّى ٱلْقُرْءَانَ مِن لَّدُنْ حَكِيمٍ عَلِيمٍ

As to you, the Qur'an is bestowed upon you from the presence of One Who is Wise and All-Knowing. (27:6)

2. **Revelation's Time**

The Revelation of the Qur'an began in the month of Ramadan. One may read in Surah Al-Baqarah (The Cow) the following:

شَهْرُ رَمَضَانَ ٱلَّذِىٓ أُنزِلَ فِيهِ ٱلْقُرْءَانُ هُدًى لِّلنَّاسِ
وَبَيِّنَٰتٍ مِّنَ ٱلْهُدَىٰ وَٱلْفُرْقَانِ

Ramadan is the (month) in which was sent down the Qur'an, as a guide to mankind, also clear (signs) for guidance, and judgement (between right and wrong). (2:185)

11

Moreover, the Qur'an was revealed in Lailatul Qadr (The Night of Power), the last ten days of the month of Ramadan. In Surah Al-Qadr Allah says the following:

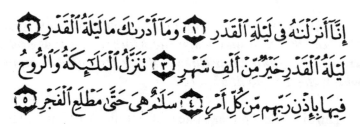

We have indeed revealed this (Message) in the Night of Power. And what will explain to you what the Night of Power is? The Night of Power is better than a thousand months. Therein come down the Angels and the Spirit by Allah's permission, on every errand: Peace! This until the rise of the Morn! (97:1-5)

3. The Book of Truth

a) The Qur'an is the Book of Truth, because it was revealed by Allah. The Qur'an says in Surah Fatir (The Originator of Creation) the following:

وَٱلَّذِىٓ أَوْحَيْنَآ إِلَيْكَ مِنَ ٱلْكِتَٰبِ هُوَ ٱلْحَقُّ مُصَدِّقًا لِّمَا بَيْنَ يَدَيْهِ إِنَّ ٱللَّهَ بِعِبَادِهِۦ لَخَبِيرُۢ بَصِيرٌ ﴿٣١﴾

That which We have reveal to you of the Book is the truth-confirming what was revealed before it: for God is assuredly with respect to His servants Well-Acquainted and Fully-Observant. (35:31)

12

b) The Qur'an also speaks about this point in Surah Younus the following:

وَمَاكَانَ هَذَا ٱلْقُرْءَانُ أَن يُفْتَرَىٰ مِن دُونِ ٱللَّهِ وَلَكِن تَصْدِيقَ ٱلَّذِى بَيْنَ يَدَيْهِ وَتَفْصِيلَ ٱلْكِتَبِ لَارَيْبَ فِيهِ مِن رَّبِّ ٱلْعَلَمِينَ ٣٧

This Qur'an is not such as can be produced by other than God; on the contrary, it is a confirmation of revelations that went before it, and a fuller explanation of the Book-wherein there is no doubt-from the Lord of the Worlds. (10:37)

4. <u>Sources other than Allah</u>

If the Qur'an were to be from any source other than Allah, many mistakes would have been found. The Qur'an states in Surah An-Nisaa' (The Women) the following:

أَفَلَا يَتَدَبَّرُونَ ٱلْقُرْءَانَ وَلَوْكَانَ مِنْ عِندِ غَيْرِ ٱللَّهِ لَوَجَدُواْ فِيهِ ٱخْتِلَفًا كَثِيرًا ٨٢

Do they not consider the Qur'an (with care)? Had it been from other than God, they would surely have been found therein much discrepancy. (4:82)

5. <u>Qur'anic Language</u>

a) The Book (Qur'an) was revealed in the Arabic language. The Qur'an states in Surah Yusuf the following:

A.L.R.   These are the Symbols or Verses of the Perspicuous Book.   We have sent it down as an Arabic Qur'an, in order that you may learn wisdom. (12:1-2)

b) The Qur'an also states in Surah Az-Zukhruf (Gold Adornments) the following:

Haa. Meem, By the Book that makes things clear, We have made it a Qur'an in Arabic, that you may be able to understand (and learn wisdom). (43:1-3)

6. <u>Other Languages</u>

If the Qur'an were to be revealed in any language other than Arabic, confusion would have been brought into the minds of people. Qur'an says in Surah Fussilat (Explained in Depth) the following:

وَلَوْجَعَلْنَٰهُ قُرْءَانًا أَعْجَمِيًّا لَّقَالُواْ لَوْلَا فُصِّلَتْ ءَايَٰتُهُۥٓ ءَا۬عْجَمِىٌّ
وَعَرَبِىٌّ قُلْ هُوَ لِلَّذِينَ ءَامَنُواْ هُدًى وَشِفَآءٌ وَالَّذِينَ
لَا يُؤْمِنُونَ فِىٓ ءَاذَانِهِمْ وَقْرٌ وَهُوَ عَلَيْهِمْ عَمًى أُوْلَٰٓئِكَ
يُنَادَوْنَ مِن مَّكَانٍ بَعِيدٍ ﴿٤٤﴾

Had We sent this Qur'an in a language other than Arabic, they would have said: Why are not its verses explained in detail? What? A Book not in Arabic and a Messenger an Arab? Say: "It is a guide and a healing to those who believe….." (41:44)

7. Wisdom of Revelation

a) The Book was revealed as a glad-tiding, as a reminder, as a mercy, and as a guidance to mankind. In this respect one may read in Qur'an the following verses in Surah Ya- Seen:

وَمَا عَلَّمْنَٰهُ ٱلشِّعْرَ وَمَا يَنۢبَغِى لَهُۥٓ إِنْ هُوَ إِلَّا ذِكْرٌ وَقُرْءَانٌ مُّبِينٌ ۝ لِّيُنذِرَ مَن كَانَ حَيًّا وَيَحِقَّ ٱلْقَوْلُ عَلَى ٱلْكَٰفِرِينَ ۝

This is no less than a Message and a Qur'an making things clear, that it may give admonition to any who are alive, and that the charge may be proved against those who reject Truth. (36:69-70)

b) The Qur'an also says in Surah Al-Israa' (Night Travel) the following:

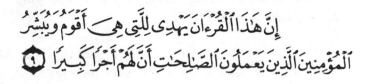

إِنَّ هَٰذَا ٱلْقُرْءَانَ يَهْدِى لِلَّتِى هِىَ أَقْوَمُ وَيُبَشِّرُ ٱلْمُؤْمِنِينَ ٱلَّذِينَ يَعْمَلُونَ ٱلصَّٰلِحَٰتِ أَنَّ لَهُمْ أَجْرًا كَبِيرًا ۝

Verily this Qur'an does guide to that which is most right or stable, and give the glad tidings to the Believers who work deeds of righteousness, that they shall have a magnificent reward. (17:9).

c) The Qur'an states also in Surah Al-Israa' that there is a healing and a mercy through the Qur'an:

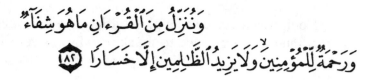

We send down stage by stage in the Qur'an that which is a healing and a mercy to those who believe: to the unjust it causes nothing but loss after loss. (17:82)

d) Allah (swt) again states in Surah An-Naml (The Ants) that there is in the Qur'an guidance and good news to the believers:

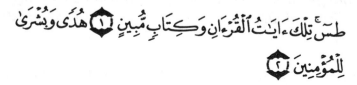

Taa. Seen. These are the verses of the Qur'an – a Book that makes things clear; a guide, and glad tidings for the believers. (27:1-2)

e) Finally, the Qur'an says in this regard in Surah Al-Baqarah, (The Cow) that Allah (swt) sent the Qur'an as a guide to mankind:

شَهْرُ رَمَضَانَ ٱلَّذِيٓ أُنزِلَ فِيهِ ٱلْقُرْءَانُ هُدًى لِّلنَّاسِ
وَبَيِّنَتٍ مِّنَ ٱلْهُدَىٰ وَٱلْفُرْقَانِ

Ramadan is the month in which was sent down the Qur'an, as a guide to mankind, also clear signs for guidance and judgment between right and wrong. (2:185)

8. Reading and Understanding

The Qur'an was revealed to be an easy book to be read and to be understood by all persons with all levels of understanding. This is one of the miracles of the Qur'an without any doubt. In this regard the Qur'an states in Surah Al-Qamar (The Moon) the following:

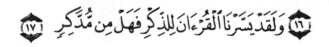

And We have indeed made the Qur'an easy to understand and remember: then is there any that will receive admonition? (54:17)

9. Preservation of Qur'an

a) The revealed Book is preserved by Allah, and no changes would occur at all in it. It is the Mercy of Allah to keep it preserved until the Day of Judgment. In this regard the Qur'an says in Surah Al-Hijr (The Rocky Tract), the following:

إِنَّا نَحْنُ نَزَّلْنَا ٱلذِّكْرَ وَإِنَّا لَهُۥ لَحَٰفِظُونَ ۝

We have, without doubt, sent down the Message;
and We will assuredly guard it from corruption (15:9)

b) The Qur'an also says similarly in Surah Al-Burooj (The
Zodiacal Signs) the following:

بَلْ هُوَ قُرْءَانٌ مَّجِيدٌ ۝ فِى لَوْحٍ مَّحْفُوظٍ ۝

Nay, this is a Glorious Qur'an inscribed in a Tablet
Preserved. (85:21-22)

c) Finally, the Qur'an says in Surah Al-Waqi'ah (The
Inevitable Event) the following:

إِنَّهُۥ لَقُرْءَانٌ كَرِيمٌ ۝ فِى كِتَٰبٍ مَّكْنُونٍ ۝ لَّا يَمَسُّهُۥٓ إِلَّا
ٱلْمُطَهَّرُونَ ۝ تَنزِيلٌ مِّن رَّبِّ ٱلْعَٰلَمِينَ ۝

That this is indeed a Qur'an most honorable, in a
Book well-guarded, which none shall touch but those
who are clean: A Revelation from the Lord of the
Worlds. (56:77-80)

10. **Challenges by the Qur'an**

The Qur'an challenged those who do not believe in it.

a) First, the Qur'an challenged the unbelievers, by asking them to make a similar book. Indeed, they were unable to do so. Allah says in Surah Al-Israa' (Night Travel) the following:

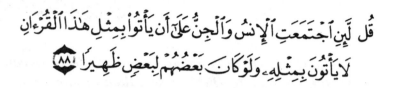

Say: If the whole of mankind and Jinns were to gather together to produce the like of this Qur'an, they could not produce the like thereof, even if they backed up each other with help and support. (17:88)

b) Secondly, the Qur'an asked them to make ten chapters like the Qur'an. In Surah Hud, the Qur'an states the following:

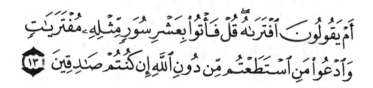

Or they may say, "He forged it". Say, "Bring you then ten suras forged, like unto it, and call (to your aid) whomsoever you can other than God! —if you speak the truth! (11:13)

c) Thirdly, the Qur'an challenged them to make even one
    chapter like the Qur'an. In Surah Al-Baqarah (The Cow)
    the Qur'an states:

وَإِن كُنتُمْ فِى رَيْبٍ مِّمَّا نَزَّلْنَا عَلَىٰ عَبْدِنَا
فَأْتُوا بِسُورَةٍ مِّن مِّثْلِهِ وَادْعُوا شُهَدَآءَكُم مِّن دُونِ ٱللَّهِ
إِن كُنتُمْ صَادِقِينَ ﴿٢٣﴾

*And if you are in doubt as to what We have revealed
from time to time to Our servant, then produce a Sura
like thereunto; and call your witnesses or helpers (if
there are any) besides God, if your doubts are
true. (2:23)*

d) Finally, the Qur'an challenged them to the extent that the
    non-believers will never be able to produce a single
    chapter. In Surah Al-Baqarah (The Cow), also the Qur'an
    states:

فَإِن لَّمْ تَفْعَلُوا وَلَن تَفْعَلُوا فَٱتَّقُوا
ٱلنَّارَ ٱلَّتِى وَقُودُهَا ٱلنَّاسُ وَٱلْحِجَارَةُ أُعِدَّتْ لِلْكَٰفِرِينَ ﴿٢٤﴾

*But if you cannot- and of a surety you cannot- then
fear the fire whose fuel is men and stones- which is
prepared for those who reject Faith. (2:24)*

20

11. Recitation of the Qur'an

a) When a believer wants to recite the Qur'an, he should seek refuge in Allah from the outcast Satan. The Qur'an states in Surah An-Nahl (The Bees) the following:

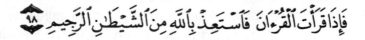

فَإِذَا قَرَأْتَ ٱلْقُرْءَانَ فَٱسْتَعِذْ بِٱللَّهِ مِنَ ٱلشَّيْطَٰنِ ٱلرَّجِيمِ ۝

When you read the Qur'an, seek God's protection from Satan, the rejected one. (16:98)

b) When the Qur'an is being recited, the believing Muslims should listen carefully and have reverence for the word of Allah. Qur'an states in Surah Al-A'raf (The Heights) the following:

وَإِذَا قُرِئَ ٱلْقُرْءَانُ فَٱسْتَمِعُوا۟ لَهُۥ وَأَنصِتُوا۟ لَعَلَّكُمْ تُرْحَمُونَ ۝

When the Qur'an is read, listen to it with attention, and hold your peace: that you may receive mercy. (7:204)

C. Final Remarks

In presenting this selection of verses from the Qur'an about the Qur'an, I hope the readers will have more incentive to read the Qur'an on a daily basis. In doing so, they will be blessed by Allah

21

for every word and for every letter they recite. It is irrelevant how many Surahs or how many Ayahs they read. The most important thing is to read it regularly and undersstand it so as to live the teachings of Allah. Moreover, one will experience the spiritual upliftment, and he will be kept under the guidance of Allah.

May Allah guide us all to the straight path. May Allah put in our hearts the love for the Qur'an as a source of guidance in our daily lives. May Allah help us act according to the teachings of the Qur'an, so as to be blessed in this world and in the Hereafter. Ameen.

V. ABOUT THE QUR'AN FROM PROPHET MUHAMMAD (pbuh)

A. General

The Qur'an was revealed in the Arabic language to Prophet Muhammad as mercy, a guide, a glad-tiding and a warning. The Prophet memorized it totally and lived it every minute of his life. He explained it to his companions and helped them live its teachings; and so they did. The Prophet spoke about the Qur'an, by advising his companions to learn it, to recite it, to memorize it, to live it, and to believe in it as a revealed book from the Ultimate Truth, namely Allah. He also advised them to deliver its message to all humanity at large. Al-Hamdu Lillah, they did their best.

In this chapter, some information about the sayings of Prophet Muhammad (pbuh) concerning the Qur'an will be brought to the attention of the readers so that they will be inspired and motivated in their daily lives. In so doing they will, Insha-Allah, be able to practice the teachings of Allah without difficulty.

B. Specifics

1. Reading And Recitation

Concerning the reading, recitation and chanting of the Qur'an, Prophet Muhammad (pbuh) said the following:

a. The Qur'an as a Savior

The Prophet encouraged the Muslims to read the Qur'an so that it will be a witness and a savior for them in the Day of Judgement. He said in this regard the following:

١٠٩٨ ــ عن أبي أُمَامَةَ رضي اللهُ عنهُ قالَ : سَمِعتُ رسولَ اللهِ صلَّى
اللهُ عليهِ وسلَّمَ يقولُ : « اقْرَؤُوا القُرْآنَ فَإِنَّهُ يَأتِي يَومَ القِيَامَةِ شَفِيعاً
لأصْحَابِهِ » رواه مسلم

Abu Umamah narrated that he heard the Messenger of Allah said:

Read the Qur'an so that it will be an intercessor for you on the Day of Judgment. [From Muslim]

b. **Reading is a Blessing**

The Prophet encouraged the Muslims to read the Qur'an so that they will be rewarded by Allah for every Surah, for every Ayah, for every word (Kalimah) and for every letter (Harf). The Prophet (pbuh) said:

١٠٠٩ـ وعن ابن مسعود رضي الله عنه قال : قالَ رسولُ اللهِ صلى الله عليه وسلم :
« مَنْ قَرَأ حَرْفاً مِنْ كِتَابِ اللهِ فَلَهُ حَسَنَةٌ ، والحَسَنَةُ بِعَشْرِ أَمْثَالِهَا لا أَقولُ :
الم حَرفٌ ، وَلـٰكِن : أَلِفٌ حَرْفٌ وَلامٌ حَرْفٌ وَمِيمٌ حَرْفٌ ، رواه الترمذي
وقال : حديث حسن صحيح .

Ibn Mas'ood narrated:

*Anyone who reads one letter from the Book of Allah will have a blessing and reward; and each good thing is equal to ten rewards; I don't say: Alif Lam Meem is a letter, but Alif is one letter; Lam is a letter and Meem is a letter.
[From 'Al-Tarmazi]*

24

c. **Chanting the Qur'an**

The Prophet encouraged Muslims to recite the Qur'an in a chanting and in a beautiful voice. He said:

Abu Lubabah 'Abdul al-Mundzir narrated that the Prophet said:

« لَيْسَ مِنَّا مَنْ لَمْ يَتَغَنَّ بِالقُرآن »

Anyone who does not recite the Qur'an with a chanting voice is not from us.

d. **Recitation with Difficulty**

The Prophet encouraged Muslims to read the Qur'an even if they find it difficult, as it is a blessing from Allah to read it. Those whose mother tongue is other than Arabic may find it difficult to recite the Qur'an. For them there is indeed a better reward. In this respect, the Prophet (pbuh) said:

١١٠١ ـ وعن عائشةَ رضيَ اللهُ عنهَا قالتْ : قالَ رسولُ اللهِ صلَّى اللهُ عليهِ وسلَّم : « الَّذي يَقرأُ القُرآنَ وَهُوَ ماهرٌ بهِ (٢) مع السَّفَرَةِ الكِرَامِ البَرَرَةِ ، وَالذي يَقرأُ القُرآنَ وَيَتَتَعْتَعُ فيهِ وَهُوَ عليهِ شَاقٌ له أجرَان » . متفقٌ عليه .

25

'Aisha Reported that Prophet Muhammad (pbuh) said:

Anyone who recites the Qur'an and is an expert in it will in the Hereafter be with the Ambassadors (Messengers) of Allah who are the noblest and the most honest; and anyone who recites the Qur'an with difficulty and hard pronunciation will have a double reward and blessing.   [Agreed upon]

2. Reading Or Not Reading

The Prophet categorized those who read the Qur'an versus those who abandon the Qur'an in similitudes and examples, some of which are the following:

a. A Reciting Believer

A believer who recites the Qur'an is like a citron having a sweet fragrance and good taste.

b. A Non-Reciting Believer

A believer who does not read the Qur'an is like a date fruit which has no fragrance but has a sweet taste.

c. A Hypocrite Reciter

A hypocrite who recites the Qur'an may impress the audience only, but not Allah. He is similar to a fruit which has a good smell but a bitter taste.

d. A Hypocrite Non-Reader

If a person is a hypocrite (or a non-believer,) who does not read the Qur'an, then he is like a colocynth. It does not have a good smell and it has a bitter taste.

26

All these four categories of people have been mentioned by Prophet Muhammad (pbuh) and have been summarized in one beautiful Hadith which is 'Agreed upon' as follows:

وعن أبى موسى الأشعري رضي الله عنه قال : قال رسول الله صلى الله عليه
وسلم : « مَثَلُ المؤمِنِ الذى يقرَأُ القرآنَ مَثَلُ الأُتْرُجَّةِ (٤) : ريحُها طَيبٌ وطعمُها
طيبٌ ، ومَثَلُ المؤمنِ الذى لا يقرأُ القرآنَ كمثلِ التمْرَةِ : لا ريحَ لها وطعمُها
حُلوٌ ،ومَثَلُ المُنافقِ الذى يقرأُ القرآنَ كمثلِ الرّيْحانةِ : ريحُها طيبٌ وطعمُها مُرٌّ ،
ومثلُ المُنافقِ الذى لا يقرأُ القرآنَ كمثلِ الحَنْظَلَةِ : ليسَ لها ريح وطعمُها مُرٌّ »
متفق عليه .

Reported by Abu Musa Al-Ash'ari that prophet Muhammad (pbuh) said:

The similitude of a believer who reads the Qur'an is like that of a citron (Atrijah) that smells good and tastes good; the similitude of a believer who does not read the Qur'an is like a date fruit which does not have a good smell but it tastes good; the similitude of an hypocrite who reads the Qur'an is like a basil (Rayhana) which does have a good smell but it does taste bitter; and the similitude of a hypocrite who does not read the Qur'an is like a colocynth (Hanzalah) which does not have good smell and it does taste bitter.

3. **Non- Memorizers**

As for those who have not memorized anything from the Qur'an, the Prophet (pbuh) said about them the following:

١١٠٥ – وعن ابنِ عباسٍ رضيَ اللهُ عَنهمَا قال : قالَ رسولُ اللهِ صلى
اللهُ عليهِ وسلَّم : « إنَّ الَّذي لَيسَ في جَوْفِهِ شَيْءٌ مِنَ القُرآنِ (١) كالبَيَتِ
الخَرِبِ » رواه الترمذي وقال : حديث حسن صحيح .

Ibn 'Abbas reported: that prophet Muhammad said:"

The one who has nothing from the Qur'an in his heart is like a deserted and demolished house. [Al-Tarmazi]

C. Final Remarks

It is recommended for Muslims to read the Qur'an daily so that it will be a savior for them and a savior in the Day of Judgment. We hope and pray that each one of us will try his/her best to be closer and closer to Allah by reading His words.

On should remember that the Qur'an is a unique message from Allah to each one of us. Allah wants each one of us to communicate with Him directly and often. Remember that the best language to communicate with Allah is His own favorite chosen language: the Qur'an. One should also remember that a Muslim lady in the early history of Islam never spoke anything for forty years in her daily life except quotations from the Qur'an. We hope and we pray that we, the contemporary Muslims of the 21st century, will realize our need for the daily reading of the Qur'an.

Since we don't have radio or T.V. stations owned and operated by Muslims in North America, we are deprived and denied the spiritual need for hearing the Qur'an. The best thing for us to do as Muslims who are living in a predominantly non-Muslim society, would be to obtain tapes or recordings to hear Allah's words in the houses, offices and cars. For those who want to benefit more, they

28

may have satellites or internet-connection in their houses. Then they will be able to see and listen at the same time all the good Islamic programs from the Muslim countries. Moreover, one may obtain Islamic softhware teaching the Qur'an.

Remember that we live in a complex society and everything is working like a machine. We might end up having mental break – downs. One of the best ways to obtain spiritual upliftment would be to read the Qur'an daily with a chanting voice.

May Allah bless us. May Allah guide us and may Allah bring us closer to Him. Ameen.

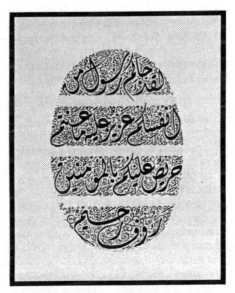

Now has come unto you a Messenger from amongst yourselves: it grieves him that you should suffer, ardently anxious is he over you: to the believers is he most kind and merciful. [Qur'an, 9:128]

VI. BLESSINGS OF THE QUR'AN

The topic of this chapter is about the Blessings of the Qur'an. These blessings are many to be counted, but here are two major categories of blessings:

A. Blessings of the Qur'an itself

However, I will do my best to enumerate some of them for the benefits of all.   In the next chapter, we will see some of the Benefits of the Qur'an.

1. The Qur'an is the Book of Blessings from Allah.   The Qur'an states in Surah Al-An'am (The Cattle) the following:

وَهَذَا كِتَبٌ أَنزَلْنَهُ مُبَارَكٌ مُّصَدِّقُ ٱلَّذِى بَيْنَ يَدَيْهِ

And this is a Book which We have sent down, bringing blessings, and confirming the revelations which came before it. (6:92)

2. The Qur'an is to get people out of darkness and lead them the way to enlightenment. Accordingly, the Qur'an states in Surah Ibrahim the following:

الٓر كِتَبٌ أَنزَلْنَهُ إِلَيْكَ لِتُخْرِجَ ٱلنَّاسَ مِنَ ٱلظُّلُمَتِ إِلَى ٱلنُّورِ بِإِذْنِ رَبِّهِمْ إِلَى صِرَطِ ٱلْعَزِيزِ ٱلْحَمِيدِ ۩

A.L.R. A Book which We have revealed unto you, in order that you might lead mankind out of the depths of darkness into light – by the leave of their Lord – to the way of Him, the Exalted in Power, worth of all Praise. (14:1).

3. The Qur'an is the Book of Verification, Purification, Summation, and Culmination of all the previous revealed books before Islam. In this regard Allah says in Surah Al-Imran, (The Family of 'Imran) the following:

نَزَّلَ عَلَيْكَ ٱلْكِتَٰبَ

بِٱلْحَقِّ مُصَدِّقًا لِّمَا بَيْنَ يَدَيْهِ وَأَنزَلَ ٱلتَّوْرَىٰةَ وَٱلْإِنجِيلَ ﴿٣﴾

It is He Who sent down to you step by step, in truth, the Book, confirming what went before it; and He sent down the Law of Moses and the Gospel of Jesus before this, as a guide to mankind, and He sent down the Criterion of Judgment between right and wrong. (3:3)

4. The Qur'an is a Blessing, and people are to rule their daily affairs by the teachings of the Qur'an. If they do so, they will get the benefits of living in peace and happiness in this world. They will also get the blessings and rewards in the hereafter. Allah revealed the Qur'an so that the Prophet will settle disputes among people with its teachings. In this regards, Allah says in Surah Al-Baqarah the following:

وَأَنزَلَ مَعَهُمُ ٱلْكِتَٰبَ بِٱلْحَقِّ لِيَحْكُمَ بَيْنَ ٱلنَّاسِ

فِيمَا ٱخْتَلَفُوا فِيهِ

*And with them He sent the Book in truth, to judge
between people in matters wherein they differed. (2:213)*

B. Blessings for reading the Qur'an

Concerning the Blessings for the one who recites the Qur'an, I
wish to mention the following:

1. Allah demands from the Muslims to read the Qur'an with
   recitation. In Surah Al-Muzzammil, Allah says the
   following:

أَوْ زِدْ عَلَيْهِ وَرَتِّلِ ٱلْقُرْءَانَ تَرْتِيلًا ﴿٤﴾

*Or a little more; and recite the Qur'an in slow,
measured rhythmic tones. (73:4)*

And in the same Surah, Allah says the following:

فَٱقْرَءُوا مَا تَيَسَّرَ مِنْهُ

*Read you, therefore, of the Qur'an as much as may be
easy for you. (73:20)*

2. Qur'an is an enlightenment to the person who recites it. In
   this respect, Prophet Muhammad (pbuh) said:

" عَلَيْكَ تِلَاوَةَ الـقُرْآنِ, فَـإِنَّـهُ نُورٌ لَكَ فِي الأَرْضِ وَذُخْـرٌ

لَكَ فِي الـسَّـمَــــــا ء . "

Be steady with recitation of the Qur'an as it is a light for you in this world and a saving in the upper heaven.

3. Qur'an is to be a mediator in the Day of Judgement for the person who recites it. The Prophet of Islam said:

عن أبي أُمَامَةَ رضي الله عنه قال : سمعت رسول الله صلى الله عليه وسلم

يقول : « أَقْرَءُوا القرْآنَ فَإِنَّهُ يَأْتى يومَ القيامةِ شَفِيعاً (٠) لأَصحابه » رواه مسلم .

Narrated by Abu Umamah that the Prophet (pbuh) said: Read the Qur'an because it comes in the Day of Judgement as a mediator. Reported by Muslim.

C. **Final Remarks**

The Blessings of the Qur'an come to people from Allah (swt). They have to read the Qur'an, undestand its meaning, and apply its teachings on them privately and publicly. The Qur'an is a comprehensive Book: it will definitely guide people to the straight path (Assiratul Mustaqeem). All what is needed is for people to be honest and sincere towards the teachings of Allah (swt).

The Blessings of Allah (swt) through the Qur'an will defintely come to people directly and indirectly. The direct blessings could be peace, happiness, tranquility, rewards in this world and then later in the Day of Judgement. The indirect Blessings could be: prevent crisis, calamities, sickness.

33

We hope and pray that we try our best to read the Qur'aan daily with good intention. We pray to Allah (swt) to send us His Blessings in this world and in the Hereafter. Ameen

VII. BENEFITS OF THE QUR'AN
FADA-IL AL-QUR'AN

Allah (swt) revealed the Qur'an to Prophet Muhammad (pbuh) in a period of (23) years. The Qur'an has many benefits to all of us, individually and collectively. Some of the major benefits from reading, reciting and listening to the Qur'an are:

1. Guidance

Allah (swt) says in Surah Al-Baqarah (The Cow) that the Qur'an was revealed in Ramadan as a guide to all mankind. The Qur'an states the following:

شَهْرُ

رَمَضَانَ ٱلَّذِىٓ أُنزِلَ فِيهِ ٱلۡقُرۡءَانُ هُدًى لِّلنَّاسِ وَبَيِّنَٰتٍ مِّنَ ٱلۡهُدَىٰ وَٱلۡفُرۡقَانِ

Ramadan is the month in which was sent down the Qur'an, as a guide to mankind, also clear signs for guidance and judgment. (2:185)

2. Glad Tidings

There are good news for those who read the Qur'an, listen to its recitation, and apply its meaning privately and publicly. Allah (swt) says in Surah Al-Israa' the following:

إِنَّ هَٰذَا ٱلْقُرْءَانَ يَهْدِى لِلَّتِى هِىَ أَقْوَمُ وَيُبَشِّرُ ٱلْمُؤْمِنِينَ ٱلَّذِينَ يَعْمَلُونَ ٱلصَّٰلِحَٰتِ أَنَّ لَهُمْ أَجْرًا كَبِيرًا ۝

Verily this Qur'an does guide to that which is most right (or stable), and gives the glad tidings to the Believers who work deeds of righteousness, that they shall have a magnificent reward. (17:9)

3. Shifaa' (Healing)

By listening, reading and reciting the Qur'an, a person will get healing. It is a spiritual as well as a biological, neurological and psychological healer. In this respect, Allah (swt) says in Surah Al-Israa' the following:

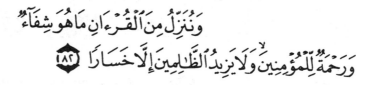

وَنُنَزِّلُ مِنَ ٱلْقُرْءَانِ مَا هُوَ شِفَآءٌ وَرَحْمَةٌ لِّلْمُؤْمِنِينَ وَلَا يَزِيدُ ٱلظَّٰلِمِينَ إِلَّا خَسَارًا ۝

We send down (stage by stage) of the Qur'an that which is a Healing and a Mercy to those who believe: To the unjust it causes nothing but loss after loss. (17:82)

4. Mercy

The above Ayah has both meaning of Healing and Mercy at the same time. This means that Qur'an has Healing effects, and it is a Mercy from Allah (swt) to all.

36

5. Witness

The Qur'an, will be a witness for those who read it in the grave as well as on the Day of Judgment. In Surah Al-Israa' Allah (swt) says the following:

$$\text{أَقِمِ ٱلصَّلَوٰةَ لِدُلُوكِ ٱلشَّمْسِ إِلَىٰ غَسَقِ ٱلَّيْلِ وَقُرْءَانَ ٱلْفَجْرِ إِنَّ قُرْءَانَ ٱلْفَجْرِ كَانَ مَشْهُودًا ﴿٧٨﴾}$$

Establish regular prayers at the sun's decline till the darkness of the night, and the recital of the Qur'an in morning prayer for the recital of dawn is witnessed. (17:78)

This means that we should read from the Qur'an daily and especially at dawn time, so that it will be a witness for us and a guide to paradise.

6. Group Benefits

Those who leave their houses and come to the House (Masjid) of Allah (swt) to read the Qur'an and to study its meaning, will please Allah (swt). As such, Allah (swt) will reward them a group of rewards and benefits at one time. These benefits are: mercy, peace, angels come down for them, and they will be put on the honor list in the Book of Allah (swt). All these benefits are summarized in the following Hadith: It was narrated by Abu Hurairah and recorded by Muslim and Abu Dawood that the Prophet (pbuh) said:

١١٠٤ – وَعَنْ أَبِي هُرَيْرَةَ رَضِيَ اللهُ عَنْهُ قَالَ : قَالَ رَسُولُ اللهِ
صلى الله عَلَيْهِ وَسَلَّمَ : « ومَا اجْتَمَعَ قَوْمٌ في بَيْتٍ من بُيوتِ اللهِ يَتْلُونَ
كتَابَ اللهِ . ويَتَدَارَسُونَهُ بَيْنَهُمْ ، إلاَّ نَزَلَتْ عَلَيْهِم السَّكِينَةُ .
وغَشِيَتْهُمُ الرَّحْمَةُ ، وحَفَّتْهُمُ المَلائِكَةُ ، وذَكَرَهُمُ اللهُ فِيمَنْ
عِنْدَهُ » رواه مسلم .

Any group of Muslims who meet at the House of Allah (swt) for the sake of reciting the Qur'an and studying its meaning, Allah (swt) will reward them with the following: The Mercy of Allah (swt) will descent upon them, peace and tranquility will cover them; Angels from heaven will encircle them; and Allah (swt) will mention their names to those who are at His Throne.

7. **Multiples of Rewards**

Those who read the Qur'an for the love of Allah (swt) will get multiples of rewards. Their rewards are counted as to the number of letters they read from the Qur'an. Our beloved prophet informed us the following Hadith: It was narrated by Abdullah Ibn Mas'ood and recorded in the book of Tarmazi that the Messenger of Allah (swt) said:

وعن ابن مسعود رضى الله عنه قال : قال رسول الله صلى الله عليه وسلم : « من
قرأ حَرْفًا من كِتابِ اللهِ فَلَهُ حَسَنَةٌ ، والحَسَنَةُ بِعَشْرِ أمثالِهَا لا أقولُ آلَم حَرْفٌ ،
ولكنْ أَلِفٌ حَرْفٌ ولاَمٌ حَرْفٌ ومِيمٌ حَرْفٌ » رواه الترمذى

38

Anyone who reads one letter from the Book of Allah (swt), he will be rewarded as a good deed; each deed is equal ten times; I don't say Alif...Laam...Meem.. is one letter; but Alif is one letter; Laam is one letter and Meem is one letter.

There are still many more Ayat and Ahadith about the benefits that we get by reading and listening to the Qur'an. In Surah Al-A'raaf (The Heights) Allah (swt) says:

وَإِذَا قُرِئَ ٱلْقُرْءَانُ

فَٱسْتَمِعُوا۟ لَهُۥ وَأَنصِتُوا۟ لَعَلَّكُمْ تُرْحَمُونَ ٢٠٤

When the Qur'an is read, listen to it with attention, and hold your peace that you may receive Mercy. (7:204)

However, in Surah Al-Nahl (The Bees) Allah (swt) says:

فَإِذَا قَرَأْتَ ٱلْقُرْءَانَ فَٱسْتَعِذْ بِٱللَّهِ مِنَ ٱلشَّيْطَٰنِ ٱلرَّجِيمِ ٩٨

When you read the Qur'an, seek Allah's protection from Satan, the rejected one. (16:98)

Let me remind myself and yourselves with the following recommendations:

1. We should try to listen to the recitation of the Qur'an as much as possible.

2. We should read the Qur'an during Salat and outside Salat. The best time is Fajr.
3. We should attend group recitation of Qur'an (Halaqah)
4. We should attend group discussion (Tafseer)
5. We should attend the session of finishing the whole Qur'an. It is called Khatm Al-Qur'an. At that time we make special Du'a' for all of us.
6. We should try to memorize as many Surahs (Chapters) from the Qur'an as possible.
7. We should try to understand the meaning of what we read or study. This could be through Muslim scholars who will elaborate to us the meaning of what we have read.
8. We should practice and apply its meaning on us privately and publicly.
9. We should deliver the Message to others so that we will be witnesses to Allah in the Day of Judgement.

Finally, let me quote the Qur'an from Surah Al-Hashr (The Gathering) the following Ayah:

لَوْ أَنزَلْنَا هَٰذَا

ٱلْقُرْءَانَ عَلَىٰ جَبَلٍ لَّرَأَيْتَهُۥ خَٰشِعًا مُّتَصَدِّعًا مِّنْ خَشْيَةِ
ٱللَّهِ وَتِلْكَ ٱلْأَمْثَٰلُ نَضْرِبُهَا لِلنَّاسِ لَعَلَّهُمْ يَتَفَكَّرُونَ ﴿٢١﴾

Had We sent down this Qur'an on a mountain, verily, you would have seen it humble itself and cleave asunder for fear of Allah (swt). Such are the similitude, which We propound to men, that they may reflect. (59:21)

40

We hope and pray that the readers will take the Qur'an seriously so as to benefit from it in their private and public life. To receive any benefit from Allah through the Qur'an means a person will live in peace and harmony throughout his life.

VIII. MIRACLES OF THE QUR'AN

A. General

The subject of this chapter is about **"Miracles of the Qur'an"** or what is called in Arabic I'jaazul Qur'an. This subject is not meant to be given in one chapter as it demands a series of them to be covered. However, I will do my best to cover the highlights of the major sections in the discussion.

The Qur'an challenged its opponents many times to reproduce a similar Qur'an, ten Surah of Qur'an, or at least one Surah. At every challenge, the opponents failed to do so, while they were among the best orators and poets. The following is a partial list of the challenges:

1. In Surah Al-Qassass (The Narration) the opponents were challenged to synthesize a similar Qur'an. Allah (swt) says the following:

قُلْ فَأْتُواْ بِكِتَبٍ مِّنْ عِندِ ٱللَّهِ هُوَ أَهْدَىٰ مِنْهُمَآ أَتَّبِعْهُ إِن كُنتُمْ صَدِقِينَ ۞ فَإِن لَّمْ يَسْتَجِيبُواْ لَكَ فَٱعْلَمْ أَنَّمَا يَتَّبِعُونَ أَهْوَآءَهُمْ وَمَنْ أَضَلُّ مِمَّنِ ٱتَّبَعَ هَوَىٰهُ بِغَيْرِ هُدًى مِّنَ ٱللَّهِ إِنَّ ٱللَّهَ لَا يَهْدِى ٱلْقَوْمَ ٱلظَّٰلِمِينَ ۞

Say: "Then bring you a Book from God, which is a better guide than either of them, that I may follow it! (Do), if you are truthful!" But if they hearken not to you, know that they only follow their own lusts: And who is more astray than one who follows his own lusts, devoid of guidance from God? For God guides not people given to wrong-doing." (28:49-50)

2. The Qur'an challenged his opponents to synthesize ten similar Surah as is seen in Surah Hud:

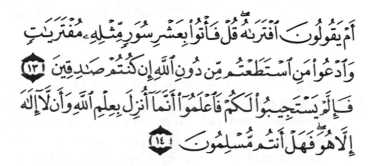

Or they may say, "He forged it," Say, "Bring you then ten Surah forged, like unto it, and call (to your aid) whomsoever you can, other than God! If you speak the truth! "If then they (your false gods) answer not your (call), know you that this Revelation is sent down (replete) with the knowledge of God, and that there is no god but He! Will you even then submit (to Islam)?! (11:13-14)

3. When the opponents failed, the Qur'an even challenged them to synthesize one single Surah similar to the Qur'an. This type of a challege seen in Surah Al-Baqarah (The Cow):

وَإِن كُنتُمْ فِي رَيْبٍ مِّمَّا نَزَّلْنَا عَلَىٰ عَبْدِنَا فَأْتُوا بِسُورَةٍ مِّن مِّثْلِهِۦ وَٱدْعُوا شُهَدَآءَكُم مِّن دُونِ ٱللَّهِ إِن كُنتُمْ صَٰدِقِينَ ﴿٢٣﴾ فَإِن لَّمْ تَفْعَلُوا وَلَن تَفْعَلُوا فَٱتَّقُوا ٱلنَّارَ ٱلَّتِي وَقُودُهَا ٱلنَّاسُ وَٱلْحِجَارَةُ أُعِدَّتْ لِلْكَٰفِرِينَ ﴿٢٤﴾

And if you are in doubt as to what We have revealed from time to time to Our servant, then produce a Surah like thereunto; and call your witnesses or helpers (if there are any) besides God, if your (doubts) are true. But if you cannot then fear the Fire whose fuel is people and stones, which is prepared for those who reject faith. (2:23-24)

B. Uniqueness of Qur'an

At this point we should summarize the uniqueness of the miracles of the Qur'an:

1. The Qur'an is unique in its tune, rhythm, and rhyme.
2. The Qur'an is unique in its similitude, metaphor, brevity, repetition, eloquence, lack of discrepancy and synonyms.
3. The Qur'an is unique in its information about the unseen and the stories it narrates.

44

4. The Qur'an is very unique in its spiritual upliftment and in its touches to the inner heart for those who are sincere and honest.
5. The Qur'an is unique in its scientific miracles. While it is not a scientific book, it surpassed science and technology in its foretelling the scientific information.

C. Scientific Information

Let me highlight some of the major scientific information mentioned in the Qur'an:

1. Oneness of the Universe and the split of the earth from its origin, its creation and its establishment as a planet of its own. In Surah Al-Anbiya' (The Prophets), Allah says:

أَوَلَمۡ يَرَ ٱلَّذِينَ كَفَرُوٓاْ
أَنَّ ٱلسَّمَٰوَٰتِ وَٱلۡأَرۡضَ كَانَتَا رَتۡقًا فَفَتَقۡنَٰهُمَاۖ وَجَعَلۡنَا
مِنَ ٱلۡمَآءِ كُلَّ شَىۡءٍ حَىٍّۚ أَفَلَا يُؤۡمِنُونَ ﴿٣٠﴾

Do not the unbelievers see that the heavens and the earth were joined together (as one Unit of Creation), before We cloved them asunder? We made from water every living thing. Will they not then believe?" (21:30)

2. Movements of the planets in the universe. In Surah Yasin, Allah says:

وَٱلشَّمْسُ تَجْرِى لِمُسْتَقَرٍّ لَّهَا

ذَٰلِكَ تَقْدِيرُ ٱلْعَزِيزِ ٱلْعَلِيمِ ﴿٣٨﴾ وَٱلْقَمَرَ قَدَّرْنَٰهُ مَنَازِلَ حَتَّىٰ

عَادَ كَٱلْعُرْجُونِ ٱلْقَدِيمِ ﴿٣٩﴾ لَا ٱلشَّمْسُ يَنۢبَغِى لَهَآ أَن تُدْرِكَ

ٱلْقَمَرَ وَلَا ٱلَّيْلُ سَابِقُ ٱلنَّهَارِ وَكُلٌّ فِى فَلَكٍ يَسْبَحُونَ ﴿٤٠﴾

*And the Sun runs its course for a period determined
for it: that is the decree of (Him), the Exalted in Might,
the All-Knowing. And the moon, We have measured for
its mansions (to traverse) till it returns like the old (and
withered) lower part of a date-stalk. It is not permitted
to the sun to catch up the moon, nor can the night
outstrip the Day: each (just) swim along in (its own)
orbit (according to Law). (36:38-40)*

3. The creation of other living creatures on the other planets.
   Those creatures are praying and worshipping Allah. If Allah
   wishes, He would bring them together with us to meet one
   another. In this respect the Qur'an is very specific when
   saying in Surah Ash-Shura (Consultation) :

وَمِنْ ءَايَٰتِهِۦ خَلْقُ

ٱلسَّمَٰوَٰتِ وَٱلْأَرْضِ وَمَا بَثَّ فِيهِمَا مِن دَآبَّةٍ وَهُوَ عَلَىٰ جَمْعِهِمْ

إِذَا يَشَآءُ قَدِيرٌ ﴿٢٩﴾

46

And among His Signs is the creation of the heavens and the earth, and every living creatures that He has scattered through them: and He has power to gather them together when He wills. (42:29)

4. The lack of oxygen in the upper atmosphere which in turn will make it hard for people to live peacefully. In this regard, the Qur'an states in Surah Al-An'am (The Cattles) :

فَمَن يُرِدِ ٱللَّهُ أَن يَهْدِيَهُ يَشْرَحْ صَدْرَهُۥ لِلْإِسْلَٰمِ وَمَن يُرِدْ أَن يُضِلَّهُۥ يَجْعَلْ صَدْرَهُۥ ضَيِّقًا حَرَجًا كَأَنَّمَا يَصَّعَّدُ فِى ٱلسَّمَاءِ كَذَٰلِكَ يَجْعَلُ ٱللَّهُ ٱلرِّجْسَ عَلَى ٱلَّذِينَ لَا يُؤْمِنُونَ ١٢٥

Those whom God (in His Plan) will guide, He opens their breast to Islam; Those whom He will to leave straying, He makes their breast close and constricted, as if they had to climb up to the skies: thus does God (heap) the penalty on those who refuse to believe. (6:125)

5. The atom or its components were mentioned in the Qur'an in such a way that Allah does know each and everything in the universe. It was He Who created them, and it was He Who knows everything about them and whereabouts they are located. In this respect, Allah says in Surah Yunus:

47

وَمَايَعْزُبُ عَن رَّبِّكَ مِن مِّثْقَالِ ذَرَّةٍ فِي ٱلْأَرْضِ وَلَا فِي ٱلسَّمَآءِ وَلَآ أَصْغَرَ مِن ذَٰلِكَ وَلَآ أَكْبَرَ إِلَّا فِي كِتَٰبٍ مُّبِينٍ ۝

Nor is hidden from your Lord (so much as) the weight of an atom on the earth or in heaven. And not the least and not the greatest of these things but are recorded in a clear record. (10:61)

6. The creation of everything in the universe is made up of pairs: human beings, plants, animals, and etc. In many places in the Qur'an Allah gives us information of pairings. The comprehensive Ayah is the one in Surah Al-Zariyat (The Winds that Scatter) :

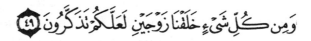

And of every thing We have created pairs: that you may receive instruction. (51:49)

7. The concept of fertilization of plants or clouds to produce the new offspring or water respectfully. The Qur'an states in Surah Al-Hijr (The Rocky Tract) about the use of wind for pollen fertilization:

وَأَرْسَلْنَا الرِّيَاحَ لَوَاقِحَ فَأَنزَلْنَا مِنَ السَّمَاءِ مَاءً فَأَسْقَيْنَاكُمُوهُ وَمَا أَنتُمْ لَهُ بِخَازِنِينَ ٢٢

And We send the fecundating winds, then cause the rain to descend from the sky, therewith providing you with water (in abundance), though you are not the guardians of its stores. (15:22)

In Surah Al-Noor (The light), Allah informs us about the production of water from the clouds through the process of fertilization of the positive and negative electric charges:

أَلَمْ تَرَ أَنَّ اللَّهَ يُزْجِي سَحَابًا ثُمَّ يُؤَلِّفُ بَيْنَهُ ثُمَّ يَجْعَلُهُ رُكَامًا فَتَرَى الْوَدْقَ يَخْرُجُ مِنْ خِلَالِهِ وَيُنَزِّلُ مِنَ السَّمَاءِ مِن جِبَالٍ فِيهَا مِن بَرَدٍ فَيُصِيبُ بِهِ مَن يَشَاءُ وَيَصْرِفُهُ عَن مَّن يَشَاءُ يَكَادُ سَنَا بَرْقِهِ يَذْهَبُ بِالْأَبْصَارِ ٤٣

See you not that God makes the clouds move gently, then joins them together, then makes them into a heap? Then will you see rain issue forth from their midst. And He sends down from the sky mountain masses (of clouds) wherein is hail: He strikes therewith whom He pleases and He turns it away from whom He pleases. The vivid flash of His lightning well-nigh blinds the sight. (24:43)

8. The creation of human being, the stages of his embryonic development and the number of layers that the embryo is embedded in, are among the fascinating information given to us in the Qur'an. Mankind should be grateful to Allah for all the scientific news. One of the series of Ayat in the Qur'an is the one in Surah Al-Mu'minoon (The Believers):

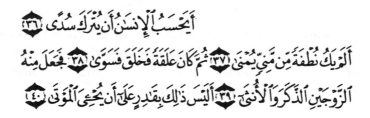

Does Man think that he will be left uncontrolled, (without purpose)? Was he not a drop of sperm emitted (in lowly form)? Then did (God) make and fashion (him) in due proportion. And of him He, made two sexes, male and female. Has not He, (the same), the power to give life to the dead? (75:36-40)

9. The science of fingerprints is a new one to mankind. Through this scientific knowledge, officials were and are still able to identify each person through his/her fingerprints. Allah made these fingerprints of special identification of every person. In the Day of Judgement, He will be able of course, to reproduce the fingerprints of every one of us. In this regard Allah says in the Qur'an in Surah Al-Qiyamah (The Resurrection) the following.

I do call to witness the Resurrection Day; and I do call to witness the self-reproaching spirit; (Eschew Evil). Does man think that We cannot assemble his bones? Nay, We are able to put together in perfect order the very tips of his fingers. (75:1-4)

The scientific miracles of the Qur'an are beyond count. There are many more miracles. The scientific wisdom of the Qur'an concerning food, health, behavior and diseases are too many to be counted. The prohibition of eating pork, and of drinking of alcohol are among the many examples to be mentioned. I refer the reader to obtain these information from my previous booklets regarding this subject. The benefits of honey are too many to be elucidated here. The production of the milk from the bellies of animals is among the blessings of Allah upon us all.

D. Final Remarks

Let us ponder and contemplate! Let us think and pause for a moment! Let us reflect and deduct through analysis! Let us start doing research and find out the answers to the questions that are asked by many. Let us remember the Ayah in the Qur'an in Surah Fussilat (Explained in Detail):

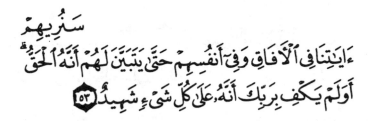

Soon will We show them Our Signs in the (furthest) regions (of the earth), and in their own souls, until it becomes manifest to them that this is the Truth. Is it not enough that your Lord does witness all things? (41:53)

Let us also remember the other Ayah in Surah Al-Zariyat (The Winds that Scatter):

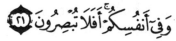

As also in your own selves: will you not then see? (51:21)

Finally, let us ask Allah to help us and guide us. Let us ask Allah to shower His blessings upon us. Let us ask Allah forgiveness. Ameen.

I seek refuge in Allah from the outcast Shaitan. In the name of Allah, the Most Gracious, the Most Merciful. O Allah! You are the Opener of the doors of blessings, please open for us the best door of blessings.

IX. THE HEALING ASPECTS OF THE QUR'AN

AL-QUR'AN SHIFAA'

A. General

The subject of this chapter is about the Qur'an to be used as a healing process, or what is called in Arabic Shifaa'. Let me quote for you what the Qur'an says about itself as a Healing Book. Allah (swt) says in Surah Al-Israa' the following:

وَنُنَزِّلُ مِنَ ٱلْقُرْءَانِ مَا هُوَ شِفَآءٌ
وَرَحْمَةٌ لِّلْمُؤْمِنِينَ وَلَا يَزِيدُ ٱلظَّـٰلِمِينَ إِلَّا خَسَارًا ۝

We send down (stage by stage) of the Qur'an that which is a healing and a mercy to those who believe: To the unjust it causes nothing but loss after loss. (17:82)

In another place in the Qur'an, Allah (swt) says in Surah Fussilat (Ha-Mim) the following:

قُلْ هُوَ لِلَّذِينَ ءَامَنُوا هُدًى وَشِفَآءٌ وَٱلَّذِينَ
لَا يُؤْمِنُونَ فِىٓ ءَاذَانِهِمْ وَقْرٌ وَهُوَ عَلَيْهِمْ عَمًى أُوْلَـٰٓئِكَ
يُنَادَوْنَ مِن مَّكَانٍ بَعِيدٍ ۝

Say: It is a guide and a healing to those who believe; and for those who believe not, there is a deafness in their ears, and it is blindness in their (eyes). They are (as it were) being called from a place far distant. (41:44)

53

Also one can find in Surah Yunus the following:

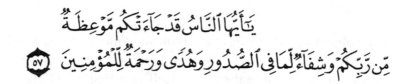

O mankind! There has come to you an admonition from your Lord and a Healing for the (diseases) in your hearts, and for those who believe, a Guidance and Mercy. (10:57)

When we talk about Shifaa', we are not specifying any particular type of sickness or disease. The Qur'an could be used as a means to heal oneself from certain types of sickness such as spiritual, psychological, biological, physical, mental, moral, as well as sickness from the unseen creatures such as Al-Jinn, or demons.

It should be understood that sickness and healing are from Allah (swt) as a mercy upon us. They come to us for one reason or another. Moreover, the Healer is Allah (swt) Alone. However, people should seek health through Halal methods. We should go to physicians for biological sickness. We should go to an 'Alim for spiritual problems. The treatment for any spiritual and mental sickness should be directly from the Qur'an and the authentic Hadith. Similarly any problem that may come from the Evil-Eye or from the Jinn should be treated from the Qur'an and Hadith.

B. Precursor of Healing

1. Before going to any physicians or 'Alim for any treatment, one has to improve his relationship with Allah (swt). A non-practicing Muslim will not be healed by the Qur'an. Healing by the Qur'an is meant for the believing Muslims, as stated previously in Surah Al-Israa' (17:82). For a believer, he has to take the initiative and pay Sadaqah (charity) before going to any physician or 'Alim. The prophet (pbuh) said:

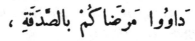

Heal your sick ones with charity.

2. There are some Muslims who usually say the following: Yah Allah (swt)! If you heal me, I will pay charity, or I will slaughter an animal and distribute the meat to the needy ones. This is totally wrong. We have to take the initiative, do good, and pay charity before we ask Allah (swt) to heal us, and before we go to the physician or to the 'Alim.

C. Healing Methods

1. For those who are having problems of drought, lack of money, deprived of children and so on, they should immediately make Istighfar: asking Allah's (swt) forgiveness. The Qur'an is very clear in this matter. In Surah Nooh, Allah (swt) informed him to instruct his people to make Istighfar. The Qur'an states the following:

55

لَكُمْ جَنَّتٍ وَيَجْعَل لَّكُمْ أَنْهَٰرًا ۝ مَّالَكُمْ لَا تَرْجُونَ لِلَّهِ وَقَارًا ۝
وَقَدْ خَلَقَكُمْ أَطْوَارًا ۝

Ask forgiveness from your Lord, for He is Oft-Forgiving. He will send rain to you in abundance, give you increase in wealth and children, and bestow on you gardens and rivers (of flowing water). What is the matter with you, that you are not conscious of Allah's (swt) Majesty, seeing that it is He Who has created you in diverse stages. (71:10-14)

The way to recite the statement of Istighfar is as follows:

أَسْتَغْفِرُ اللَّهَ الَّذِي لَا إِلَٰهَ إِلَّا هُوَ الْحَيُّ الْقَيُّومُ
وَأَتُوبُ إِلَيْهِ

I seek refuge in Allah (swt), the Magnificent. There is no deity except Him. He is the Living and oversees everything. I repent back to Him.

2. There is another version of Istighfar. It was narrated by Jubair Ibn Mat'am and reported in the Book of Nasaa-ee, Tabarani, and Al-Hakim that the Messenger (pbuh) of Allah (swt) said:

سُبْحَانَكَ اللَّهُمَّ وَبِحَمْدِكَ، أَشْهَدُ أَنْ لَا إِلَٰهَ إِلَّا
أَنْتَ، أَسْتَغْفِرُكَ وَأَتُوبُ إِلَيْكَ   (ثلاثًا) .

Glory be to You O Allah (swt)! Praise be to You! I bear witness that there is no other god except You. I seek Your forgiveness and I come back to You with repentance.

56

3. For those who are attacked by the Evil-Eye due to jealousy, they have to read Ayat Al-Kursi (2:255), Surah Al-Falaq (113:1-5) and Surah Al-Naas (114:1-6) daily. They are to wipe their faces and bodies after reading them. Reciting the verses should be in multiples of 3, 5, or 7 times each.

4. For those who are sick from Jinns, they should read the same verses from the Qur'an, as well as the following Du`aa` from the Prophet (pbuh):

a. It was reported by Abu Bakr (R) that the Prophet (pbuh) used to say:

اللّهُمَّ عَـافِني فِي بَدَنِـي، اللّهُمَّ عَـافِني فِي سَمْـعِي، اللّهُمَّ عَافِني فِي بَصَـرِي

O Allah (swt)! give me healing in my body. O Allah (swt)! give me good health in my hearing. O Allah (swt)!, give me good health in my sight.

b. The Second Du`aa` is narrated by Aisha® that the Prophet (pbuh) used to say:

١١٧٧ ــ وعن عائشة أن النبيَّ ، صلى اللهُ عليه وسلَّم كَان يَعُودُ بَعْضَ أهْلِه يَمْسَحُ بِيَدِه اليُمْنَى ويقولُ : « اللّهُمَّ رَبَّ النّاسِ ، أذْهِب البْأَسَ ، واشْفِ ، أنْتَ الشّافي لا شِفَاءَ إلاَّ شِفَاؤُكَ ، شِفَاءً لا يُغَادِرُ سَقَمَاً »

57

Ya Allah (swt)! You are The Healer. There is no healing except from You. Please Ya Allah (swt! give me health and healing that stay with me till I am completely healed from any sickness or disease.

c. The Third Du`aa` as narrated by Uthman Ibn 'Affan that the Messenger of Allah (swt)) said:

«بسم الله الذي لا يضرُّ مَعَ اسمِهِ شَيْءٌ في الأرْضِ وَلَا فِي السماءِ وَهُوَ السَّمِيعُ العَلِيمُ»

In the Name of Allah (swt) nothing will hurt with His Name on this earth as well as in the heavens. Indeed He is the All-Healer and All-Knowing.

d. The Fourth Du`aa` (as narrated by Abu Hurairah) that the Prophet (pbuh) used to say:

أَعُوذُ بِكَلِمَاتِ اللَّهِ التَّامَّاتِ مِنْ شَرّ مَا خَلَقَ

I seek refuge with the words of Allah (swt) totally and completely from all the evil creatures that He created.

D. **Final Remark**

There are still many situations where one can read the Qur'an and make a Du`aa` for healing from sickness and disease. Healing by the Qur'an therefore, is good for everyone, Muslims and non-Muslims. One has to know when to use it, how to use it and how to benefit from it. Ameen.

X. SUBJECTS OF THE QUR'AN.

A. Introduction

There is no person in the world who would be able to understand the Qur'an as much as the one who received it, namely Prophet Muhammad. To understand and appreciate the meaning and the subjects of the Qur'an, one has to go to Hadith, Sunnah, Sirah, Companions of the Prophet, as well as to the Books of Tafseer. Even with all these sources, one has to have a series of Muslim Scholars, Ulamaa', Professors and teachers to help him understand some parts of the Qur'an.

B. General Categories

As far as the subjects of the Qur'an are concerned, they can be grouped into the following categories:

1. Creed, Tawheed, Aqeeda, obedience to God, Allegiance to God, and the Oneness of God as He revealed it in the Qur'an in Surah Al-Samad or Al-Ikhlas (The Purity of Faith). It is chapter 112. The subject of this Surah covers one-third of the Qur'anic subjects. For this reason, chapter 112 is considered to be equal to one-third of the Qur'an in its meanings.

2. 'Ibaadaat or Religious practices. This section covers the five pillars of Islam: Declaration of Faith (Shahada), Salat, Sawm (Fasting), Zakat, and Hajj (Pilgrimage) to Makkah. This section does include also the six pillars of Iman: Belief in one God, the belief in all angels, the divine revealed books, the whole prophets and messengers of Allah, the Day of Judgement, and destiny from Allah.

3. The third category is Human Relationships and business transactions. Under this subject one may find the following major categories: personal, family, society, government, and business transactions.

C. Specific Categories

1. In the field of family as a sub-topic, it includes: courtship, marriage, divorce, khul'ah, inheritance, custody, fostering (not adoption), waleema, 'Aqeeqa, Eelaa', Zihar, etc.

2. In the field of government, the Islamic transactions may include: politics, business transactions, education systems, economic banking, relationship with other governments, social welfare, jurisprudence, legal matters, halal and haram, rewards or penalties, etc.

3. There are other categories that mushroom from the previous ones. In order to appreciate life as a whole, Allah (swt) revealed other information that will undoubtedly help people to enjoy life, and to appreciate the creation of Allah in the whole universe. Some of these topics would be:

a. History and stories of previous nations along with their prophets and messengers that Allah sent. It is a good idea for every new generation to take a lesson from their ancestors.

b. The future of this life, the life in the grave, and the life in the hereafter: Paradise, hell or A'raaf (custody).

c. The concepts of morality, modesty, manners, behavior and ethics that are needed in every society so as to live in peace and harmony.

d. The subjects about cosmos and the universe are explained. The presence of other planets and living creatures outside our own planet and outside our own orbit has been revealed in the Qur'an.

e. The concept of the creation of people from soil through the fertilization of the sperm to the ova. This concept of creation is compared with the creation of Adam who had no father and no mother. This concept has also been compared with the creation of Eve from the rib of Adam. The other creation is that of Jesus from a mother without a father. All these methods are the miracle of Allah to teach us a lesson.

f. There are many scientific facts in the Qur'an being mentioned such as: Embryology, Cosmos, water, cloud, rain, thunder, rivers, oceans, navigation, the north pole, solar system, lunar system, honey, milk, etc.

g. Allah (swt) has explained to us the halal foods, and drinks that we are to utilize. At the same time, He informed us about the haram consumption of foods and drinks. Anything that is halal is good for the health, nutritionally is good, and is delicious and very tasty as well.

D. Specific Topics

In order to study the Qur'an, one has also to find out the different subjects and topics that have been revealed in the Qur'an. By studying them, one may be able to understand or at least may appreciate the Qur'an, and the wisdom of such information revealed in the Qur'an. The following is a partial list of topics, subjects and titles that one has to study with a group of Muslim Scholars before being able to open his mouth and talk about the Qur'an. These topics are summarized as follows:

1. Revealed in Makkah or Madeenah
2. In the city or Travelling
3. During the Days or the Nights
4. The Summer or the Winter
5. In Bed or Sleeping
6. On the Earth or in Heaven
7. First of What Was Revealed
8. Last Revelation
9. Reasons of Revelation
10. Revealed About Sahabah
11. Repeated Revelation
12. Wisdom for Delayed Revelations and Decisions
13. Revealed Separately or Totally
14. Revealed Collectively or Individually
15. Revealed to Some Prophets
16. Never Revealed to Any Prophets Before Muhammad (saw)
17. How It Was Revealed
18. Names of the Qur'an and the Surahs
19. Compilation and Sequential Order
20. Number of Surahs, Ayat, Words, and Letters
21. Memorizers and Reporters

22. The High and the Low
23. Sequential Order
24. The Most Famous Ayat and Surahs
25. The Unique Ayat
26. The Exceptional Ayat
27. Subjects
28. Classifications
29. Stopping and Starting
30. United Pronunciation and Meaning
31. Elongation and Shortening
32. Pronunciations with Noonation
33. Hamzah
34. How to Handle the Qur'an
35. Manners of Reading
36. Knowing the Strange Meanings
37. Outside Language of Hijaz
38. Inside Language of Hijaz
39. Similarities and Opposites
40. Items Needed for the One Who is Giving Tafseer
41. Grammar
42. Basics for Tafseer
43. Fundamentals and Similarities
44. Starting and Ending
45. Specifics and Generalities
46. In Summary and Detail
47. Replacement of Certain Ayat
48. The So-Called "Confusions"
49. Restricted an Non-Restricted
50. Logical and Understood
51. Different Ways of Addressing Issues
52. Explicit and Implicit
53. Similitudes
54. Nicknames

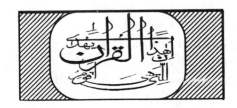

XI. SPECIFIC TOPICS OF THE QUR'AN

In a previous chapter some discussion was presented about **Subjects of the Qur'an**. In that chapter it was mentioned that there are many topics and subjects that a person can find in the Qur'an. The minimum ones reported were 76 subjects. Each and every topic cannot be picked up from one Surah only. One has to go to different Surahs in order to get the complete picture about that particular subject. For example:

A. Topic of Fasting

1. If one selects the topic of fasting in the Qur'an, he has to realize that the rules and regulations are the same, i.e., one has to abstain completely from dawn to sunset. Fasting the month of Ramadan is a pillar of Islam, and it is for a whole month.

2. There are compensatory fasting in case someone has to break any day (s) in Ramadan for being sick, travelling, or for the menstruating women, etc. However, there are other types of fasting; compensation outside the fasting month of Ramadan.

3. During Hajj for example: Those who could not sacrifice an animal during their presence in Mina, have to fast three (3) days in Mina, and seven (7) days after they come back home.

4. If someone by accident killed someone, he has to pay compensation to the family of the dead person and liberate a slave. Otherwise he pays the monetary compensation and has to fast two consecutive months as a Kaffarah (Repentance).

5. For those who make oath and could not fulfill their promises, have to feed ten needy persons, or fast three (3) consecutive days as a Kaffarah.

6. For those who defame their wives, and say: You are to me like my own mother(Zihaar). They have to fast sixty (60) consecutive days as a Kaffarah (Repentance). There are still other situations regarding this topic of fasting. Therefore, one will not be able to find all these subjects in one Surah in the Qur'an. The Qur'an is not meant to be topics with specific titles. It is a comprehensive Book from Allah (swt), and as a Guide and a Mercy to all mankind. Hence, what has been discussed in this chapter about the topic of fasting can be found in the following chapters of the Qur'an.

TABLE I FASTING

Fasting Situation	Surah Name	Surah No.	Verses No
1. Fasting of Ramadan	Al-Baqarah The Cow	2	183-187
2. Hajj Sacrifice	Al-Baqarah The Cow	2	196
3. Marital relation during the fasting month of Ramadan	An-Nisaa' (The Women)	4	92
4. Oath not fulfilled	Al-Maidah (The Table Spread)	5	89
5. Defaming wife as a mother (Zihaar)	Al-Mujadalah (The Woman who pleads)	58	4

Whatever has been mentioned about the topic of fasting is also to be said about the other topics in the Qur'an. Therefore, one has to go to the Index of the Qur'an and find the topic that he is interested to read, study and understand. One good source of that would be an Arabic text called: Al-Mu'jam Al-Mufahrass Li-Alfaaz Al-Qur-an. It was compiled and prepared by Muhammad Fuad Abdel Baqi. It was published by Dar Al-Hadith in Cairo, Egypt, 1987. It is really one of the best book to search any topic in the Qur'an.

B. Topic of Allah

To let the reader feel better, another word is selected here. For example the name of Allah is found in the Qur'an in three (3) different tenses: Subject (Nominative Case); Object (Accusative Case); and Object of Preposition.

1. If it is as a subject, it is to be pronounced as Allahu (اللهُ). This name of Allahu is mentioned in the Qur'an (980) times in 73 Surahs.
2. The word Allaha (اللهَ) is found (592) times in the Qur'an in (56) Surahs.
3. The word Allahi (اللهِ) is found in the Qur'an (1125) times in (74) Surahs . The reader is requested to see the information in detail at the end of this chapter.

Therefore, in order to study the Qur'an and to understand its meaning one has to have a series of Muslim scholars whose specialties are the Qur'an. He has to have a series of books, references, encyclopedia of the Qur'an, and so on.

We hope and pray that no one should start explaining any subject of the Qur'an unless he knows what he his talking about. Otherwise, he will be in trouble in the Day of Judgement in front of Allah (swt).

TABLE II ALLAHU

Surah Name	English Meaning	Surah No.	Fre- quency
1. Al–Baqarah	The Cow	2	107
2. Al-Imran	The Family of Imran	3	83
3. An-Nisaa'	The Women	4	87
4. Al-Maidah	The Table Spread	5	67
5. Al –An'am	The Cattle	6	30
6. Al-A'raf	The Heights	7	18
7. Al-Anfal	The Booties	8	30
8. Al-Tawbah	Repentance	9	72
9. Yunus	Yunus	10	20
10. Hood	Hud	11	5
11. Yusuf	Joseph	12	15
12. Al-Ra'ad	Thunder	13	14
13.	Abraham	14	10
14. Al-Nahl	The Bees	16	29
15. Al-Israa'	Night Travel	17	3
16. Al-Kahf	The Cave	18	8
17. Mariam	Mary	19	2
18. Taha	Taha	20	5
19. Al-Anbiyaa'	The Prophets	21	1
20. Al-Hajj	Pilgrimage	22	15
21. Al-Mu'minoon	The Believers	23	4
22. Al-Noor	The Light	24	37
23. Al-Furqan	The Criterion	25	4
24. Al-Naml	The Ants	27	7
25. Al-Qasass	Narrations	28	9
26. Al- `Ankaboot	Spider	29	13
27. Al-Room	The Romans	30	9
28. Luqman	Luqman	31	3
29. Al-Sajdah	Prostration	32	1

TABLE II ALLAHU

Surah Name	English Meaning	Surah No.	Fre-quency
30. Al-Ahzab	The Confederates	33	34
31. Saba'	Saba'	34	2
32. Fatir	The Originator of Creation	35	7
33. Yaseen	Abbreviated Letter	36	2
34. Al-Saaffaat	Those Ranged in Ranks	37	4
35. Saad	Abbreviated letter	38	1
36. Al-Zumar	The Groups	39	24
37. Ghafir	The Forgiver	40	18
38. Fussilat	Explained in Details	41	2
39. Al-Shura	Consultation	42	19
40. Al-Zuhkruf	Gold Adornment	43	1
41. Al-Dukhan	Smoke	44	1
42. Al-Jathiyah	Bowing the Knees	45	6
43. Al-Ahqaaf	Winding Sand-Tracts	46	1
44. Muhammad	Prophet Muhammad	47	15
45. Al-Fath	Victory	48	21
46. Al-Hujurat	The Inner Apartments	49	7
47. Al-Toor	The Mount	52	1
48. Al-Najm	The Star	53	2
49. Al-Hadeed	Iron	57	8
50. Al-Mujadalah	The Woman Who Pleads	58	18
51. Al-Hashr	The Gathering	59	9
52. Al-Mumtahana	The Woman to Be Examined	60	9
53. Al-Saff	Battle Array	61	4
54. Al-Jumu'ah	Friday	62	4
55. Al-Munafiqoon	The Hypocrites	63	6
56. Al-Taghabun	Mutual Loss & Gain	64	9

Continuation TABLE II ALLAHU

Surah Name	English Meaning	Surah No.	Fre-quency
57. Al-Talaq	Divorce	65	8
58. Al-Tahreem	Holding To Be Forbidden	66	8
59. Al-Mulk	Dominion	67	2
60. Nooh	Noah	71	3
61. Al-Jinn	The Jinn	72	1
62. Al-Muzzammil	Folded in Garment	73	1
63. Al-Muddathir	One Wrapped Up	74	3
64. Al-Insan	Mankind	76	2
65. Al-Nazi'aat	Those Who Tear Out	79	1
66. Al-Takweer	The Folding Up	81	1
67. Al-Inshiqaq	The Rending Asunder	84	1
68. Al-Burooj	The Zodiacal Signs	85	2
69. Al-A'laa	The Most High	87	1
70. Al-Ghashiyah	The Overwhelming Event	88	1
71. Al-Teen	The Fig	95	1
72. Al-Baiynah	The Clear Evidence	98	1
73. Al-Ikhlas	Purity of Faith	112	2

TABLE III ALLAHA

Surah Name	English Meaning	Surah No.	Fre-quency
1. Al–Baqarah	The Cow	2	75
2. Al-Imran	The Family of Imran	3	41
3. An-Nisaa'	The Women	4	33
4. Al-Maidah	The Table Spread	5	21
5. Al –An'am	The Cattle	6	6

Continuation

TABLE III ALLAHA

Surah Name	English Meaning	Surah No.	Fre-quency
6. Al-A'raf	The Heights	7	8
7. Al-Anfal	The Booties	8	3
8. Al-Tawbah	Repentance	9	33
9. Yunus	Prophet Yunus	10	8
10. Hood	Prophet Hud	11	8
11. Yusuf	Joseph	12	3
12. Al-Ra'ad	Thunder	13	4
13. Ibrahim	Prophet Abraham	14	8
14. Al-Hijr	The Rocky Tract	15	1
15. Al-Nahl	The Bees	16	14
16. Al-Israa'	Night Travel	17	2
17. Al-Kahf	The Cave	18	1
18. Mariam	Mary	19	1
19. Al-Hajj	Pilgrimage	22	35
20. Al-Mu'minoon	The Believers	23	2
21. Al-Noor	The Light	24	17
22. Al-Shu'araa'	The Poets	26	10
23. Al-Naml	The Ants	27	2
24. Al-Qasass	Narrations	28	6
25. Al-`Ankaboot	Spider	29	8
26. Al-Room	The Romans	30	1
27. Luqman	Luqman	31	15
28. Al-Ahzab	The Confederates	33	26
29. Fatir	The Originator of Creation	35	11
30. Al-Saaffaat	Those Ranged in Ranks	37	1

Continuation   TABLE III ALLAHA

Surah Name	English Meaning	Surah No.	Fre-quency
31. Al-Zummar	The Groups	39	12
32. Ghafir	The Forgiver	40	7
33. Fussilat	Explained in Detail	41	3
34. Al-Shura	Consultation	42	2
35. Al-Zuhkruf	Gold Adornment	43	2
36. Al-Ahqaaf	The Winding Sand	46	4
37. Muhammad	Prophet Muhammad	74	7
38. Al-Fath	Victory	48	3
39. Al-Hujurat	The Inner Apartments	49	12
40. Al-Zariyat	The Winds	51	1
41. Al-Hadeed	Iron	57	7
42. Al-Mujadalah	The Woman who Pleads	58	11
43. Al-Hashr	The Gathering	59	12
44. Al-Mumtahana	The Women to be Examined	60	6
45. Al-Saff	Battle Array	61	1
46. Al-Jumu'ah	Friday	62	1
47. Al-Munafiqoon	The Hypocrites	63	1
48. Al-Taghabun	Mutual Loss and Gain	64	4
49. Al-Talaq	Divorce	65	9
50. Al-Tahreem	Holding to be Forbidden	66	2
51. Nooh	Noah	71	1
52. Al-Jinn	The Jinn	72	2

Continuation   **TABLE III ALLAHA**

Surah Name	English Meaning	Surah No.	Fre-quency
53. Al-Muzzammil	Folded in Garment	73	3
54. Al-Insan	Mankind	76	1
55. Al-'Alaq	The Leech- Like Clot	96	1
56. Al-Baiynah	The Clear Evidence	98	1

TABLE IV ALLAHI

Surah Name	English Meaning	Surah No.	Fre-quency
1. Al-Fatihah	The Opening	1	1
2. Al–Baqarah	The Cow	2	99
3. Al-Imran	The Family of Imran	3	85
4. An-Nisaa'	The Women	4	91
5. Al-Maidah	The Table Spread	5	41
6. Al –An'am	The Cattle	6	50
7. Al-A'raf	The Heights	7	35
8. Al-Anfal	The Booties	8	22
9. Al-Tawbah	Repentance	9	64
10. Yunus	Yunus	10	33
11. Hood	Hud	11	25
12. Yusuf	Joseph	12	26
13. Al-Ra'ad	Thunder	13	16
14.	Abraham	14	19
15. Al-Hijr	The Rocky Tract	15	1
16. Al-Nahl	The Bees	16	41
17. Al-Israa'	Night Travel	17	5
18. Al-Kahf	The Cave	18	7

Continuation

TABLE IV ALLAHI

Surah Name	English Meaning	Surah No.	Fre-quency
19. Mariam	Mary	19	5
20. Taha	Taha	20	1
21. Al-Anbiyaa'	The Prophets	21	5
22. Al-Hajj	Pilgrimage	22	25
23. Al-Mu'minoon	The Believers	23	7
24. Al-Noor	The Light	24	26
25. Al-Furqan	The Criterion	25	4
26. Al-Shu'araa'	The Poets	26	3
27. Al-Naml	The Ants	27	18
28. Al-Qasass	Narrations	28	12
29. Al-`Ankaboot	Spider	29	21
30. Al-Room	The Romans	30	14
31. Luqman	Luqman	31	14
32. Al-Ahzab	The Confederation	33	30
33. Saba'	Saba'	34	6
34. Fatir	The Originator of Creation	35	18
35. Yaseen	Abbreviated Letter	36	1
36. Al-Saaffaat	The Groups	37	10
37. Saad	Abbreviated letter	38	2
38. Al-Zumar	The Groups	39	23
39. Ghafir	The Forgiver	40	28
40. Fussilat	Explained in Details	41	6
41. Al-Shura	Consultation	42	11
42. Al-Dukhan	Smoke	44	2
43. Al-Jathiyah	Bowing the Knees	45	12
44. Al-Ahqaaf	Winding Sand-Tracts	46	11

Continuation

TABLE IV ALLAHI

Surah Name	English Meaning	Surah No.	Fre-quency
45. Muhammad	Prophet Muhammad	47	5
46. Al-Fath	Victory	48	15
47. Al-Hujurat	The Inner Apartments	49	8
48. Qaf	Abbreviated Letter	50	1
49. Al-Zariyat	The Winds That Scatter	51	2
50. Al-Toor	The Mount	52	2
51. Al-Najm	The Star	53	4
52. Al-Hadeed	Iron	57	17
53. Al-Mujadalah	The Woman Who Pleads	58	11
54. Al-Hashr	The Gathering	59	8
55. Al-Mumtahana	The Woman to Be Examined	60	6
56. Al-Saff	Battle Array	61	12
57. Al-Jumu'ah	Friday	62	7
58. Al-Munafiqoon	The Hypocrites	63	7
59. Al-Taghabun	Mutual Loss & Gain	64	7
60. Al-Talaq	Divorce	65	8
61. Al-Tahreem	Holding To Be Forbidden	66	3
62. Al-Mulk	Dominion	67	1
63. Al-Haaqqah	The Sure Reality	69	1
64. Al-Ma'arij	The Ways of Ascent	70	1
65. Nooh	The Prophet Noah	71	3

Continuation

TABLE IV ALLAHI

Surah Name	English Meaning	Surah No.	Frequency
66. Al-Jinn	The Jinn	72	7
67. Al-Muzzammil	Folded in Garment	73	3
68. Al-Insan	Mankind	76	2
69. Al-Infitar	The Cleaving Asunder	82	1
70. Al-Burooj	The Zodiacal Signs	85	1
71. Ash-Shams	The Sun	91	2
72. Al-Baiynah	The Clear Evidence	98	1
73. Al-Humazah	The Scandal Monger	104	1
74. Al-Nasr	Help	110	2

XII. NAMES OF THE QUR'AN (Part I)

A. General

Qur'an is the Book from Allah revealed to Prophet Muhammad in Arabic language for a period of twenty-three years. This Book is meant to all human beings including Christians, Jews, Hindus, Buddhists, Agnostics, Atheists, and Muslims. This Book also is meant for non-human beings such as Jinns and other living creatures in the universe (Qur'an 72:1-17 and 46:29).

In order to appreciate the Qur'an, the power of its Message and its effects on human beings, one should read it in its original language. Its originality, totality and language are all documented and authenticated. Millions of people, Arabs and non-Arabs have memorized it by heart. One has to read the following Ayah to recognize its power, its impact and its influence in the universe. In Surah Al-Hashr (The Gathering), Allah says the following:

لَوۡ أَنزَلۡنَا هَٰذَا الۡقُرۡءَانَ عَلَىٰ جَبَلٍ لَّرَأَيۡتَهُۥ خَٰشِعًا مُّتَصَدِّعًا مِّنۡ خَشۡيَةِ اللَّهِ وَتِلۡكَ الۡأَمۡثَٰلُ نَضۡرِبُهَا لِلنَّاسِ لَعَلَّهُمۡ يَتَفَكَّرُونَ ۞

Had We sent down this Qur'an on a mountain, verily, you would have seen it humble itself and cleave asunder for fear of God. Such are the similitude which We propound to people, that they may reflect. (59:21)

Muslims are instructed by Allah to read the Qur'an at dawn (Fajr) time on a daily basis so that it will be a witness for them in

this life and the life after. In Surah Al-Israa' (The Night Journey)
Allah says the following:

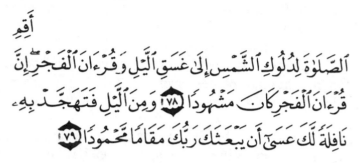

*Establish regular prayers at the sun's decline till
the darkness of the night, and the recital of the Qur'an
in morning prayer, for the recital of dawn is witnessed.
And as for the night, keep awake a part of it as an
additional prayer for you: soon will Your Lord raise you
to a station of Praise and Glory! (17:78 –79)*

The early Muslims paid extreme attention to the study of the
Qur'an. They memorized it and were able to analyze each and
every Ayah, each word and even each letter. They were able to
calculate the total number of Ayat, words and letters. They came
up with the following:

1. Total number of Surahs, (Chapters) : 114
2. Total number of Ayat, (Sentences) : 6,236
3. Total number of Kalimah, (Words) : 77,437
4. Total number of Harf, (Letters) : 323,671

B. Names of Qur'an

To recognize the Qur'an, one has to know the different names
this Book is known with. These names are taken directly from the
Qur'an itself. By going through the list of names of the Qur'an,
one will be able to:

1. Recognize what type of a Book it is.
2. Understand the Message of the Book.
3. Acknowledge its Wisdom and its Universality.
4. Appreciate the Unanimity of all the Prophets and Messengers that were sent by God.
5. Comprehend the Legislative System that came with it.
6. Enjoy the beauty of its melody, rhyme, and rhythm of its words and sentences.

The Qur'an has fifty names all taken directly from the Qur'an. The 51st name has been given by Khalifah Abu Bakr. This listing is grouped under three columns: Transliteration, English meaning and Arabic Names. To know more about each name, you may read next chapter.

TABLE I   NAMES OF THE QUR'AN

Transliteration	English Meaning	Arabic Names
1. Al-Qur'an	The Reading	القـــرآن
2. Al-Kitab	The Book	الكتـاب
3. Al-Furqan	The Criterion	الفـرقـان
4. Al-Zikr	The Reminder	الذكـر
5. Al-Tanzeel	The Revelation	التـنزيـل
6. Ahsan Al-Hadeeth	The Most Beautiful Message, the fairest statements	أحسـن الحـديث
7. Al-Maw'izah	The Exhortation	الموعظـة
8. Al-Hukm	The Judgment of Authority, the Decisive Utterance	الحكـم
9. Al-Hikmah	The Effective Wisdom, Mature Wisdom	الحكـمة
10. Al-Hakeem	The Wise, Full of Wisdom	الحكـيم

Continuation   TABLE I   NAMES OF THE QUR'AN

11. Al-Muhkam	The Basic, Fundamental	المحكم
12. Al-Mutashabah	The Allegoric	المتشابه
13. Al-Shifa'	The Healing	الشفاء
14. Al-Huda	The Guidance	الهدى
15. As-Sirat Al-Mustaqeem	The Straight Path	الصراط المستقيم
16. Habl Allah	The Cable of Allah	حبل اسه
17. Al-Rahmah	The Mercy	الرحمة
18. Al-Rooh	The Spirit	الروح
19. Al-Bayan	The Declaration	البيان
20. Al-Basa'ir	The Insight	البصائر
21. Al-Fasl	The Conclusive Word	الفصل
22. Al-Mufassal	The Fully Explained	المفصل
23. Al-Mathani	The Consistent	المثاني
24. Al-Ni'mah	The Bounty	النعمة
25. Al-Burhan	The Proof	البرهان
26. Al-Qayyim	The Rightly Directing, the Straight	القيم
27. Al-Basheer	The Good Tidings, the Good News	البشير
28. Al-Natheer	The Warner	النذير
29. Al-Muhaymin	The Guardian	المهيمن
30. Al-Noor	The Light	النور
31. Al-Haqq	The Truth	الحق
32. Al-'Azeez	The Invincible, the Unassailable, the One with Exalted Power	العزيز

Continuation **TABLE I   NAMES OF THE QUR'AN**

33. Al-Kareem	The Bounteous, the Noble	الكريم
34. Al-'Azeem	The Grant, the Great	العظيــم
35. Al-Mubarak	The Blessed	المبارك
36. Al-Majeed	The Glorious	المجــد
37. Al-'Ilm	The Knowledge	العلــم
38. Al-'Arabi	The Arabic	العــربى
39. Kalamullah	The Word of Allah	كلام الله
40. Al-Wahy	The Inspiration, the Revelation	الوحى
41. Al-Imam	The Record, the Leader, the Imam	الإمــام
42. Al-Naba'	The News, the Tidings, the Announcement	النــبأ
43. Haqqul Yaqeen	The Certain Truth, the Absolute Truth	حق اليقـين
44. Al-Risalah	The Message	الرســالـة
45. Al-Sidq	The Truth	الصـدق
46. Al-'Ajab	The Marvelous, the Wonderful	العجـب
47. Al-Ayat Al-Bayyinat	The Clear Messages, the Clear Revelations, Signs	آيات بينات
48. Fadlullah	The Bounty of Allah, the Grade of Allah	فضـل الله
49. Al-Kawthar	The Abundance	الكـوثر
50. Al-Munadee	The Crier, the One Calling	المنَادى
51. Al-Mus-haff *	The Bound Sheets	المصحف

* This word was used by Abu Bakr.

81

XIII. NAMES OF THE QUR'AN (Part II)

The title of this chapter is: **"The Names of the Qur'an in the Qur'an"**. There are about fifty (50) different names for the Qur'an, each of which reflects an aspect of its miracle from Allah to us. These names are directly mentioned in the Qur'an. I will try to enumerate most of these names so that they will be of great help to us in our daily lives. The following is a list of the most common names used in the Qur'an about the word Qur'an itself:

A. <u>Qur'an</u>

The first name of course, is Qur'an. The word Qur'an is mentioned in the Qur'an sixty nine (69) times in thirty eight (38) Surahs. For the sake of abbreviation, I will mention few verses related to the word of Qur'an:

1. Allah says in the Qur'an in Surah Al-Baqarah the following:

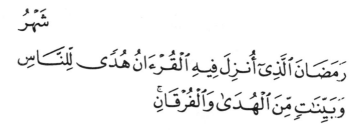

Ramadan is the month in which was sent down the Qur'an, as a guide to mankind, also clear signs for guidance and judgment (between right and wrong). (2:185)

2. Allah also says in the Qur'an about the word Qur'an in Surah Taha the following:

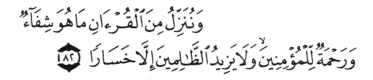

Taha. We have not sent down the Qur'an to you to be (an occasion) for your distress. (20:1-2)

3. In Surah Al-Israa' Allah says the following:

And We reveal of the Qur'an that which is healing and a mercy for believers through it increase the evildoers in naught save ruin. (17:82)

4. Allah also says in Surah Yussuf about the Qur'an:

A.L.R. These are the symbols or verses of the Perspicuous Book. We have sent it down as an Arabic Qur'an in order that you may learn wisdom. (12:1-2).

5. Last but not the least, Allah says about the word Qur'an in the Qur'an in Surah Al-Rahman the following:

God, Most Gracious. It is He Who has taught the Qur'an. He has created man. (55:1-3)

You may read the rest of the verses related to the word Qur'an itself. The following is a list of the verses related to the word of Qur'an:

Surah #	Verses #	Surah #	Verses #
2	185	36	69, 106
4	81	38	1
5	104	39	27, 28
6	19	41	3, 26, 44
7	203	42	7
9	112	43	3, 31
10	15, 37, 61	46	29
12	2,3	47	24
13	33	50	1, 45
15	1, 87, 91	54	17, 22, 32 40
16	98	55	2
17	41, 45, 46, 60, 78, 82, 88, 89, 106	56	77
18	55	59	21
20	2, 113, 114	72	1
25	30, 32	73	4, 20
27	1, 6, 76, 92	75	17, 18
28	85	76	23
30	58	84	21
34	31	85	21

B. The Book

The second word is The Book, Al-Kitab. This word Book has been mentioned in the Qur'an 238 times. Most of them are related to the Qur'an. The following verses are some of them:

1. Allah says in the Qur'an in Surah Al-Baqarah, the following:

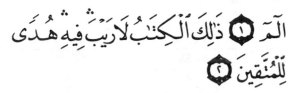

A.L.M. This is the Book; in it is guidance sure, without doubt, to those who fear God. (2:1-2)

2. Allah also says in the Qur'an in Surah Al-Baqarah the following:

الٓمٓ ذَٰلِكَ بِأَنَّ ٱللَّهَ نَزَّلَ ٱلْكِتَٰبَ بِٱلْحَقِّ وَإِنَّ ٱلَّذِينَ ٱخْتَلَفُواْ فِى ٱلْكِتَٰبِ لَفِى شِقَاقٍۭ بَعِيدٍ ﴿١٧٦﴾

Their doom is because God sent down the Book in truth, but those who seek causes of dispute in the Book are in a schism far (from the purpose) (2:176)

3. Allah says in Surah Al-Nissa' (The Women) the following:

إِنَّآ أَنزَلْنَآ إِلَيْكَ ٱلْكِتَٰبَ بِٱلْحَقِّ لِتَحْكُمَ بَيْنَ ٱلنَّاسِ بِمَآ أَرَىٰكَ ٱللَّهُ وَلَا تَكُن لِّلْخَآئِنِينَ خَصِيمًا ﴿١٠٥﴾

We have sent down to you the Book in truth, that you might judge between people, as guided by God; so be not used as an advocate by those who betray their trust. (4:105)

The rest of the verses may be read from the Qur'an if you are interested. Some of which are the following:

Surah #	Verses #	Surah #	Verses #
2	85,89,101	10	1
3	7, 23	29	45
4	122, 136	35	31
5	51	42	14
6	38		

Because the subject of this task is vast and beyond the scope of this presentation, I will mention some of the verses and forms used related to the different names of the Qur'an. The following is a partial list:

C. Al-Furqan

*The third word for the meaning of the Qur'an is:

Furqan; *(Criterion)* *Al-Furqan;* *Furqanan*

Allah says in the Qur'an in Surah Al-Furqan that He revealed the Qur'an to be a criterion so as to be a warner. In this respect Allah says the following:

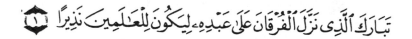

Blessed is He Who has revealed unto His servant the Criterion of right and wrong, that he may be a warner to the people. (25:1)

The rest of the verses related to this word are:

Surah #	Verses #	Surah #	Verses #
2	53, 185	8	29, 41
3	3	21	48

D. Al-Zikr

*The fourth name for the Qur'an is:

Zikr, (Reminder) *Al-Zikr* *Zikri* *Zikrina*

Allah says in the Qur'an in Surah Al-Imran that the Qur'an is a wise reminder. Allah says:

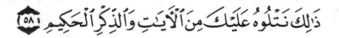

This which We recite unto you is a revelation and a wise reminder. (3:58)

Some other verses are: (15:6), (15:9), 16:44), (36:11), and (38:1).

E. Al-Tanzeel

*The fifth name for the Qur'an is:
Tanzeel (Revelation) *Al-Tanzeel* *Tanzeelan*
Tanzeela *Tanzeelun*

Allah says in the Qur'an in Surah Ash-Shu'ara' that the Qur'an is a revelation from Allah Who is the Lord of the Universe.

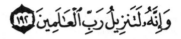

And lo! It is a revelation of the Lord of the world. (26:192)

Some other verses are: (36:5), (41:2), and (41:42).

F. Ah-sanul Hadeeth

*The sixth name for the Qur'an is:

Ahsanul Hadeeth (Best statement)

Allah says in the Qur'an in Surah Az-Zumar that the Qur'an is the best statement from Allah to people. For those who believe in Allah, will benefit from it tremendously. Allah says:

اللَّهُ نَزَّلَ أَحْسَنَ الْحَدِيثِ كِتَابًا مُّتَشَابِهًا مَّثَانِيَ تَقْشَعِرُّ مِنْهُ جُلُودُ الَّذِينَ يَخْشَوْنَ رَبَّهُمْ ثُمَّ تَلِينُ جُلُودُهُمْ وَقُلُوبُهُمْ إِلَىٰ ذِكْرِ اللَّهِ ذَٰلِكَ هُدَى اللَّهِ يَهْدِي بِهِ مَن يَشَاءُ وَمَن يُضْلِلِ اللَّهُ فَمَا لَهُ مِنْ هَادٍ ﴿٢٣﴾

Allah has revealed (From time to time), the most beautiful Message in the form of a Book, consistent with itself, (yet) repeating (its teaching in various aspects): The skins of those who fear their Lord tremble threat; then their skins and their hearts do soften to the remembrance of Allah. Such is the guidance of Allah; He guides therewith whom He pleases, but such as Allah leaves to stray, can have none to guide. (39:23)

G. Al-Maw'izah

*The seventh name for the Qur'an is:

Maw'izatun   (Admoniation)   Al-Maw'izah   Maw'izatan

Allah says in the Qur'an in Surah Al-Imran that the Qur'an is an admonition from Allah to those who heed in Him:

هَٰذَا بَيَانٌ لِّلنَّاسِ وَهُدًى وَمَوْعِظَةٌ لِّلْمُتَّقِينَ ﴿١٣٨﴾

This is a declaration for mankind, a guidance and an admonition unto those who ward off (evil). (3:138)

H. Al-Hukm

*The eighth name for the Qur'an is:

Hukm   (Decisive Utterance)   *Al-Hukm   Hukman*

Allah says in the Qur'an in Surah Al-Ra'ad that the Qur'an was revealed as a law to be enforced. He says:

وَكَذَٰلِكَ أَنزَلْنَٰهُ حُكْمًا عَرَبِيًّا

Thus have We revealed it, a decisive utterance in Arabic...(13:37)

89

The other verses are (3:79). (5:53), (6:89),

I. Al-Hikmah

*The ninth name for the Qur'an is:

Hikmah (Wisdom) *Al-Hikmah*

Allah says in the Qur'an in Surah Al-Qamar that the Qur'an was revealed as an effective wisdom to guide mankind. He says:

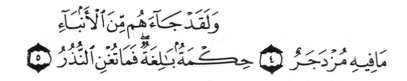

And surely there has come unto them news whereof the purport should deter, effective wisdom; but warnings avail not. (54:4-5)

Some of the other verses are (2:231), (3:81), (17:39), and (33:34).

J. Al-Hakeem

*The tenth name for the meaning of the Qur'an is:

Hakeem (Wise) *Al-Hakeem*

Allah says in Surah Yasin that the Qur'an is the wise Book sent from Allah to all mankind:

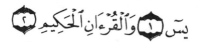

Ya Sin. By the wise Qur'an. (36:1-2)

K. Al-Muhkam

*The eleventh name for the meaning of the Qur'an is:

Muhkam   (Perfection)   *Uhkimat*

Allah says in the Qur'an in Surah Hud that the Qur'an is the most perfect Book ever revealed to mankind.

الٓرۚ كِتَٰبٌ أُحْكِمَتْ ءَايَٰتُهُۥ ثُمَّ فُصِّلَتْ مِن لَّدُنْ حَكِيمٍ خَبِيرٍ ۝

Alif. Lam. Ra. This is a Scripture the revelations whereof are perfected and then expounded it comes from One Wise, Informed. (11:1)

Some other verses are (3:7) and (47:20).

L. Al-Mutashabah

*The twelfth name for the Qur'an is:

Al-Mutashabah   (Allegoric)

Allah says in the Qur'an in Surah Al-'Imran that the Qur'an is a perfect book which has similar or allegoric verses:

هُوَ

ٱلَّذِىٓ أَنزَلَ عَلَيْكَ ٱلْكِتَٰبَ مِنْهُ ءَايَٰتٌ مُّحْكَمَٰتٌ هُنَّ أُمُّ ٱلْكِتَٰبِ وَأُخَرُ مُتَشَٰبِهَٰتٌ فَأَمَّا ٱلَّذِينَ فِى قُلُوبِهِمْ زَيْغٌ فَيَتَّبِعُونَ مَا تَشَٰبَهَ

He is Who has revealed unto you (Muhammad) the Scripture wherein are clear revelations- they are the substance of the Book- and others (which are) allegorical..."(3:7)

M. Shifaa'

*The thirteenth name for the Qur'an is:

Shifaa'   (Healer)

Allah says in the Qur'an in Surah Al-Israa' that the Qur'an is a healer and a mercy to the believers:

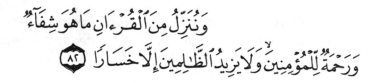

And We reveal of the Qur'an that which is a healing and a mercy for believers though it increases the evil-doers in naught save ruin. (17:82)

Some other verses are (10:57), (16:69), (17:82) and (41:44).

N. Al-Huda

*The fourteenth name for the Qur'an is:

Hudan   (Guidance)   Hudaya   Al-Huda

Allah says in the Qur'an in Surah Al-Baqarah that the Qur'an was revealed as a guidance to those who believe in Allah:

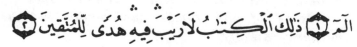

Alif. Lam. Meem. This is the Scripture wherein there is no doubt, a guidance unto those who ward off (evil). (2:1-2)

The other verses are (2:38), (2:97), (9:34) and (17:94).

O. As-Sirat Al-Mustaqeem

*The fifteenth name for the Qur'an is:

As-Sirat Al-Mustaqeem   (Straight path)

Allah says in the Qur'an in Surah Al-An'am that this Qur'an is the straight path of Allah to be followed:

$$وَأَنَّ هَٰذَا صِرَٰطِى مُسْتَقِيمًا فَٱتَّبِعُوهُ وَلَا تَتَّبِعُوا۟ ٱلسُّبُلَ فَتَفَرَّقَ بِكُمْ عَن سَبِيلِهِۦ ذَٰلِكُمْ وَصَّىٰكُم بِهِۦ لَعَلَّكُمْ تَتَّقُونَ ١٥٣$$

And He commands you, saying: This is My Straight Path, so follow it. Follow not other ways, lest you be parted from His way. This has He ordained for you, that you may ward off (evil). (6:153)

P. Habl Allah

*The sixteenth name of the Qur'an is:

Habl Allah   (The Rope of Allah)

Allah says in the Qur'an in Surah Al-'Imran that believers should hold all together to the rope of Allah so as to be successful.

$$وَٱعْتَصِمُوا بِحَبْلِ ٱللَّهِ جَمِيعًا وَلَا تَفَرَّقُوا$$

And hold fast, all of you together, to the cable (rope) of Allah, and do not separate. (3:103)

Q. <u>Rahmah</u>

*The seventeenth name of the Qur'an is:

Rahmah   (Mercy)

Allah says in the Qur'an in Surah Al-Israa' that the Qur'an was revealed as a mercy and as a healer to the believers:

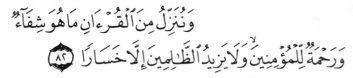

And We reveal of the Qur'an that which is a healing and a Mercy for believers though it increases the evil-doers in naught save ruin. (17:82).

R. <u>Rooh</u>

*The eighteenth name of the Qur'an is:

Rooh   (Spirit)

Allah says in the Qur'an in Surah Ash-Shura that the Qur'an is a spirit from Allah and a light to guide mankind.

$$وَكَذَٰلِكَ أَوْحَيْنَا إِلَيْكَ رُوحًا مِّنْ أَمْرِنَا مَا كُنتَ تَدْرِى مَا ٱلْكِتَٰبُ$$
$$وَلَا ٱلْإِيمَٰنُ وَلَٰكِن جَعَلْنَٰهُ نُورًا نَّهْدِى بِهِۦ مَن نَّشَآءُ مِنْ عِبَادِنَا$$
$$وَإِنَّكَ لَتَهْدِىٓ إِلَىٰ صِرَٰطٍ مُّسْتَقِيمٍ ٥٢$$

94

And thus have We inspired in you (Muhammad) a Spirit of Our Command. You knew not what the Scripture was, nor what the Faith. But We have made it a light whereby We guide whom We will of our bondmen. And lo! You verily do guide unto a right path. (42:52).

S. Bayan

*The nineteenth name for the Qur'an is:

Bayan   (Declaration)

Allah says in Surah Al-Imran that the Qur'an is a declaration to people to guide them and to advise them:

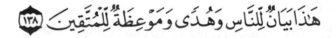

This is a declaration for mankind, a guidance and an admonition unto those who ward off (evil). (3:138).

T. Basaa-irr

* The twentieth name for the Qur'an is:

Basaa-irr   (Proofs, Insight)

Allah says in the Qur'an in Surah Al-A'raf that the Qur'an is sent as a proof, as a mercy and as a guide to mankind.

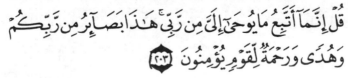

Say: I follow only that which is inspired in me from your Lord. This Qur'an is Insight (as these verses are clear proofs) from your Lord, and a guidance and a mercy for a people that believe. (7:203)

U. Fassl

The twenty-first name for the Qur'an is: Fassl   (Conclusive)

Allah says in the Qur'an in Surah Al-Tariq that the Qur'an is a conclusive word and a decisive word of Allah:

Lo! This Qur'an is a conclusive word.   It is no pleasantry. (86:13-14)

V. Mufassal

*The twenty-second name for the Qur'an is:

Mufassal	Mufassalan
Tafseel	Fussilat (Fully explained)

Allah says in the Qur'an in Surah Al-An'am that the Qur'an was revealed with detailed explanation to every thing we ask. Those who are believers will appreciate it well:

أَفَغَيْرَاللَّهِ

أَبْتَغِي حَكَمًا وَهُوَالَّذِى أَنزَلَ إِلَيْكُمُ الْكِتَبَ مُفَصَّلًا

وَالَّذِينَ ءَاتَيْنَهُمُ الْكِتَبَ يَعْلَمُونَ أَنَّهُۥ مُنَزَّلٌ مِّن رَّبِّكَ بِالْحَقِّ

فَلَا تَكُونَنَّ مِنَ الْمُمْتَرِينَ ۝

96

Shall I seek other than Allah for Judge, when He it is Who has revealed unto you this Scripture, fully explained: Those unto whom We gave the Scripture (aforetime) know that it is revealed from your Lord in truth. So be not you O Muhammad of the waverers. (6:114).

Some other verses are (6:97,98,126), (10:37), (11:1), (17:12), and (41:3),

W. Al-Mathani

*The twenty-third name for the Qur'an is:

Mathani   (Repeated injunctions)   Al-Mathani

Allah says in Qur'an in Surah Al-Hijr that the other name for the Qur'an is the oft-repeated verses:

We have given you seven of the oft-repeated verses and the Great Qur'an. (15:87).

X. Ni'mah

*The twenty-fourth name for the Qur'an is:

Ni'mah   (Bounty)

Allah says in the Qur'an in Surah Al-Duha that the Qur'an is a bounty from Allah:

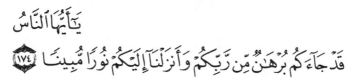

وَأَمَّا بِنِعْمَةِ رَبِّكَ فَحَدِّثْ ﴿١١﴾

Therefore of the bounty of your Lord be your discourse. (93:11)

Y. Burhan

*The twenty-fifth name of the Qur'an is:

Burhan   (Proof)

Allah says in the Qur'an in Surah An-Nisaa' that the Qur'an is a proof from Allah:

يَٰٓأَيُّهَا ٱلنَّاسُ

قَدْ جَآءَكُم بُرْهَٰنٌ مِّن رَّبِّكُمْ وَأَنزَلْنَآ إِلَيْكُمْ نُورًا مُّبِينًا ﴿١٧٤﴾

O mankind! Manifest proof has indeed come to you from your Lord and We have sent down to you a clear light. (4:174).

Z. Qaiyem

*The twenty-sixth name of the Qur'an is:

Qaiyem   (Rightly directing)

Allah says in the Qur'an in Surah Al-Kahf that the Qur'an is the rightly directing Book and a very valuable one:

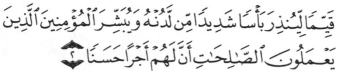

قَيِّمًا لِّيُنذِرَ بَأْسًا شَدِيدًا مِّن لَّدُنْهُ وَيُبَشِّرَ ٱلْمُؤْمِنِينَ ٱلَّذِينَ
يَعْمَلُونَ ٱلصَّٰلِحَٰتِ أَنَّ لَهُمْ أَجْرًا حَسَنًا ﴿٢﴾

Book...Rightly directing, to give warning of severe punishment from Him and to give good news to the believers. (18:2).

AA. Basheer & Natheer

*The twenty-seventh and twenty-eighth names of the Qur'an are:

Basheer & Natheer   (Glad Tidings and Warning)

Allah says in the Qur'an in Surah Fussilat that the Qur'an is meant to be a Book of glad tidings and a warning:

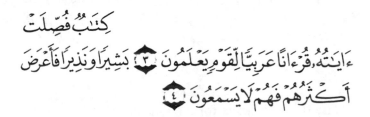

A Scripture whereof the verses are expounded, a lecture in Arabic for people who have knowledge: good tidings and a warning. But most of them turn away so that they hear not. (41:3-4).

BB. Muhaymin

*The twenty-ninth name for the Qur'an is:

Muhaymin   (Guardian over, Watcher over)

Allah says in the Qur'an in Surah Al-Ma'idah that the Qur'an was sent as a Guardian over and a watcher over so that we may use it as a guide in our daily lives:

$$وَأَنزَلْنَآ إِلَيْكَ ٱلْكِتَٰبَ$$

$$بِٱلْحَقِّ مُصَدِّقًا لِّمَا بَيْنَ يَدَيْهِ مِنَ ٱلْكِتَٰبِ وَمُهَيْمِنًا$$

$$عَلَيْهِ فَٱحْكُم بَيْنَهُم بِمَآ أَنزَلَ ٱللَّهُ وَلَا تَتَّبِعْ أَهْوَآءَهُمْ$$

$$عَمَّا جَآءَكَ مِنَ ٱلْحَقِّ لِكُلٍّ جَعَلْنَا مِنكُمْ شِرْعَةً وَمِنْهَاجًا$$

And unto you have We revealed the Scripture with the truth, confirming whatever Scripture was before it, and a watcher over it. So judge between them by that which Allah has revealed, and follow not their desires away from the truth which has come unto you. (5:48).

CC. Noor

*The thirtieth name for the Qur'an is:

Noor   (Light)

Allah says in the Qur'an in Surah Al-A'raf that the Qur'an is the light from Allah:

$$فَٱلَّذِينَ ءَامَنُوا بِهِۦ وَعَزَّرُوهُ وَنَصَرُوهُ وَٱتَّبَعُوا$$

$$ٱلنُّورَ ٱلَّذِىٓ أُنزِلَ مَعَهُۥٓ أُوْلَٰٓئِكَ هُمُ ٱلْمُفْلِحُونَ ١٥٧$$

Then those who believe in him and honor him, and help him, and follow the light which is sent down with him; they are the successful ones.(7:157).

100

DD. <u>Haqq</u>

*The thirty-first name of the Qur'an is: Haqq   (Truth)

Allah says in the Qur'an in Surah Al-Anbiya' that the Qur'an is the truth from Allah which breaks the heads of the false:

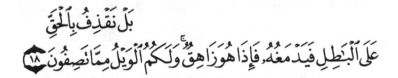

Nay, but We hurl the true against the false, and it does break its head and lo! It vanishes. And yours will be woe for that which you ascribe unto Him. (21:18)

EE.   'Azeez

*The thirty-second name of the Qur'an is:

'Azeez   (Unassailable, Invincible)

Allah says in the Qur'an in Surah Fussilat that the Qur'an is a mighty and unassailable book:

Those who disbelieve in the Reminder when it comes to them, and surely it is an Invincible Book. (41:41)

FF.   <u>Kareem</u>

*The thirty-third name of the Qur'an in the Qur'an is:

Kareem   (Noble, Bounteous)

Allah says in the Qur'an in Surah Al-Waqi'ah that the Qur'an is a noble and bounteous Book from Allah:

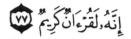

Surely it is a bounteous noble Qur'an. (56:77)

GG. 'Atheem ' Azeem

*The thirty-fourth name of the Qur'an in the Qur'an is:

'Atheem 'Azeem   (Grand, great)

Allah says in the Qur'an in Surah Al-Hijr that the Qur'an is a grand and a great Book:

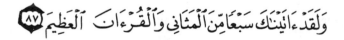

And certainly We have given you seven oft-repeated verses and the grand great Qur'an. (15:87)

HH. Mubarak

*The thirty-fifth name of the Qur'an from the Qur'an is:

Mubarak   (Blessed)

Allah says in the Qur'an in Surah Al-Anbiya' that the Qur'an is a Blessed Book to remind people of their duties towards Allah:

وَهَٰذَا ذِكْرٌ مُّبَارَكٌ أَنزَلْنَٰهُ أَفَأَنتُمْ لَهُۥ مُنكِرُونَ ۝

And this is a blessed Reminder, which We have revealed. Will you then deny it? (21:50)

II. Majeed

*The thirty-sixth name of the Qur'an is:

Majeed   (Glorious)

Allah says in the Qur'an in Surah Qaf that the Qur'an is a Glorious Book from Allah:

قٓ ۚ وَٱلْقُرْءَانِ ٱلْمَجِيدِ ۝

Qaf, by the glorious Qur'an. (50:1).

JJ. 'Ilm

*The thirty-seventh name of the Qur'an is:

'Ilm   (Knowledge)

Allah says in the Qur'an in Surah Al-'Imran that the Qur'an is a Book of the True Knowledge from Allah.

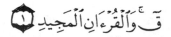

Whoever then disputes with you in this matter after the knowledge that has come to you - - - - (3:61)

KK. 'Arabi

*The thirty-eighth name of the Qur'an is:

'Arabi   (Arabic)   'Arabiyyan   'Arabiyyun   Al-'Arabi

Allah affirms that the Qur'an was revealed in Arabic language so as we get the real knowledge. In this respect Allah says in the Qur'an in Surah Yussuf:

A.L.R. These are the Symbols or verses of the Perspicuous Book. We have sent it down as an Arabic Qur'an, in order that you may learn wisdom. (12:1-2)

LL. Kalamullah

*The thirty-ninth name of the Qur'an is:

Kalamullah   (The Word of Allah)

Allah has already approved that the Qur'an is the word of Allah Himself, and Allah says in the Qur'an in Surah Tawbah the following:

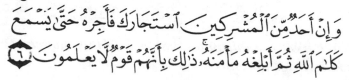

If one amongst the Pagans ask you for asylum, grant it to him, so that he may hear the Word of God; and then escort him to where he can be secure. That is because they are men without knowledge. (9:6).

MM. <u>Wahy</u>

*The fortieth name of the Qur'an from the Qur'an:

Wahy   (Revelation)

Allah says in the Qur'an in Surah Al-Najm that this Qur'an is indeed a Revelation of Allah on Prophet Muhammad (pbuh). In this respect Allah says:

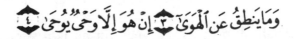

Nor does he say (aught) of (his own) Desire. It is no less than Inspiration sent down to him. (53:3-4)

NN. <u>Imam</u>

*The forty-first name of the Qur'an is:

Imam   (Leader)

Allah informs us that in the Day of Judgement each one of us will be called upon with his leader, referring to their books. For the Muslims, their book is of course the Holy Qur'an. In this regard Allah says in the Qur'an in Surah Al-Israa':

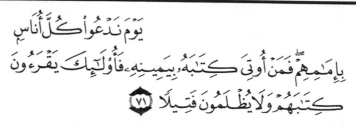

One day We shall call together all human beings with their respective Imams: those who are given their record in their right hand will read it (with pleasure), and they will not be dealt with unjustly in the least. (17:71).

OO.   Naba'

*The forty-second name of the Qur'an is:

Naba'   (News, Tidings, Announcement)   Al-Naba'

Allah informs us that the Qur'an is a very important Book of statements and information. We should accept it and take it as a source of happiness and mercy from Allah. In this regard Allah says in the Qur'an in Surah Saad the following:

Say: That is a Message Supreme (above all), from which you do turn away. (38:67-68)

PP. Haqqul Yaqeen

*The forty-third name of the Qur'an is:

Haqqul Yaqeen   (The Truthful Revelation)

106

The Qur'an is the ultimate truth from Allah. This truthful Book is the one to be believed in because it is the book of Reason and Logic. In this respect, Allah says in the Qur'an in Surah Al-Haaqqah:

وَإِنَّهُ لَحَقُّ ٱلْيَقِينِ ۞ فَسَبِّحْ بِٱسْمِ رَبِّكَ ٱلْعَظِيمِ ۞

But verily it is Truth of assured certainty. So glorify the name of your Lord Most High. (69:51-52).

QQ.   Resalah

*The forty-fourth name of the Qur'an is:

Resalah   (Message)   Resalat   Resalata

The Qur'an is considered to be a letter and a message from Allah to all mankind, revealed unto Prophet Muhammad (pbuh). The Prophet in turn delivered it and is going to be a witness for Allah in the Day of Judgement. In this regard we read in the Qur'an in Surah Al-Ma'idah:

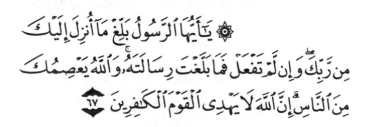

O Apostle! Proclaim the Message which has been sent to you from your Lord. If you did not, you would not have fulfilled and proclaimed His Mission. And God will defend you from men (who mean mischief). For God guided not those who reject faith. (5:67).

RR. Sidq

*The forty-fifth name of the Qur'an is: Sidq (Truth) Assidq

We are told that the Qur'an is really the Book of Truth. Whoever does not believe in it, will be taken to hell in the Day of Judgement. While those who believed in it are the ones who heed in God. In this respect Allah says in Surah Al-Zumar the following:

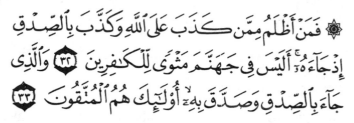

Who then, do more wrong than one who utters a lie concerning Allah, and rejects the Truth when it comes to him: is there not in Hell an abode for unbelievers? And he who brings the Truth and he who confirms (and supports) it-such are the men who do right. (39:32-33)

SS. 'Ajab

*The forty-sixth name of the Qur'an is:

'Ajab   (Fascinating)   'Ajaban   Al 'Ajab

The Qur'an is a fascinating book. Whoever believes in it, will be guided to the straight path. It is very fascinating to the extent that if you listen to its recitation you will be attracted to it as if it has magic, charm and beauty. Even the Jinns have been attracted to it and some of them believed in it. Allah says in Surah Al-Jinn:

108

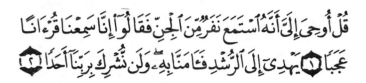

Say it has been revealed to me that a company of Jinns listened to the Qur'an. They said, 'We have really heard a wonderful recital. It gives guidance to the Right, and we have believed therein: we shall not join (in worship) any (gods) with our Lord. (72:1-2)

TT. Ayat Baiyinat

*The forty-seventh name of the Qur'an is:

Ayat Baiyinat   (Clear Miracles)

The Qur'an is sent with clear miracles so that the believers will appreciate its contents.   In this regard Allah says in Surah Al'Ankaboot:

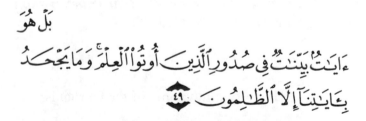

But it is clear revelations in the hearts of those who have been given knowledge, and none deny our revelations save wrongdoers. (29:49)

UU. <u>Fadlullah</u>

*The forty-eighth name of the Qur'an is:

Fadlullah   (Bounty of Allah)

The Qur'an is said to be a bounty of Allah sent to the believers so that they will be happier than all what they obtain in their daily lives. Allah says in Surah Yunus:

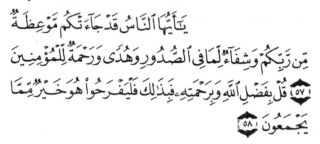

O mankind! There has come to you an admonition from your Lord and a healing for the (diseases) in your heart,- and for those who believe, a Guidance and Mercy. Say: "In the Bounty of Allah. And in His Mercy,-in that let them rejoice": that is better than the (wealth) they hoard.   (10:57-58)

VV. <u>Kawthar</u>

*The forty-ninth name of the Qur'an is:

Kawthar   (Abundance)

The name of the Qur'an was given by Allah as Abundance or (Kawthar). One of the meanings of Kawthar is a name of the Qur'an. Allah revealed a Surah in the Qur'an under this name in particular. The name of the Surah is Kawthar. Allah says to Prophet Muhammad (pbuh):

Lo! We have given you Abundance; so pray unto your Lord, and sacrifice. Lo! It is your insulter (and not you) who is without posterity. (108:1-3)

WW. Munadi

*The fiftieth name of the Qur'an from the Qur'an is:

Munadi   (The Call of One)

The Qur'an was given the name of a caller, a crier or the call of one. The Qur'an calls for belief in Allah. In this respect Allah says in Surah Al-'Imran:

رَبَّنَا إِنَّنَا سَمِعْنَا مُنَادِيًا يُنَادِى لِلْإِيمَٰنِ أَنْ
ءَامِنُوا بِرَبِّكُمْ فَـَٔامَنَّا رَبَّنَا فَٱغْفِرْ لَنَا ذُنُوبَنَا وَكَفِّرْ عَنَّا
سَيِّـَٔاتِنَا وَتَوَفَّنَا مَعَ ٱلْأَبْرَارِ ۝١٩٣

Our Lord! Lo! We have heard a crier calling unto Faith: 'Believe you in your Lord!' Some believed. Our Lord! Therefore forgive us our sins and remit from us our evil deeds, and make us die the death of the righteous. (3:193)

XX. Al-Musshaff

*The fifty-first name of the Qur'an is:

Al-Musshaff   (The Bound Sheets)

The word Musshaff or Al-Musshaff as such has not been used in the Qur'an to mean the Qur'an. The words of Suhuff, Al-Suhuff and Suhufan are used in the Qur'an to either mean the Qur'an or the previous scriptures revealed to Prophets Ibrahim and Musa. However, it was the first caliph, Abu Bakr (may Allah be pleased with him) who used the word Al-Musshaff to refer to the Qur'an. Allah says in the Qur'an in Surah Al-Baiyyinah:

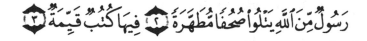

A Messenger from Allah, reading purified pages, containing correct scriptures. (98:2-3)

The previous account is a list of the different beautiful names of the Qur'an given by Allah so that we may be able to appreciate it and to value it tremendously in our daily lives. This means that the Qur'an is a bounty book and a criterion, revealed from Allah in Arabic to be a reminder, a mercy, a guide, an information with truth, a message with the ultimate knowledge, a glad tidings, a warner, a proof fully explained, a noble, a glorious, a healer, a blessed record, a marvelous declaration of news, a fundamental proof, and etc. If we read these adjectives and characteristics about the Qur'an in detail, we will indeed appreciate what the Qur'an is meant by Allah to us. Accordingly we will do our sincere and utmost best to give great reverence and respect to the Qur'an by reading it everyday so that we will be blessed by Allah.

May I request you to start reading the Qur'an as it should be read so that you will please Allah Subhanahu wa Ta'ala. You will then be pleased every minute of your lives. We hope and pray that we take the Qur'an as a personal letter from Allah to us. Ameen.

Let us ask Allah forgiveness.

"The Most beautiful names belong to Allah: so call on Him by them."
(Qur'an 7:180)

113

XIV. MEMORIZERS OF THE QUR'AN

إِنَّا نَحْنُ نَزَّلْنَا ٱلذِّكْرَ وَإِنَّا لَهُۥ لَحَٰفِظُونَ ۝

We have, without doubt, sent down the Qur'an; and
We will assuredly guard it (from corruption). (15:9)

The Qur'an was revealed to Prophet Muhammad for a period of 23 years. It was revealed Ayah by Ayah or a group of Ayat or even Surah by Surah. Every time Angel Jibreel revealed these sections to the Prophet, the latter memorized them immediately. Then he recited them to his companions. They in turn, memorized whatever was recited to them.

Those who stayed with him, lived with him and professed to be with him daily, were able to memorize whatever was revealed to him. The other Muslims who were living far distances did not have the privilege to be among the pioneers of memorizing the Qur'an.

The Qur'an is meant to be memorized, to be recited, to live and to practice its teachings, and to be preached to others. It is to be applied in the private and public life, as well as to be applied on the individual and society levels.

Certain individuals volunteered themselves to be close to the Prophet so that they will be among the pioneers to receive the Message of Islam, to memorize it, to live it, to practice it and to deliver it to others. Those pioneers were small in number. The

Prophet delegated some of them to be the pioneers of memorizing the whole Qur'an. Allah blessed them to devote their lives to be the memorizers of the Qur'an in totality, in pronunciation, in recitation, in its sequential order, and to a certain extent in explaining the meaning of the Ayat in the Qur'an.

Before the death of the Prophet, there were few thousands who memorized the Qur'an. Nowadays, the Qur'an is being memorized by millions of Muslim men and women, as well as by boys and girls of the ages 5-7 years old, and from different parts of the world.

There is no one single book in the history of mankind that has been memorized by millions of people of different language backgrounds as much as the Qur'an. There is no best seller book in the world that has been memorized by anyone at all. The only book that was and is memorized in totally is the Qur'an. It has been memorized from its original language, namely Arabic. The amazing thing is that people who are non-Arabic speakers, were able to read, recite and memorize the Qur'an in Arabic without much difficulty.

The following is a partial list of the companions (men and women) who were among the pioneers who memorized the whole Qur'an. Their efforts gave fruits in preserving the Qur'an through memory and through writings. Nowadays, with the new and advanced technology, the Qur'an is being preserved also through recording on audio and video tapes. It is also being preserved through CD Rom, satellites, World Web, computer and the like.

May Allah bless them all, and we pray to Allah to reward them the best reward in paradise. Our utmost salat and Tassleem are on Prophet Muhammad who was the key personality who received the Qur'an and memorized it before anyone could be able to do so. His inspiration, motivation and his personality inspired thousands in his life time to do the same. He is still inspiring and motivating millions of Muslims to memorize the Qur'an. Indeed, there is special spiritual attraction towards the Qur'an that helped those millions of individuals to love the Qur'an and to memorize it completely.

TABLE I   MEMORIZERS OF THE QUR'AN

Name (Transliteration)	Arabic
1. Abdullah Ibn Masood	عبد الله ابن مسعود
2. Mu'az Ibn Jabal	معاذ ابن جبل
3. Zayd Ibn Thabit	زيد ابن ثابت
4. Huthayfa	حنيفة
5. Abu Musa Al-Ash-'Ari	ابو موسى الاشعرى
6. Abu Hurayrah	ابو هريرة
7. Abu Dardaa'	ابو الدرداء
8. Abdullah Ibn Abbas	عبد الله ابن عباس
9. Abdullah Ibn 'Amr Ibn Al-'Aas	عبد الله ابن عمرو ابن العاص
10. Abdullah Ibn Umar	عبد الله ابن عمر
11. Abdullah Ibn Al-Zubayr	عبد الله ابن الزبير

Name (Transliteration)	Arabic
12. Talha Ibn Al-Zubayr	طلحة ابن الزبير
13. Ubadah Ibn Al-Samit	عبادة ابن الصامت
14. Sa'ad Ibn Abi Waqqass	سعد بن ابي وقاص
15. Abdullah Ibn Al-Saaib	عبد الله ابن السائب
16. Fudalah Ibn 'Ubaid	فضالة ابن عبيد
17. Sa'eed Ibn 'Ubaid	سعيد ابن عبيد
18. Musslamah Ibn Makhlid	مسلمة ابن مخلد
19. Ubayy Ibn Ka'ab	ابيّ ابن كعب
20. Majma' Ibn Jariyah	مجمع بن جارية
21. Abu Zayd Ibn Al-Sakan	ابو زيد ابن السكن
22. Salem Ibn Ma'qal	سالم ابن معقل
23. A'iysha, wife of the Prophet	عائشة زوجة الرسول
24. Hafsa, daughter of Abu Bakr	حفصة ، بنت عمر
25. Umm Salamah, Hind Bint Abi Umaya	ام سلمة ، هند بنت ابي امية

XV. MAKKAH AND MADINAH SURAHS

وَقَالَ ٱلَّذِينَ كَفَرُواْ لَوْلَا نُزِّلَ عَلَيْهِ ٱلْقُرْءَانُ جُمْلَةً

وَٰحِدَةً ۚ كَذَٰلِكَ لِنُثَبِّتَ بِهِۦ فُؤَادَكَ ۖ وَرَتَّلْنَٰهُ تَرْتِيلًا ٣٢

Those who reject faith say: Why is not the Qur'an revealed to him all at once? Thus (is it revealed) that We may strengthen your heart thereby, and We have rehearsed it to you in slow, well-arranged stages, gradually (25:32)

Qur'an was revealed to Prophet Muhammad for a period of 23 years from the age of forty till he died at the age of sixty-three. A total of 114 Chapters (Surahs) were revealed. These Surahs were revealed at different places, times, occasions, situations, etc.

To study the Qur'an one has to realize all these situations so as to appreciate the teachings and the message of the Qur'an. Some of the major topics would be:

1. The Makkah and Madinah Surahs;
2. Those Surahs that were revealed in a city or on the way between the two cities;
3. Some Surahs were revealed in summers, while others were revealed in winters;
4. Some were revealed on earth while others during Israa' and Mi'raaj;
5. Some were revealed during nights, and others during days;
6. Some were revealed as a simple Ayah, while others were revealed as a group of Ayat or even as a whole Surah at one time; and

7.   Other areas of specialties can be studied more in a course by itself and in more detail.

In this section the author is presenting the Makkah and the Madinah Surahs. They are grouped accordingly along with some more information as to their revelations and to their sequential numbering. As one may realize, there are 86 Surahs revealed in Makkah, while 28 Surahs were revealed in Madinah. The Makkah Surahs are short with short verses, contrary to the Madinah Surahs. The latter are long with long verses. Makkah Surahs deal with 'Aqeeda, Tawheed, and Obedience to Allah. They speak about creations of the universe, especially about mankind, angels, jinns, animals, plants, vegetation, planets, rains, mountains, oceans, and other creations. A special emphasis is on the history of the past generations of mankind who refused to obey Allah and how they were destroyed. These Makkah Surahs remind us of our future life in graves, on the Day of Resurrections, the Assembly Day, the Day of Judgement, the A'raf Station, Life in Hell and the final Life in Paradise.

There is still more information to be said about the recognition of the Makkah Surahs. Some of the major observations are the following:

(1) There are fifteen prostrations (sajdah) in fourteen Surahs. All the Surahs that have prostration are Makkah Surahs.

(2) Every Surah that has the word Kallaa is a Makkah Surah. Most of these Surahs that have such a word are found in the last half of the Qur'an. The following is a list of what is said:

119

Surahs Names	English Meaning	Surah & Ayat #
Mariam	Mary	19:79;82
Al –Mu'minoon	The Believers	23:100
Al-Shu'araa'	The Poet	26:15;62
Saba'	The City of Saba	34:27
Al-Ma'aarij	The Ways of Ascent	70:15; 39
Muddathir	One Wrapped Up	74:16;32,53,54
Al-Qiyamah	The Resurrection	75:11; 20;26
Al-Naba'	The Great News	78:4;5
'Abasa	He Frowned	80:11; 23
Al-Infitar	The Cleaving Asunder	82:9
Al-Mutaffifeen	Dealing in Fraud	83:7; 14; 15; 18
Al-Fajr	The Break of Day	89: 17; 21
Al-'Alaq	Read, Proclaim	96:6; 15; 19
Al-Takathur	Piling Up	102:3; 4; 5
Al-Humazah	The Scandal-Monger	104:4

(3) Almost all the Surahs where Allah is addressing people as O mankind! Instead of O you who believe! are considered Makkah Surahs. However, Surah Al-Hajj has O mankind, and it is considered as Madinah or as Makkah Surah.

(4) Most of the Surahs that have stories of prophets are considered Makkah Surah except Surah Al-Baqarah.

(5) All those Surahs that have the story of Adam and Ibliss are Makkah Surahs except Surah Al-Baqarah. Examples to this effect are the following Surahs:

Al-A'raf.................... 7: 11-35
Al-Israa'.................... 17: 61
Al-Kahf.................... 18:50
Taha........................ 20:115-121

(6) Almost all Surahs that start with the Luminous letters are considered Makkah Surah except Al-Baqarah and Al-Imran.

Madinah Surahs are usually long with long verses. The theme of those Surahs are related to legislations of Halal and Haram, establishment of a solid society, establishment of the families, establishment of a state, and the relationship of Muslims with non-Muslims.

These Makkah and Madinah Surahs are listed here for the benefit of the readers. The author wishes to encourage the readers to do more research on the Qur'an.

MAKKAH SURAH

No.	English	Transliteration	Sequen-tial #	Revel-ation#
1.	The Opening	Fatiha	1	5
2.	The Cattle	Al-An'am	6	55
3.	The Heights	Al-A'raf	7	39
4.	Yunus	Yunus	10	51
5.	Hud	Hood	11	52
6.	Joseph	Yusuf	12	53
7.	Abraham	Abraham	14	72
8.	The Rocky Track	Al-Hijr	15	54
9.	The Bees	Al-Nahl	16	70
10.	Night Travel	Al-Israa'	17	50
11.	The Cave	Al-Kahf	18	69
12.	Mary	Mariam	19	44
13.	Taha	Taha	20	45
14.	The Prophets	Al-Anbiya'	21	73
15.	The Believers	Al-Mu'minum	23	74
16.	The Criterion	Al-Furqan	25	42

No.	English	Transliteration	Sequen -tial #	Revela -tion #
17.	The Poets	Al-Shu'ara	26	47
18.	The Ants	Al-Naml	27	48
19.	The Narrators	Al-Qasas	28	49
20.	The Spider	Al-'Ankaboot	29	85
21.	The Romans	Al-Room	30	84
22.	Luqman	Luqman	31	57
23.	Prostration	Al-Sajdah	32	75
24.	Saba	Saba'	34	58
25.	The Originator of Creation	Fatir	35	43
26.	Yaseen	Yasin	36	41
27.	Those Ranged in Ranks	Al-Saffat	37	56
28.	Saad	Sad	38	38
29.	The Crowds	Al-Zumar	39	59
30.	The Believer	Al-Mu'mim	40	60
31.	Ha-Mim Sajdah	Fussilat	41	61
32.	Consultation	Ash-Shura	42	62
33.	Gold Adornments	Az-Zukhruff	43	63
34.	Smoke	Al-Dukhan	44	64
35.	Bowing the knee	Al-Jathiyah	45	65
36.	Winding Sand Tracks	Al-Ahqaf	46	66
37.	Qaf	Qaaf	50	34
38.	Winds that Scatter	Al-Zariyat	51	67
39.	The Mount	Al-Toor	52	76
40.	The Star	Al-Najm	53	23
41.	The Moon	Al-Qamar	54	37
42.	The Inevitable Event	Al-Waqi`ah	56	46
43.	Dominion	Al-Mulk	67	77
44.	The Pen	Al-Qalam	68	2
45.	The Sure Reality	Al-Haqqaq	69	78

No.	English	Transliteration	Sequen -tial #	Revela -tion #
46.	The Ways of Ascent	Al-Ma'arij	70	79
47.	Noah	Nooh	71	71
48.	The Spirit	Al-Jinn	72	40
49.	Folded in Garments	Al-Muzammil	73	3
50.	One Wrapped Up	Al-Muddathir	74	4
51.	The Resurrection	Al-Qiyamah	75	31
52.	Those Sent Forth	Al-Mursalat	77	33
53.	The Great News	Al-Naba'	78	80
54.	Those Who Tear Out	Al-Naazi'aat	79	81
55.	He Frowned	'Abasa	80	24
56.	The Folding Up	Al-Takweer	81	7
57.	The Clearing Asunder	Al-Infitar	82	82
58.	Dealing in Fraud	Al-Mutaffifeen	83	86
59.	The Rending Asunder	Al-Inshiqaq	84	83
60.	The Zodiacal Signs	Al-Burooj	85	27
61.	The Night Visitant	Al-Taariq	86	36
62.	The Most High	Al-A'laa	87	8
63.	The Over-whelming Event	Al-Ghashiyah	88	68
64.	The Dawn	Al-Fajr	89	10
65.	The City	Al-Balad	90	35
66.	The Sun	Al-Shams	91	26
67.	The Night	Al-Lail	92	9
68.	The Glorious Morning Light	Al-Duha	93	11
69.	The Expansion	Al-Inshirah	94	12
70.	The Fig	Al-Teen	95	28
71.	The Clot Congealed Blood	Al-`Alaq	96	1
72.	The Night Power	Al-Qadr	97	25
73.	Those that Run	Al-'Aadiyat	100	14
74.	Day of Noise and Clamor	Al-Qaari`ah	101	30

No.	English	Transliteration	Sequen -tial #	Revela -tion #
75.	Piling Up	Al-Takathur	102	16
76.	Time Through Ages	Al'Assr	103	13
77.	Scandal Monger	Al-Humazah	104	32
78.	The Elephant	Al-Feel	105	19
79.	Quraish	Quraish	106	29
80.	Neighborly Needs	Al-Maa'oon	107	17
81.	Abundance	Al-Kawthar	108	15
82.	Those Who Reject Faith	Al-Kaafiroon	109	18
83.	The Father of Flame	Al-Lahab	111	6
84.	Purity	Al-Ikhlas	112	22
85.	The Dawn	Al-Falaq	113	20
86.	Mankind	Al-Naas	114	21

MADINAH SURAHS

No	English	Transliteration	Sequen -tial #	Reve- lation #
1.	The Heifer (Cow)	Al-Baqarah	2	87
2.	The Family of 'Imran	Al-'Imran	3	89
3.	The Women	An-Nisaa''	4	92
4.	The Table Spread	Al-Maidah	5	112
5.	The Spoils of War	Al-Anfaal	8	88
6.	The Repentance of The Disavowal	Al-Tawbah Baraa-ah	9	113
7.	The Thunder	Al-Ra'd	13	96
8.	The Pilgrimage	Al-Hajj	22	103
9.	The Light	Al-Noor	24	102
10.	The Confederates	Al-Ah-zaab	33	90
11.	Muhammad	Muhammad	47	95
12.	The Victory	Al-Fath	48	111

No.	English	Transliteration	Sequen -tial #	Revela -tion #
13.	The Inner Apartments	Al-Hujuraat	49	106
14.	The Merciful	Al-Rahman	55	97
15.	Iron	Al-Hadeed	57	94
16.	The Woman Who Pleads	Al-Mujaadalah	58	105
17.	The Gathering	Al-Hashr	59	101
18.	The Woman to be Examined	Al-Mumtahanah	60	91
19.	The Battle Array	Al-Saff	61	109
20.	Friday/Assembly	Al-Jumu'ah	62	110
21.	The Hypocrites	Al-Munafiqoon	63	104
22.	Mutual Loss or Gain	Al-Taghaabun	64	108
23.	Divorce	Al-Talaaq	65	99
24.	Prohibition	Al-Tahreem	66	107
25.	Man Or The Time	Al-Insaan/ Al-Dahr	76	98
26.	The Clear Evidence	Al-Bayyinah	98	100
27.	The Convulsion (Earthquake)	Al-Zalzalah	99	93
28.	The Help	Al-Nassr	110	114

XVI. LUMINOUS LETTERS OF THE QUR'AN

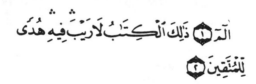

A.L.M. This is the Book; in it is guidance sure, without doubt, to those who fear Allah (2:1-2)

Qur'an is the miracle of Allah to Prophet Muhammad till the Day of Judgement. It was revealed in Arabic to Muhammad who was unlettered. He did not study anywhere, nor was he tutored by any teacher.

The people in the Arabian Peninsula were prolific in the Arabic language, and highly opinionated in composition, prose and poetry. Among other miracles of the Qur'an, it was a challenge to all those who mastered the Arabic language. The Qur'an challenged all those people to synthesize a book similar to the Qur'an (17:88). However, they failed. Then the Qur'an challenged them to formulate ten chapters (Surahs) similar to anyone in the Qur'an (11:13). They automatically failed. Finally, the Qur'an challenged all the poets and the teachers of the Arabic language to bring one chapter (Surah) similar to the Qur'an (2:23). They failed completely.

The final challenge came to them in a simple way. The Arabic alphabets are composed of 28 letters. The Arabs were writing compositions, poetry and prose of so many books and articles. The Qur'an challenged their wisdom with single letters or a combination of letters. They were shocked and baffled with the power of the Qur'anic language: style, composition, contents, rhyme, rhythm, melody, lyric and brevity. A large number became Muslims.

There are twenty-nine Surahs in the Qur'an that have such opening shining or luminous letters. Some are composed of one letter, while others are composed of two, three, four or five letters. They can be classified as follows:

CLASSIFICATION OF LUMINOUS LETTERS IN THE QUR'AN

# of Letter	Arabic	English	Fre-quency	Surah #
1	ص	Saad	(1)	38
	ق	Qaaf	(1)	50
	ن	Noon	(1)	68
2	طه	Ta-ha	(1)	20
	يس	Ta-seen	(1)	27
	طس	Ya-seen	(1)	36
	حم	Ha-meem	(6)	40, 41, 43, 44, 45, and 46
3	الم	Alif. Lam. Meem.	(6)	2, 3, 29, 30, 31, and 32
	الر	Alif. Lam. Ra.	(5)	10, 11, 12, 14, 15
	طسم	Ta-seen-Meem	(2)	26, 28

CLASSIFICATION OF LUMINOUS LETTERS
IN THE QUR'AN (Cont.)

# of Letter	Arabic	English	Frequency	Surah #
4	المص	Alif. Laam. Meem. Saad.	(1)	7
	المر	Alif. Laam. Meem. Raa.	(1)	13
5	كهيعص	Kaaf. Haa. Yaa. Ayn. Saad.	(1)	19
	حمعسق	Haa. Meem. Ayn. Seen. Qaf	(1)	42: 1-2

If one tries to calculate the different luminous letters used in these Surahs (without duplication of any letter), he will find out that they are 14 letters. These are:

1. Alif..
2. Laam..
3. Meem..
4. Saad..
5. Raa..
6. Kaaf..
7. Haa..
8. Yaa..
9. 'Ayn..
10. Taa..
11. Seen..
12. Haa..
13. Qaaf..
14. Noon..

These letters are half of the total number of the Arabic alphabets.

Many 'Ulama' tried to explain the meaning of these letters. Since there is no unanimity among their explanations, the author of this book prefers not to indulge himself into the discussion except the fact that they are signs and miracles from Allah.

These shining letters stand now as outstanding challenge to all those who speak or master the Arabic language. These luminous letters are listed as they appear sequentially and chronologically in the Qur'an. As one reads the list, he recognizes that they are arranged as to Surah name, number of the Surah and the Ayah, English name of the Surah, the Arabic List of the Luminous Letters, and the Transliteration.

LIST OF LUMINOUS LETTERS

Surah Name	Surah Ayah #	English	Arabic Transliteration
1. Al-Baqarah	2:1	The Cow	Alif. Laam. Meem.
2. Al-Imran	3:1	Family of Imran	Alif. Laam. Meem.
3. Al-A'raaf	7:1	The Heights	Alif.Laam. Meem. Saad.
4. Yunus	10:1	Younus	Alif.Laam. Raa.
5. Hood	11:1	Hud	Alif. Laam. Raa.
6. Yusu f	12:1	Joseph	Alif. Laam. Raa.
7. Al-Ra'ad	13:1	Thunder storm	Alif.Laam. Meem.Raa.
8. Ibrahim	14:1	Abraham	Alif.Laam. Raa.
9. Al-Hijr	15:1	The Rocky Tract	Alif.Laam. Raa.
10. Mariam	19:1	Mary	Kaaf. Haa. Yaa.'Ayn. Saad.
11. Taha	20:1	Taha	Taa.Haa.

Surah Name	Surah Ayah #	English	Arabic Transliteration
12.Al-Shu-'araa'	26:1	The Poets	Taa.Seen. Meem.
13. Al-Naml	27:1	The Ants	Taa.Seen.
14. Al-Qasass	28:1	The Narrations	Taa.Seen Meem.
15. Al-'Ankaboot	29:1	The Spider web	Alif.Laam. Meem.
16. Al-Room	30:1	The Romans	Alif.Laam.Meem.
17. Luqman	31:1	Luqman	Alif.Laam.Meem.
18.Al-Sajdah	32:1	Prostration	Alif.Laam Meem.
19. Yaseen	36:1	Yaseen	Yaa.Seen.
20. Saad	38:1	Saad	Saad
21.Ghafir	40:1	Forgiving	Haa.Meem.
22.Fussilat	41:1	Clearly Spelled Out	Haa. Meem.
23.Al-Shura	42:1-2	Consultation	Haa.Meem. Ayn.Seen.Qaaf
24.Al-Zukhruf	43:1	Ornaments	Haa.Meem.
25.Al-Dukhan	44:1	The Smoke	Haa.Meem.
26.Al-Jathiya	45:1	Kneeling Down	Haa.Meem.
27.Al-Ahqaf	46:1	The Sand Dunes	Haa.Meem.
28.Qaaf	50:1	Qaaf	Qaaf
29.Al-Qalam	68:1	The Pen	Noon.

Which none shall touch (The Qur'an) but
those who are clean. [Qur'an, 56:79]

130

XVII. PROSTRATION IN THE QUR'AN

The concept and action of prostration are very important in Islam and in everyone's life. It is important physically, medically, morally, spiritually and biologically. Because of its importance and of its significance, the topic is to be explained through the Qur'an and the Hadith.

The word prostration is mentioned in the Qur'an 92 times in 22 forms and in 32 different Surahs. Allah (swt) revealed a Surah in the Qur'an with the title of Al-Sajdah (Prostration). Allah (swt) says in this Surah the following:

إِنَّمَا يُؤْمِنُ

بِآيَٰتِنَا ٱلَّذِينَ إِذَا ذُكِّرُوا بِهَا خَرُّوا سُجَّدًا وَسَبَّحُوا بِحَمْدِ

رَبِّهِمْ وَهُمْ لَا يَسْتَكْبِرُونَ ۩ ﴿١٥﴾

Only those who believe in Our Signs, who, when they are recited to them, fall down in prostration, and celebrate the praises of their Lord, nor are they (ever) puffed up with pride. (32:15)

Allah (swt) created Adam and taught him all the knowledge that he needed to understand. Then Allah (swt) demanded from all the angels to prostrate to Adam. It seems the prostration was a sign of obedience to Allah (swt), and respect for Adam. As you are aware, all the angels prostrated except Satan (Ibliss), who was from Jinn. Jinns were created from fire, while angels were created from light. Satan was later outcast from heaven and from the Mercy of Allah (swt). This story of prostration of the angels to Adam was mentioned in the Qur'an 21 times. One place in the Qur'an in Surah Al-Hijr (The Rocky Tract) the following is stated:

وَإِذْ قَالَ رَبُّكَ لِلْمَلَٰٓئِكَةِ إِنِّى خَٰلِقٌۢ بَشَرًا مِّن

صَلْصَٰلٍ مِّنْ حَمَإٍ مَّسْنُونٍ ۝ فَإِذَا سَوَّيْتُهُ وَنَفَخْتُ فِيهِ مِن

رُّوحِى فَقَعُوا۟ لَهُۥ سَٰجِدِينَ ۝ فَسَجَدَ ٱلْمَلَٰٓئِكَةُ كُلُّهُمْ

أَجْمَعُونَ ۝ إِلَّآ إِبْلِيسَ أَبَىٰٓ أَن يَكُونَ مَعَ ٱلسَّٰجِدِينَ ۝

قَالَ يَٰٓإِبْلِيسُ مَا لَكَ أَلَّا تَكُونَ مَعَ ٱلسَّٰجِدِينَ ۝ قَالَ لَمْ أَكُن

لِّأَسْجُدَ لِبَشَرٍ خَلَقْتَهُۥ مِن صَلْصَٰلٍ مِّنْ حَمَإٍ مَّسْنُونٍ ۝

Behold! your Lord said to the angels, "I am about to create man, from sounding clay from mud molded into shape; when I have fashioned him (in due proportion) and breathed into him of My Spirit, fall down in obeisance unto him." So the angels prostrated themselves, all of them together, not so Ibliss: he refused to be among those who prostrated themselves. (God) said: "O Ibliss! What is your reason for not being among those who prostrated themselves?" (Ibliss) said: "I am not one to prostrate myself to man, whom You did create from sounding clay, from mud moulded into shape. (15:28-33)

These few verses reflect the story of Adam, the Angels and Satan in relation to prostration to Adam. It should be noted here that everything in the universe (animate and inanimate objects) do prostrate to Allah (swt) willingly. As far as the prostration of the living creatures in the universe to Allah (swt) is concerned, the Qur'an informs us in both Surah Al-Ra'ad (The Thunder) and of Al-Hajj (The Pilgrimage) that every living creature does prostrate to Him. In Surah Al-Ra'ad Allah (swt) says the following:

132

$$\text{وَلِلَّهِ يَسْجُدُ مَن فِى ٱلسَّمَوَتِ وَٱلْأَرْضِ طَوْعًا}$$

$$\text{وَكَرْهًا وَظِلَلُهُم بِٱلْغُدُوِّ وَٱلْأَصَالِ ﴿١٥﴾}$$

Whatever beings there are in the heavens and the earth do prostrate themselves to God (acknowledging subjection), with good will, or in spite of themselves, so do their shadows in the mornings and evenings. (13:15)

As far as the non-living matter is concerned, Allah (swt) informs us in Surah An-Nahl (The Bees) and in Surah Al-Rahman, that inanimate matters do prostrate to Allah (swt). We do not know how they do it, but we do know that they make glorifications (Tasbeeh), and prostration (Sujood). In Surah An-Nahl, Allah (swt) says the following:

$$\text{وَلِلَّهِ يَسْجُدُ مَا فِى ٱلسَّمَوَتِ وَمَا فِى ٱلْأَرْضِ مِن دَآبَّةٍ}$$

$$\text{وَٱلْمَلَٰٓئِكَةُ وَهُمْ لَا يَسْتَكْبِرُونَ ﴿٤٩﴾}$$

And to God does prostrate all that is in the heavens and on earth, whether moving (living) creatures or the angels: for none are arrogant (before their Lord). (16:49)

In this Ayah and similar Ayat, we are told that animals, plants, matter, and angels all do prostrate to Allah (swt). In Surah Al-A'raf (The Heights) Allah (swt) informs us that the creatures He has at His disposal do obey Him, do glorify Him and do prostrate to Him. The Qur'an state the following:

133

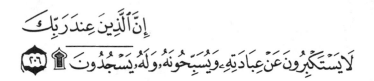

Those who are near to your Lord, disdain not to worship Him; they celebrate His praises, and prostrate before Him. (7:206)

It should be stated here that everyone throughout the history of mankind was instructed to prostrate to Allah (swt) as a sign of obedience, loyalty and allegiance. Even Prophet Muhammad (pbuh) was instructed to prostrate to Allah (swt). In Surah Al- Hijr (The Rocky Tract), Allah (swt) demanded from His Prophet Muhammad to make Sujood:

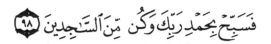

But celebrate the praises of your Lord, and be of those who prostrate themselves in adoration. (15:98)

One may also read (76:26) and (96:19). Moreover, Allah (swt) demanded from Mary, the mother of Jesus to make prostration. The Qur'an states in Surah Al-Imran the following:

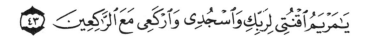

O Mary! Worship your Lord devoutly: prostrate yourself, and bow down (in prayer) with those who bow down.(3:43)

134

It should be understood that Sujood is only to Allah (swt). A Muslim should never ever try to submit himself to slavery to any human being. His prostration is to Allah (swt) and Allah (swt) alone. Allah (swt) says the following in Surah Fussilat (They Are Expounded):

وَمِنْ ءَايَٰتِهِ ٱلَّيْلُ وَٱلنَّهَارُ وَٱلشَّمْسُ وَٱلْقَمَرُ لَا تَسْجُدُوا۟ لِلشَّمْسِ وَلَا لِلْقَمَرِ وَٱسْجُدُوا۟ لِلَّهِ ٱلَّذِى خَلَقَهُنَّ إِن كُنتُمْ إِيَّاهُ تَعْبُدُونَ ۝

Among His signs are the Night and the Day, and the Sun and the Moon. Prostrate not to the Sun and the Moon, but prostrate to God, Who created them, if it is Him you wish to serve. (41:37)

Moreover, we are instructed by Allah (swt) to prostrate to Him while our intention should be for His pleasure, and as a sign of obedience. In Surah Al-Hajj (The Pilgrimage) Allah (swt) says the following:

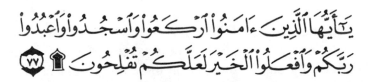

O you who believe! Bow down, prostrate yourselves, and adore your Lord; and do good; that you may prosper. (22:77)

135

There is no excuse for a Muslim not to prostrate to Allah (swt) even if he is to be in the battlefields. Muslims are to pray and to prostrate to Allah (swt) while they are in the battlefields. Allah (swt) says in Surah An-Nisaa'' (The Women) the following:

وَإِذَا كُنتَ فِيهِمْ فَأَقَمْتَ لَهُمُ الصَّلَوٰةَ فَلْتَقُمْ طَآئِفَةٌ مِّنْهُم مَّعَكَ وَلْيَأْخُذُوٓا أَسْلِحَتَهُمْ فَإِذَا سَجَدُوا فَلْيَكُونُوا۟ مِن وَرَآئِكُمْ وَلْتَأْتِ طَآئِفَةٌ أُخْرَىٰ لَمْ يُصَلُّوا۟ فَلْيُصَلُّوا۟ مَعَكَ وَلْيَأْخُذُوا۟ حِذْرَهُمْ وَأَسْلِحَتَهُمْ وَدَّ ٱلَّذِينَ

When you (O Apostle) are with them, and stands to lead them in prayer, let one party of them stand up (in prayer) with you, taking in their arms with them: when they finish their prostration, let them take their position in the rear. And let the other party come up which has not yet prayed – and let them pray with you, taking all precautions, and bearing arms......(.4:102)

It should be stated here the following: we are instructed to prostrate anytime we read or hear verses of the Qur'an that are related to Sujood. In the Qur'an there are 15 places where we are advised to prostrate to Allah (swt). This means that a Muslim is to stop reading the Qur'an till he/she makes one Sajdah to Allah (swt). These 15 places are the following:

TABLE I LIST OF SAJDAH IN QUR'AN

Surah Name	English Meaning	Surah/Ayah
1. Surah Al A'raf	(The Heights)	(7:207)
2. Surah Al-Ra'ad	(The Thunder)	(13:15)
3. Surah Al-Nahl	(The Bees)	(16:49)
4. Surah Al-Israa'	(The Children of Israel)	(17:107)
5. Surah Maryam	(Mary)	(19:58)
6. Surah Al-Hajj	(The Pilgrimage)	(22:18)
7. Surah Al-Hajj	(The Pilgrimage)	(22:77)
8. Surah Al Furqan	(The Criterion)	(25:60)
9. Surah Al Naml	(The Ants)	(27:25)
10. Surah Al-Sajdah	(The Prostration)	(32:15)
11. Surah Saad	(The Abbreviated Letter)	(38:24)
12. Surah Fussilat	(They Are Expounded)	(41:38)
13. Surah Al-Najm	(The Star)	(53:62)
14. Surah Al-Inshiqaq	(The Rending Asunder)	84:21)
15. Surah Al-'Alaq	(The Clot Congealed Blood)	(96:19)

Allah (swt) gave credit to all those believers who prostrate willingly to Him. Some of whom are the following:

1. In Surah Al-Furqan (The Criterion), Allah (swt) defined the characteristics of Ibadur Rahman, and praised them for prostrating to Him. The Qur'an states the following in Surah Al-Furqan:

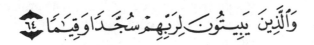

137

Those who spent the night in prostration of their Lord prostrate and standing. (25:64)

2. In Surah Al-Fath (The Victory), Allah (swt) informed us about the companions of the Prophet (pbuh) and their characteristics; among which is that they prostrate regularly, sincerely and effectively. The Qur'an states the following in Surah Al-Fath:

مُّحَمَّدٌ رَّسُولُ ٱللَّهِ وَٱلَّذِينَ مَعَهُۥٓ أَشِدَّآءُ عَلَى ٱلْكُفَّارِ رُحَمَآءُ بَيْنَهُمْ تَرَىٰهُمْ رُكَّعًا سُجَّدًا يَبْتَغُونَ فَضْلًا مِّنَ ٱللَّهِ وَرِضْوَٰنًا سِيمَاهُمْ فِى وُجُوهِهِم مِّنْ أَثَرِ ٱلسُّجُودِ

Muhammad the Apostle of God; and those who are with him are strong against the unbelievers, (but) compassionate amongst each other. You will see them bow and prostrate themselves (in prayer), seeking grace from God and (His) Good Pleasure. On their faces are their marks, (being the traces of their prostration...(48:29)

3. In Surah Al-Tawbah (Repentance), Allah (swt) praised those who prostrate to Him and considered them among the believers. He also gave them glad-tidings. The Qur'an states the following:

138

ٱلتَّٰٓئِبُونَ ٱلۡعَٰبِدُونَ ٱلۡحَٰمِدُونَ ٱلسَّٰٓئِحُونَ ٱلرَّٰكِعُونَ ٱلسَّٰجِدُونَ ٱلۡءَامِرُونَ بِٱلۡمَعۡرُوفِ وَٱلنَّاهُونَ عَنِ ٱلۡمُنكَرِ وَٱلۡحَٰفِظُونَ لِحُدُودِ ٱللَّهِ وَبَشِّرِ ٱلۡمُؤۡمِنِينَ ۝

Those that turn (to God) in repentance; that serve Him, and praise Him; that wander in devotion to the cause of God; that bow down and prostrate themselves in prayer; that enjoin good and forbid evil; and observe the limits set by God; (these do rejoice). So proclaim the glad tidings to the believers. (9:112)

The name of the mosque in Arabic is Al-Masjid. Allah (swt) gave it this name to reflect Sujood or prostration. Allah (swt) mentioned in the Qur'an the name of Al-Ka'bah mosque as Al-Masjid Al-Haram or the Sacred Mosque. He also gave the name of the mosque in Jerusalem as Al-Masjid Al-Aqsa or the Farthest Mosque. Allah (swt) took the Prophet (pbuh) on a journey for Israa' and Mi'raaj from the First Mosque to the Other. The Qur'an states the following in Surah Al-Israa' (Night Journey):

سُبۡحَٰنَ ٱلَّذِىٓ أَسۡرَىٰ بِعَبۡدِهِۦ لَيۡلًا مِّنَ ٱلۡمَسۡجِدِ ٱلۡحَرَامِ إِلَى ٱلۡمَسۡجِدِ ٱلۡأَقۡصَا ٱلَّذِى بَٰرَكۡنَا حَوۡلَهُۥ لِنُرِيَهُۥ مِنۡ ءَايَٰتِنَآ إِنَّهُۥ هُوَ ٱلسَّمِيعُ ٱلۡبَصِيرُ ۝

Glory to (God) Who did take His servant for journey
by night from the Sacred Mosque to the Farthest
Mosque, whose precincts We did bless, in order that We
might show him some of Our Signs; for He is the One
Who hears and sees (all things). (17:1)

Therefore one of the purposes of having a Masjid is for Sujood or Prostration. We come to the Masjid to obey Allah (swt), and to demonstrate our obedience, our loyalty and our allegiance to Him. We come to the Masjid to make sujood physically, mentally, spiritually, morally and medically. If we make sujood perfectly, we will attain peace, tranquility, concord, harmony and happiness. Along with all these we will get the rewards from Allah (swt) too.

It should be mentioned here that we are exposed daily to many problems. We are also propounded with too many electrostatic charges from the atmosphere. These charges are precipitated on the Central Nervous System (CNS) which in turn is being supersaturated. One has to get rid of these charges, otherwise he will be in trouble by having headaches, neckaches, muscle spasms, etc...One has to take tranquilizers and other types of drugs in order to reduce the pressure on the brain. One may become schizophrenic. Finally one may have to go to a mental institution where he will be stuck at for the rest of his life.

The best way to get rid of these electrostatic charges is to dissipate them by discharging them out of the body. In as much as an electrical appliance is in need to be grounded and earthed through the electric cord, a human being has to earth himself on the ground. He has to put his forehead on the ground because the thinking capacity of the brain is the forehead and not the tip top of the head. The Yoga and the Transcendental Meditation programs use the tip of the head by flipping upside down.

In Islam one has to prostrate by putting his forehead on the ground while the nose, the arms, the knees and the toes are still touching the floor. By so doing, there will be maximum dissipation of the extra electrostatic charges from the brain and the central nervous system into the ground. Hence, one will receive the peace of mind and soul. By doing prostration five times a day, and in each time one prostrates several times, he will undoubtedly earn peace, concord, happiness and relaxation. This type of approach does not cost any money and does not have any side reactions. It is the best method to allow a person to continue to live in peace, obedience and happiness for the rest of his life.

Moreover, the best position to ask Allah (swt) and to make Du`aa' is while in Sujood. During Sujood the Du`aa' is accepted by Allah (swt). The best time, place, and position to dialogue with Allah (swt) is during Sujood. The best position to meet Allah (swt) (i.e. to die) is while in Sujood. For this reason the Prophet (pbuh) said the following (as narrated by Abder Rahman Thawban, servant of the Prophet (pbuh) the following:

عَنْ عَبْدِ الرَّحْمَنِ ثَوْبَانَ مَوْلَى رَسُولِ اللهِ صلى الله عليه
وَسَلَّمَ ،قَالَ : سَمِعْتُ رَسُولَ اللهِ صلى اللهُ عَلَيْهِ وَسَلَّمَ
يَقُولُ : "عَلَيْكَ بِكَثْرَةِ السُّجُودِ فَإِنَّكَ لَنْ تَسْجُدَ لِلهِ سَجْدَةً
إِلَّا رَفَعَكَ اللهُ بِهَا دَرَجَةً ،وَحَطَّ عَنْكَ بِهَا خَطِيئَةً" .

I heard the Messenger of Allah say: Perform Sujood (prostration) in abundance. Anytime you prostrate to Allah one Sujood, Allah will elevate you one step, and erase one mistake for you.

141

Finally, let me recite this Ayah from Surah Al-Hajj (The Pilgrimage):

أَلَمْ تَرَ أَنَّ ٱللَّهَ

يَسْجُدُ لَهُۥ مَن فِى ٱلسَّمَـٰوَٰتِ وَمَن فِى ٱلْأَرْضِ وَٱلشَّمْسُ وَٱلْقَمَرُ

وَٱلنُّجُومُ وَٱلْجِبَالُ وَٱلشَّجَرُ وَٱلدَّوَآبُّ وَكَثِيرٌ مِّنَ ٱلنَّاسِ

وَكَثِيرٌ حَقَّ عَلَيْهِ ٱلْعَذَابُ وَمَن يُهِنِ ٱللَّهُ فَمَا لَهُۥ مِن مُّكْرِمٍ

إِنَّ ٱللَّهَ يَفْعَلُ مَا يَشَآءُ ۩ ۞ ﴿١٨﴾

Seest you not that to God prostrate in worship all things that are in the heavens and on earth: the sun, the moon, the stars, the hills, the trees, the animals; and a great number among mankind?...(22:18)

Let us ask Allah (swt) for His forgiveness. Ameen.

142

XVIII. LIST OF SAJDAH
IN THE QUR'AN

The following section is a collection of the Ayat that are in the Qur'an where a Muslim is commanded to prostrate to Allah (swt) when he/she hears or recites any one of them. A Muslim is supposed to be in a state of ablution (wudu'). If he/she is not in a state of ablution, and/or if he/she is in a place where Sujood can't be performed, the person is to say three (3) times in the Arabic language:

$$\text{،أَحَبُّ الكَلاَمِ إلَى اللهِ تَعَالَى أَرْبَعٌ:}$$
$$\text{سُبْحَانَ اللهِ ،وَالْحَمْدُ لِلّهِ ،وَلَا إلَهَ إلاَّ اللّهُ ،وَاللّهُ أكْبَرُ}$$
$$\text{لاَ يَضُرُّكَ بِأَيِّهِنَّ بَدَأْتَ، .}$$
(رواه مُسلِم)

Glory be to Allah. Praise be to Allah. There is no one worthy to be worshipped except Allah, and Allah is the Greatest.

THE FIRST SAJDAH

The First Sajdah is found in Surah Al-A'raaf (The Heights). Allah (swt) informs us that all creatures that He created and especially Angels are to prostrate for Him. The Qur'an states the following:

$$\text{إِنَّ ٱلَّذِينَ عِندَ رَبِّكَ}$$
$$\text{لَا يَسْتَكْبِرُونَ عَنْ عِبَادَتِهِ وَيُسَبِّحُونَهُ وَلَهُ يَسْجُدُونَ ۩}$$

Lo! Those who are with your Lord are not too proud to do Him service, but they praise Him and prostrate to Him. (7:206)

THE SECOND SAJDAH

The Second Sajdah is found in Surah Al-Ra'ad (The Thunder). Allah (swt) informs us that every living creature in the heavens and the earth does prostrate to Him willingly, or unwillingly. The Qur'an states the following:

وَلِلَّهِ يَسْجُدُ مَن فِى ٱلسَّمَوَٰتِ وَٱلْأَرْضِ طَوْعًا

وَكَرْهًا وَظِلَالُهُم بِٱلْغُدُوِّ وَٱلْآصَالِ ۩ ⟨١٥⟩

And unto Allah fall prostrate whoever is in the heavens and the earth, willingly or unwillingly, so as do their shadows in the morning and evening hours. (13:15).

THE THIRD SAJDAH

The Third Sajdah is found in Surah An-Nahl (The Bees), where Allah (swt) informs us that all living and non-living creatures, even the angels, do prostrate to Allah (swt), as follows:

⟨٤٧⟩ أَوَلَمْ يَرَوْا إِلَىٰ مَا خَلَقَ ٱللَّهُ مِن شَىْءٍ

يَتَفَيَّؤُا ظِلَالُهُ عَنِ ٱلْيَمِينِ وَٱلشَّمَآئِلِ سُجَّدًا لِّلَّهِ وَهُمْ دَاخِرُونَ

⟨٤٨⟩ وَلِلَّهِ يَسْجُدُ مَا فِى ٱلسَّمَوَٰتِ وَمَا فِى ٱلْأَرْضِ مِن دَآبَّةٍ

وَٱلْمَلَٰٓئِكَةُ وَهُمْ لَا يَسْتَكْبِرُونَ ⟨٤٩⟩ يَخَافُونَ رَبَّهُم مِّن فَوْقِهِمْ

وَيَفْعَلُونَ مَا يُؤْمَرُونَ ۩ ⟨٥٠⟩

Have they not observed all things that Allah has created, how their shadows incline to the right and to the left, making prostration unto Allah, and they are lowly? And unto Allah make prostration whatsoever is in the heavens and whatsoever is in the earth of living creatures, and the angels (also) and they are not proud. They fear their Lord above them, and do what they are bidden. (16:48-50).

THE FOURTH SAJDAH

The Fourth Sajdah is found in Surah Al-Israa' (The Night Travel). Allah (swt) tells us that all the previous people of knowledge used to prostrate to Allah (swt) as soon a they hear the verses of Allah (swt). Every person has to prostrate to Allah (swt), whether he/she believes or not; otherwise he/she is to live in a vacuum. Such a person will live in problems psychologically, socially, and spiritually. The Qur'an states the following:

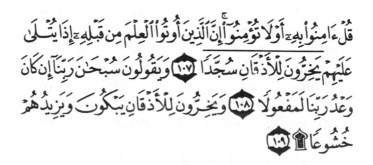

Say: Believe therein or believe not, lo! Those who were given knowledge before it, when it is read unto them, fall down prostrate on their faces, adoring. Saying" Glory to our Lord! Verily the promise of our Lord must be fulfilled. They fall down on their faces, weeping, and it increases humility in them (17:107-109).

THE FIFTH SAJDAH

The Fifth Sajdah is found in the Qur'an in Surah Mariam. Allah (swt) reminds us that all the Prophets that He sent used to prostrate to Him. They prostrated every time an Ayah was revealed to them. Allah (swt) says about them the following:

145

أُوْلَٰٓئِكَ ٱلَّذِينَ
أَنْعَمَ ٱللَّهُ عَلَيْهِم مِّنَ ٱلنَّبِيِّـۧنَ مِن ذُرِّيَّةِ ءَادَمَ وَمِمَّنْ حَمَلْنَا مَعَ نُوحٍ
وَمِن ذُرِّيَّةِ إِبْرَٰهِيمَ وَإِسْرَٰٓءِيلَ وَمِمَّنْ هَدَيْنَا وَٱجْتَبَيْنَآ إِذَا تُتْلَىٰ عَلَيْهِمْ
ءَايَٰتُ ٱلرَّحْمَٰنِ خَرُّوا۟ سُجَّدًا وَبُكِيًّا ۩ ۞ (٥٨)

*These are they unto whom Allah showed favour
from among the Prophets, of the seed of Adam and of
those whom We carried (in the ship) with Noah, and of
the seed of Abraham and Israel, and from among those
whom We guided and chose. When the revelations of
the Beneficent were recited unto them, they fell down,
adoring, in prostration and weeping. (19:58).*

THE SIXTH SAJDAH

The Sixth Sajdah is found in Surah Al-Hajj (The Pilgrimage).
Allah (swt) reaffirms to us that everything in the universe (living
and non-living) does make sajdah as a sign of obedience to Him.
The Qur'an states the following:

أَلَمْ تَرَ أَنَّ ٱللَّهَ
يَسْجُدُ لَهُۥ مَن فِي ٱلسَّمَٰوَٰتِ وَمَن فِي ٱلْأَرْضِ وَٱلشَّمْسُ وَٱلْقَمَرُ
وَٱلنُّجُومُ وَٱلْجِبَالُ وَٱلشَّجَرُ وَٱلدَّوَابُّ وَكَثِيرٌ مِّنَ ٱلنَّاسِ
وَكَثِيرٌ حَقَّ عَلَيْهِ ٱلْعَذَابُ وَمَن يُهِنِ ٱللَّهُ فَمَا لَهُۥ مِن مُّكْرِمٍ
إِنَّ ٱللَّهَ يَفْعَلُ مَا يَشَآءُ ۩ ۞ (١٨)

Have you not seen that unto Allah pay adoration whosoever is in the heavens and whosoever is in the earth, and the sun and the moon, and the stars, and the hills, and the trees, and the beasts and many of mankind, while there are many unto whom the doom is justly due. He whom Allah scorns, there is none to give him honor. Lo! Allah does what He will (22:18).

THE SEVENTH SAJDAH

The Seventh Sajdah is found in the same Surah as the sixth sajdah, in the Surah of Al-Hajj (The Pilgrimage). In this Surah, Allah (swt) is demanding from all of the believers to bow forward (Rukoo'), to make Sujood (Prostration), to worship Allah (swt) alone, and to do the best. The Qur'an states the following:

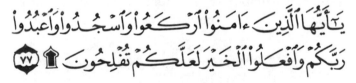

O, you who believe! Bow down and prostrate yourselves, and worship your Lord, and do good, that happily you may prosper. (22:77).

THE EIGHTH SAJDAH

The Eighth Sajdah is found in Surah Al-Furqan (The Criterion). Allah (swt) demanded from every human being to make Sajdah to Allah (swt). It seems that the unbelievers (Kafiroon) always refuse to do so. Their arrogance stops them from being humble and from being obedient to Allah the Creator. The Qur'an states the following:

وَإِذَا قِيلَ لَهُمُ اسْجُدُوا لِلرَّحْمَنِ قَالُوا وَمَا الرَّحْمَنُ
أَنَسْجُدُ لِمَا تَأْمُرُنَا وَزَادَهُمْ نُفُورًا ۩ ٦٠

*And when it is said unto them; Adore the
Beneficent! They say; and what is the Beneficent? Are
we to adore whatever you (Muhammad) bid us? And it
increased aversion in them. (25:60).*

THE NINTH SAJDAH

The Ninth Sajdah is found in Surah An-Naml (The Ants). In
this particular Surah, Allah (swt) is informing us about the early
people of Saba. They used to worship the sun. He demanded them
to worship Him as being the Creator Himself. They were not
supposed to worship any creatures at all. The Qur'an emphasizes
this idea explicitly as follows:

وَجَدتُّهَا وَقَوْمَهَا يَسْجُدُونَ لِلشَّمْسِ مِن
دُونِ اللهِ وَزَيَّنَ لَهُمُ الشَّيْطَانُ أَعْمَالَهُمْ فَصَدَّهُمْ عَنِ السَّبِيلِ
فَهُمْ لَا يَهْتَدُونَ ٢٤ أَلَّا يَسْجُدُوا لِلَّهِ الَّذِي يُخْرِجُ الْخَبْءَ
فِي السَّمَوَاتِ وَالْأَرْضِ وَيَعْلَمُ مَا تُخْفُونَ وَمَا تُعْلِنُونَ ٢٥ اللهُ
لَا إِلَهَ إِلَّا هُوَ رَبُّ الْعَرْشِ الْعَظِيمِ ۩ ٢٦

*I found her and her people worshipping the sun
instead of Allah; and Satan made their works fair-
seeming unto them, and debars them from the way (of
Truth), so that they go not aright: So that they worship
not Allah, Who brings forth the hidden in the heavens*

148

*and the earth, and knows what you hide and what you
proclaim. Allah; there is no god save Him, the Lord of
the tremendous Throne. (27:24-26)*

THE TENTH SAJDAH

The Tenth Sajdah is found in Surah Al-Sajdah (Prostration).
Allah (swt) is praising the believers who do prostrate anytime they
hear the words of Allah (swt). They rush to obey and bow forward
and prostrate as a sign of obedience to Allah (swt). The Qur'an
states the following:

إِنَّمَا يُؤْمِنُ بِآيَاتِنَا الَّذِينَ إِذَا ذُكِّرُوا بِهَا خَرُّوا سُجَّدًا وَسَبَّحُوا بِحَمْدِ رَبِّهِمْ وَهُمْ لَا يَسْتَكْبِرُونَ ۩ ﴿١٥﴾ تَتَجَافَىٰ جُنُوبُهُمْ عَنِ الْمَضَاجِعِ يَدْعُونَ رَبَّهُمْ خَوْفًا وَطَمَعًا وَمِمَّا رَزَقْنَاهُمْ يُنفِقُونَ ﴿١٦﴾

*Only those who believe in Our revelations who,
when they are reminded of them fall down prostrate and
hymn the praise of their lord, and they are not scornful:
Who forsake their beds to cry unto their Lord in fear
and hope, and spend of what We have bestowed on
them. (32:15-16)*

THE ELEVENTH SAJDAH

This Sajdah is found in Surah Saad. In this Ayah, Allah (swt) is
informing us that Prophet Dawood (David) (pbuh), thought he was
being tested by Allah (swt). He asked forgiveness and prostrated
to Allah (swt). The Qur'an explains the story as follows:

قَالَ

لَقَدْ ظَلَمَكَ بِسُؤَالِ نَعْجَتِكَ إِلَى نِعَاجِهِۦ وَإِنَّ كَثِيرًا مِّنَ ٱلْخُلَطَآءِ لَيَبْغِى بَعْضُهُمْ عَلَىٰ بَعْضٍ إِلَّا ٱلَّذِينَ ءَامَنُوا۟ وَعَمِلُوا۟ ٱلصَّٰلِحَٰتِ وَقَلِيلٌ مَّا هُمْ وَظَنَّ دَاوُۥدُ أَنَّمَا فَتَنَّٰهُ فَٱسْتَغْفَرَ رَبَّهُۥ وَخَرَّ رَاكِعًا وَأَنَابَ ۩ ﴿٢٤﴾

(David) said: He has wronged you in demanding your ewe in addition to his ewes, and lo! Many partners oppress one another, save such as believe and do good works, and they are few. And David guessed that We had tried him, and he sought forgiveness of his Lord, and he bowed himself and fell down prostrate and repented.(38:24).

THE TWELFTH SAJDAH

This type of Sajdah is found in Surah Fussilat (Explained). In this Surah, Allah (swt) is explaining that He created the whole universe. Everything that we see is among His miracles. He instructed us not to prostrate to any of His Creation, including the sun and the moon. We are demanded to prostrate to Him. The Qur'an explains this type of instruction as follows:

وَمِنْ ءَايَٰتِهِ

ٱلَّيْلُ وَٱلنَّهَارُ وَٱلشَّمْسُ وَٱلْقَمَرُ لَا تَسْجُدُوا۟ لِلشَّمْسِ وَلَا لِلْقَمَرِ وَٱسْجُدُوا۟ لِلَّهِ ٱلَّذِى خَلَقَهُنَّ إِن كُنتُمْ إِيَّاهُ تَعْبُدُونَ ﴿٣٧﴾ فَإِنِ ٱسْتَكْبَرُوا۟ فَٱلَّذِينَ عِندَ رَبِّكَ يُسَبِّحُونَ لَهُۥ بِٱلَّيْلِ وَٱلنَّهَارِ وَهُمْ لَا يَسْـَٔمُونَ ۩ ﴿٣٨﴾

150

And of His portents are the night and the day and the sun and the moon. Adore not the sun nor the moon but adore Allah Who created them if it is in truth Him Whom you worship. But if they are too proud-still those who are with your Lord glorify Him night and day, and tire not. (41:37-38).

THE THIRTEENTH SAJDAH

This Sajdah is found in Surah Al-Najm (The Star). In this Surah, Allah (swt) is warning people not to worship anyone or anything except He Himself as the Creator of the whole universe. He is telling us that this Qur'an is also a warning to those who refuse to obey Him. For those who believe in Allah, they should demonstrate their love, their loyalty, their obedience, and allegiance to Him. One of the physical demonstrations of such worship is to bow down and prostrate to Him. Th Qur'an is explicit about this type of instruction. The Ayat goes a follows:

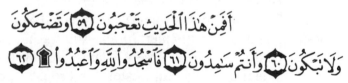

Marvel you then at this statement. And laugh and not weep. While you amuse yourselves? Rather prostrate yourselves before Allah and serve Him. (53:59-62)

THE FOURTEENTH SAJDAH

This Sajdah is found in Surah Al-Inshiqaq (Split Asunder). In this particular Makkah Surah, Allah (swt) is expressing His unhappiness and unsatisfaction with those people who refused to believe in Him. It seems that they closed their eyes, ears, brains and hearts from seeing and recognizing the Creation and the Miracles of Allah (swt) that He created in the universe. The

151

Qur'an was revealed in their own tongues and it was recited for them by the Prophet (pbuh). They even refused to believe, to obey, to listen, to bow down and to prostrate to Allah (swt). The Qur'an explains this tragedy about the unbelievers as follows:

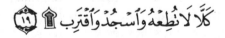

وَإِذَا قُرِئَ عَلَيْهِمُ ٱلْقُرْءَانُ لَا يَسْجُدُونَ ۩

What ails them, then, that they believe not. And, when the Qur'an is recited unto them, worship not (Allah)? (84:21).

THE FIFTEENTH SAJDAH

The last recorded Sajdah in the Qur'an is found in the first revealed Surah to the Prophet (pbuh). It is called Surah Al-'Alaq (The Blood clot). In this particular Surah, Abu Lahab, the uncle of the Prophet (pbuh) refused to accept Islam. He even fought the Prophet (pbuh) and tried his best to stop the Prophet (pbuh) from delivering the Message of Allah (swt). He went too far to the extent that he did not like to see his nephew praying in the Ka'bah. However, Allah (swt) instructed the Prophet (pbuh) not to listen to his uncle. Allah (swt) encouraged the Prophet (pbuh) to continue to pray at Ka'bah, and to make sajdah. The Qur'an explains this situation as follows:

كَلَّا لَا تُطِعْهُ وَٱسْجُدْ وَٱقْتَرِب ۩

No! Obey him not! But prostrate yourself, and draw near (unto Allah) (96:19).

152

TABLE I: LIST OF SAJDAH IN THE QUR'AN

No	Surah	English Meaning	Surah/ Verse #
1.	Al-A'raf	The Heights	7:206
2.	Al-Ra'ad	The Thunder	13:15
3.	Al-Nahl	The Bees	16:49
4.	Al-Israa'	Night Travel	17:107
5.	Maryam	Mary	19:58
6.	Al-Hajj	The Pilgrimage	22:18
7.	Al-Hajj	The Pilgrimage	22:77
8.	Al-Furqan	The Criterion	25:60
9.	Al-Naml	The Ants	27:25
10.	Al-Sajdah	The Prostration	32:15
11.	Saad	The Arabic Letter	38:24
12.	Fussilat	They Were Expounded	41:38
13.	Al-Najm	The Star	53:62
14.	Al-Inshiqaq	The Rending Asunder	84:21
15.	Al-'Alaq	Clot of Congealed	96:19

XIX. RECITING THE QUR'AN
Tilawatul Qur'an

A. General

The subject of this chapter is the Manners for Reading and Reciting the Qur'an, or what is called in Arabic Tilawatul Qur'an. Allah (swt) says the following in Surah Al-Nahl (The Bees):

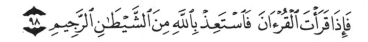

When you do read the Qur'an, seek Allah's (swt)
protection from Satan, the rejected one. (16:98)

This means that we have to read the Qur'an, and that we should seek refuge in Allah (swt) from the outcast Satan. However in Surah Al-A'raf (The Heights), Allah (swt) demands from us to listen to the Qur'an when it is recited by someone.

When the Qur'an is read, listen to it with attention,
and hold your peace, so that you may receive Mercy.
(7:204)

This means that we should listen to the recitation of the Qur'an whenever it is being recited by someone else. We have to open our minds and hearts while we are listening to its recitation.

As far as the Ahadith are concerned, it was narrated by Abu-Harairah ® and it was recorded in the Sahih Book of Muslim, that the Prophet (pbuh) said:

١١٠٤ - وَعَنْ أَبِي هُرَيْرَةَ رَضِيَ اللهُ عَنْهُ قَالَ : قَالَ رَسُولُ اللهِ صلى الله عَلَيْهِ وَسَلَّمَ : « وَمَا اجْتَمَعَ قَوْمٌ فِي بَيْتٍ مِن بُيوتِ اللهِ يَتْلُونَ كِتَابَ اللهِ ، وَيَتَدَارَسُونَهُ بَيْنَهُمْ ، إلاَّ نَزَلَتْ عَلَيهِم السَّكِينَةَ ، وَغَشِيَتْهُمُ الرَّحْمَةَ ، وَحَفَّتْهُمُ الْمَلائِكَةَ ، وذَكَرَهُمُ اللهُ فِيمَنْ عِندَهُ » رواه مسلم .

Any group of people who meet in a House of Allah (swt) to recite from the Book of Allah (swt), and to study it among themselves, then Allah (swt) will descend upon them Peace, Mercy will cover them, Angels will encircle them, and Allah (swt) will remember them to those at His Throne.

The other Hadith narrated by Uthman Ibn Affan ® and recorded in the Sahih Book of Bukhari, that the Prophet (pbuh) said:

٩٩٩ وعن عثمان بن عفان رضى اللهُ عنه قال : قال رسول اللهُ صلى الله عليه وسلم : « خَيْرُكُمْ مَنْ تَعَلَّمَ الْقُرْآنَ وَعَلَّمَهُ ، رواه البخارى .

The best among you are those who study the Qur'an and teach it to others.

B. Etiquette and Manners

From these Ayat and Ahadith, the following is a summary about the etiquette and manners for reading and reciting the Qur'an:

1. We should read the Qur'an for the love of Allah (swt). We are to seek the Mercy, Blessing and Guidance from Allah (swt) too.
2. To read the Qur'an we should be in a state of cleanliness from janabah, or from menses for women.
3. We should have wudoo' (ablution.)
4. If we are to read directly from the Qur'an, it should not be put on the floor or on our legs, but to be carried in our hands or being put on a Qur'an stand.
5. We should be facing the Ka'bah as well.
6. While reading the Qur'an, we should concentrate on its beautiful meaning and relate those teachings to our daily life.
7. When reading the Qur'an we should read it with rules and regulations, i.e. the Makharij (pronunciation) and Tarteel (noonation).
8. If and when we come at an Ayah where there is a Tassbeeh, we should glorify Allah (swt). This means that whenever there is an Ayah where Allah (swt) demands us to be thankful, we should be grateful to Him.

Let me quote for you a few more Ayat concerning the recitations of the Qur'an. In Surah Al-Muzzammil (Folded in Garments), Allah (swt) says to all of us the following:

156

إِنَّ رَبَّكَ يَعْلَمُ أَنَّكَ تَقُومُ أَدْنَىٰ مِن ثُلُثَيِ ٱلَّيْلِ وَنِصْفَهُ وَثُلُثَهُ وَطَآئِفَةٌ مِّنَ ٱلَّذِينَ مَعَكَ وَٱللَّهُ يُقَدِّرُ ٱلَّيْلَ وَٱلنَّهَارَ عَلِمَ أَن لَّن تُحْصُوهُ فَتَابَ عَلَيْكُمْ فَٱقْرَءُوا مَا تَيَسَّرَ مِنَ ٱلْقُرْءَانِ عَلِمَ أَن سَيَكُونُ مِنكُم مَّرْضَىٰ وَءَاخَرُونَ يَضْرِبُونَ فِى ٱلْأَرْضِ يَبْتَغُونَ مِن فَضْلِ ٱللَّهِ وَءَاخَرُونَ يُقَٰتِلُونَ فِى سَبِيلِ ٱللَّهِ فَٱقْرَءُوا مَا تَيَسَّرَ مِنْهُ

He knows that you are unable to keep count thereof.
So He has turned to you (in Mercy): read it therefore, of
the Qur'an as much as may be easy for you. He knows
that there may be (some) among you in ill-health; others
traveling through the land, seeking of Allah's (swt)
bounty; yet others fighting in Allah's (swt) Cause. Read
it therefore, as much of the Qur'an as may be easy (for
you). (73:20)

Also in the same Surah, Allah (swt) wants us to read the
Qur'an with recitation and with rhythmic tones. He says the
following:

أَوْ زِدْ عَلَيْهِ وَرَتِّلِ ٱلْقُرْءَانَ تَرْتِيلًا

And recite the Qur'an in slow, measured rhythmic
tones. (73:4)

Finally, the following is quoted from the Prophet (pbuh):

1. As reported by Dailami and Baihaqi on behalf of the Prophet
saying :

157

١١١٢ ـ أَفْضَلُ عِبَادَةِ أُمَّتِيْ قِرَاءَةُ الْقُرْآنِ .

(الديلمي واليهقي)

The best worship of my followers is the recitation of the Qur'an.

2. As reported by Dailami and Al-Khatib on behalf of the Prophet (pbuh) saying:

١١١١ ـ إِذَا أَحَبَّ أَحَدُكُمْ أَنْ يُحَدِّثَ رَبَّهُ فَلْيَقْرَأِ الْقُرْآنَ .

(الديلمي والخطيب)

If anyone of you likes to speak to Allah (swt), he should read the Qur'an.

C. **Final Remarks**

Muslims try their best to read the Qur'an on a daily basis. They also try to finish reading the whole Qur'an every lunar month. Moreover, Muslims all over the world read, recite, and listen to the recitation of the whole Qur'an in the month of Ramadan. Reading, reciting, and listening to Qur'an is good, but understanding its meaning is more important. However, trying to practice what has been learned is expected from every honest and sincere Muslim. Therefore, one has to look for the teachers, scholars, and Imams to learn from them, and to find out the best way to read, recite, and memorize the Qur'an. They should try to understand the Qur'an and then deliver it to others. More importantly is that they should try to apply its meaning on a daily basis: privately and publicly. If and when we do this, then and only then Allah (swt) will be pleased with us. Ameen.

XX. RULES OF RECITING THE QUR'AN

To read the Qur'an, one has to study the rules and regulations so that reading the Qur'an will be perfect without any defaults. The following is a partial list of the Rules:

First: A person has to know how to pronounce each and every letter in the Arabic language. This is called the study of Makhaarij. One has to differentiate between Seen (س) and Saad (ص); between Ta (ت) and Taa (ط); between Ha (ه) and Haa (ح); between Daal (د) and Daad (ض); and between A (ا) and 'Ayn (ع); etc. The science of Makhaarij cannot be studied in books without teachers. The latter group of scholars of Qur'an are the ones who will be able to help the students to pronounce each letter properly.

Second: The student has to learn the proper pronunciation of the words. Examples: Qur'an, Surah, Ayah, Kalimah, Harf, Rasool, Nabi, Allah, Muhammad, Salat, Siyam, Zakat, Hajj, Islam, Muslim, Muslimoon, Muslimeen, etc.

Third: The third level for the study of Reciting the Qur'an, would be how to pronounce those words and others if the word has a definite article. The Arabic Alphabets are composed of 28 letters. Half of them have the characteristics of being pronounced clearly without assimilating the definite article with the letter. These are called: The Moon letters or Al-Ahruf Al-Qamariyah. See Chapter XXIV

The Second half of the Alphabet letters are called The Sun Letters or Al-Ahruf Ash-Shamsiyah. When the definite article is being used, it loses its independence. It will not be pronounced separately, but it will merge itself with the letter that comes immediately after it. See Chapter XXIV

Fourth: The Fourth Level is that a person has to recognize the Qalqalah pronunciation. These are Qaaf; Taa; Ba; Jeem; and Daal. Anytime there is a silent pronunciation on these letters, they have to be pronounced as if they are composed of one-and-a half letter.

Fifth: The Fifth Level is to study the signs of stops. One has to know when to stop, where to stop, and how to stop. See Chapter XXVI

Sixth: The Sixth Level of Reciting Qur'an properly is the study of the Accuracy of Punctuation. See Chapter XXVI

Seventh: The Seventh Level of Reciting Qur'an is the study of the end of each Ayah, the place of Prostration, the division of the Qur'an into 30 volumes (Juzu'), sixty Hizb, and so on. See Chapter XXVI

Eighth: The Eighth Level of Reciting Qur'an is to study the meaning of the Ayat. This means that one has to study Qur'anic Tafseer for each Surah and for each Ayah. This has to be done through a Muslim Scholars who are specialized in Tafseer, the Sirah and the Sunnah of the Prophet as well.

Ninth: The Ninth Level for Studying and Reciting Qur'an is to apply its meaning in our private and public life. Knowledge of the Qur'an is one thing, but application of its meaning is much more important. Therefore, one has to be honest and sincere that he is studying Qur'an, not only to enjoy the melodic voice of its recitation, but to practice what has been learned. Yes indeed! Qur'an has to be recited with Rhyme, Rhythm, and with a melodic voice, but all these terminologies should be for the love of Allah. If a Reciter is to recite Qur'an so as to attract the attention of the audience, and hence they praise him, he is automatically a loser.

However, if he does it for the love of Allah, he is the winner in this life and in the hereafter.

Tenth: The Tenth level of learning how to read and recite Qur'an is to teach it to others. Our beloved Prophet (pbuh) informed us the following:

٩٩٩ وعن عثمان بن عفان رضى الله عنه قال : قال رسول الله صلى الله عليه
وسلم : « خَيْرُكُمْ مَنْ تَعَلَّمَ الْقُرْآنَ وَعَلَّمَهُ ، رواهالبخارى .

Uthman Ibn Affan ® narrated that the Messenger of Allah said:

The Best among you are those who learn the Qur'an, and teach it to others. (Bukhari)

161

XXI. READING FROM THE QUR'AN

A. First Level

Muslims are to read the whole Qur'an and they are to memorize it too. Since not all Muslims can memorize the whole Qur'an, they try to memorize certain Surahs and special verses to be read during Salat. Some Surahs and verses are to be recited on certain events, and/or for special occasions. Examples:

1. For protection from satan and human sneakers, one has to read Ayat Kursi , in Surah Al-Baqarah, Chapter 2, and Ayah 255. Moreover, one has to read Al-Mu'awwazatain (Al-Falaq, Al-Nass), chapters 113 and 114.

2. To release a dying person from the hardships of soul-taking by the angels, one has to read Surah Yaseen (Chapter 36)

3. If a person cannot make Tahajjud /Qiyam Al-Lail, he should read the last three Ayat of Surah Al-Baqara. (2:284-286)

4. At the time of sunrise and sunset, one is to read the Ayat in Surah Al-Imran (3:26-27)

B. Second Level

At the same time, there are certain Surahs and verses to be read to help Muslims improve their relationship among themselves as well as among their family members. Examples:

1. One has to read from Surah Al-Israa' those Ayat regarding respect to parent, and how to behave in the society. (17:23-39)

2. Reading of Ayat in Surah Luqman is important to teach parents how to advise their children in being good Believers and obedient to Allah. (31:12-19)

3. To remember our obligations to Allah in having good manners, behaviors, and attitude towards one another, one has to read Surah Al-Hujurat (49)

4. To behave well morally within the same family, one has to read those Ayat of Surah Al-Noor (24:58-64)

5. To know the qualities of believers (Mu'minoon) one has to read Surah Al-Mu'minoon (23:1-11)

6. To realize the qualities of Ibadur Rahman, one has to read Surah Al-Furqan (25:61-77)

C. Third Level

There are other Surahs that need to be read for other benefits. The following is a partial list:

1. To prevent oneself from poverty or need, one has to read daily and at night Surah al-Waqi'ah (The Inevitable). It is chapter (56.)

2. To protect oneself from the penalty in the grave, one has to read Surah Al-Mulk: The Dominion, chapter (67).

3. In Surah Nooh (71:10-14) we are instructed to make Istighfar (to ask Allah Forgiveness). For those who request Allah to forgive them, will get: Forgiveness, rain will come down; Allah will give them wealth, and good children. The best time for Istighfar is at Sahar time: one hour before Fajr (Dawn or first twilight).

4. For those who want to protect themselves for one whole day from Shaitan not to bother them or to harm them, a person should read from Surah Al-Baqarah Ayat (1-5), Ayat (255-257) and Ayat (284-286).

5. To protect oneself from Shaitan for three days so that he will not do any harm, one has to read the whole Surah al-Baqarah, chapter (2.)

6. Reading from Qur'an should be done daily, and the best time is at time of Fajr (Dawn). Allah (swt) says in surah Al-Israa' (Night Journey) the following:

أَقِمِ ٱلصَّلَوٰةَ لِدُلُوكِ ٱلشَّمْسِ إِلَىٰ غَسَقِ ٱلَّيْلِ وَقُرْءَانَ ٱلْفَجْرِ إِنَّ قُرْءَانَ ٱلْفَجْرِ كَانَ مَشْهُودًا ﴿٧٨﴾

Establish regular prayers – at the sun's decline till the darkness of the night, and the recital of the Qur'an in morning prayer for the recital of dawn is witnessed. (17:78)

7. A Muslim is to read from Qur'an daily. He has to start with Ta'weeza: To seek protection from Shaitan. In Surah Al-Nahl (The Bees) Allah (swt) says the following:

فَإِذَا قَرَأْتَ ٱلْقُرْءَانَ فَٱسْتَعِذْ بِٱللَّهِ مِنَ ٱلشَّيْطَانِ ٱلرَّجِيمِ ﴿٩٨﴾ إِنَّهُ لَيْسَ لَهُ سُلْطَانٌ عَلَى ٱلَّذِينَ ءَامَنُوا وَعَلَىٰ رَبِّهِمْ يَتَوَكَّلُونَ ﴿٩٩﴾ إِنَّمَا سُلْطَانُهُ عَلَى ٱلَّذِينَ يَتَوَلَّوْنَهُ وَٱلَّذِينَ هُم بِهِ مُشْرِكُونَ ﴿١٠٠﴾

164

*When you do read the Qur'an, seek Allah's
protection from Satan the rejected One. No authority
has he over those who believe and put their trust in their
Lord. His authority is over those only, who take him as
patron and join partners with Allah (16:98-100)*

8. A Muslim has also to listen to the recitation of Qur'an being recited by others. He should open his ears, mind and heart so as to enjoy the meaning of Qur'an, as well as its melodic rhyme and rhythm. Allah (swt) says in Surah Al-A'raaf (The Heights) the following:

وَإِذَا قُرِئَ ٱلْقُرْءَانُ فَٱسْتَمِعُوا۟ لَهُۥ وَأَنصِتُوا۟ لَعَلَّكُمْ تُرْحَمُونَ ۝

*When the Qur'an is read, listen to it with attention,
and hold your peace: that you may receive Mercy.
(7:204)*

D. Final Remark

As a final remark, there are many more things to state here about reading from Qur'an. The latter is a Sacred Book revealed from God Almighty. It is the Last Revealed Book. It has all the previous revelations from God to all His Prophets such as Noah, Abraham, Ishmael, Issaq, Jacob, David, Moses, Jesus and finally Muhammad. Therefore, the Qur'an is the Summation, Purification, and Culmination of all the revealed books from Allah, the Most Merciful.

XXII. QUR'ANIC TAFSEER
(Interpretation of the Meaning of the Qur'an)

The best person who knows how to explain the meaning of the Qur'an is the one who received it by Wahy from Allah. He is indeed Prophet Muhammad (pbuh). The Prophet explained the Qur'an to his people and especially to those who devoted their life to associate themselves with him. He explained the Qur'an using the Qur'an. This means that the Qur'an explains itself from the Qur'an. Many verses in one Surah cannot be understood by themselves unless we look in other Surahs to find the meaning of those verses. The Prophet made certain Du`a` for some of his immediate followers so that Allah will give them the knowledge to explain the Qur'an to others.

The following section is a summary of the sequential order of those whom Allah (swt) has blessed with some knowledge about the meaning of the Qur'an. It should be stated here that no one will be able to comprehend the full meaning of the Qur'an, even if he studied all the previous books of those authors who devoted all their lives for the sake of the Qur'an. Moreover, one has to state here that the Qur'an is The Living Book of Allah: It will be understood more and more as long as science, technology and other scientific information are at our disposal. The more people advance in science and technology, the more the Qur'an is understood and appreciated. For that reason one can observe that a good number of highly educated non-Muslims have accepted Islam after they read the general meaning of the Qur'an.

Therefore, the following is a partial list of names whom Allah has blessed. They tried their best to explain the Qur'an after the Prophet.

1. **Prophet's (saw) Tafseer**

2. **Companions' Tafseer:**

   a. Four Khulafaa' Rashidoon (Abu Bakr, Omar, Uthman & Ali)
   b. Abdullah ibn Mass'ood
   c. Abdullah ibn 'Abbas (Prophet's Cousin)
   d. Ubay ibn Ka'ab
   e. Zeyd ibn Thabit
   f. Abu Musa Al-Ash`aree
   g. Abdullah ibn Al-Zubayr

3. **Tabi`oon Tafseer:**

   a. Using the Method of Ma`thoor (reported):

      1. Tabari   2. Ibn Katheer   3. Al-Siyooti

   b. Using the Method of Opinions:

      1. Al-Raazi   4. Al-Nasafi
      2. Al-Baydawi`   5. Al-Khaazin
      3. Ibn Mass`ood

   c. Others:

      1. Al-Zamakhshari   4. Al-Aaloosi
      2. Sufis   5. Ibn Hayan
      3. Al-Mu'tazilah

4. **Contemporary Tafseer:**

   a.) Muhammad Rashid Rida   d.) Mawdoodi
   b.) Tantawi – Jawhari   e.) Al-Saabooni
   c.) Syed Qutub

XXIII. CLASSIFICATIONS OF QUR'ANIC CHAPTERS

A. General Information

In this chapter, the Surahs are to be arranged into different groups according to the similarity of their titles and to the themes that they belong to. By so doing, it will make it easy for the readers to understand the whole Qur'an: its themes, its subjects and its meaning. The more a person gets to know the Qur'an, the more his heart will be attached to it. To make this discussion easy to be understood, there are some Surahs that their names are related to Allah Himself; other are related to the Day of Judgement, while others are related to Prophets and Messengers; and still others are about people , nations and so on.

B. Specific Information

The following is a list of these groups of Surahs:

Section I   Surahs   Related   to   Allah.

The following Surahs are entitled after the Names and Attributes of Allah (swt). Their number is (13) thirteen.

No.	Name of Surah	English Meaning	Surah #
1	An-Noor	The Light	24
2	Fatir	The Originator of Creation	35
3	Ghafir	The Forgiver	40
4	Ar-Rahman	The Most Merciful	55
5	Al-A'laa	The Most High	87
6	Al –Fatiha	The Opening Chapter	1

No.	Name of Surah	English Meaning	Surah #
7	As-Sajdah to Allah	Prostration	32
8	Al-Mulk of Allah	Dominion	67
9	Al-Fath from Allah	Victory	48
10	Al-Inshirah from Allah	The Expansion	94
11	An-Nasr from Allah	Help	110
12	Saad from Secrets of Allah	Saad	38
13	Qaaf from Secrets of Allah	Qaaf	50

Section II Surahs Related to Prophets

The following Surahs are after the names of Prophets and Messengers. Also are related to their qualities and their mission in life . Their number is (16) sixteen.

No.	Name of Surah	English Meaning	Surah #
1	Al-Imran	The Family of Imran	3
2	Yunus	Prophet Yunus	10
3	Hood	Prophet Hood	11
4	Yusuf	Prophet Yusuf	12
5		Prophet	14
6	Mariam	Mary	19
7	Taha	Taha	20
8	Al-Anbiyaa'	The Prophets	21
9	Al-Qasass	The Narrations	28
10	Luqman	Luqman the Wise man	31
11	Yaseen	Yaseen	36

No.	Name of Surah	English Meaning	Surah #
12	Muhammad	Prophet Muhammad	47
13	Nooh	Prophet Nooh	71
14	Muzzammil	Folded in Garments	73
15	Muddathir	One Wrapped up	74
16	Al-Baiyna	The Clear Evidence	98

Section III Surahs Related to Angels

The following Surahs are after the names of angels and/or their attributes. Their number is only (3).

No	Name of Surah	English Meaning	Surah #
1	Assaaffaat	Those Ranged in Ranks	37
2	Ma'arij	The Ways of Ascent	70
3	Naazi'aat	Those Who Tear Out	79

Section IV Surahs Related to Qur'an

The following are two Surahs related to the attributes of Qur'an itself.

No	Name of Surah	English Meaning	Surah #
1	Al-Furqan	The Criterion	25
2	Fussilat	Explained in Detail	41

Section V Surahs Related to Day of Judgement

The following is a list of Surahs related to the Day of Judgement. Their total number is (13) thirteen.

No.	Name of Surah	English Meaning	Surah #
1	Al-Dukhan	Smoke	44
2	Al-Waqi'ah	The Inevitable Event	56
3	Al-Hashr	The Gathering	59
4	Al-Taghabun	Mutual Loss and Gain	64
5	Al-Haaqqah	The Sure Reality	69
6	Al-Qiyamah	The Resurrection	75
7	Al-Naba'	The Great News	78
8	Al-Takweer	The Folding Up	81
9	Al-Infitar	The Cleaving Asunder	82
10	Al-Inshiqaaq	The Rending Asunder	84
11	Al-Ghashiyah	The Overwhelming	88
12	Al-Zalzalah	The Convulsion	99
13	Al-Qari`ah	The Day of Clamour	101

Section VI Surahs Related to Sky

This group of Surahs are related to the Sky and to whatever is there, such as the stars, the moon, the sun, etc. their total number is (8) eight.

No.	Name of Surah	English Meaning	Surah #
1	Al Zaariyaat	The Winds that Scatter	51
2	Al-Najm	The Star	53
3	Al-Ra'ad	Thunder	13
4	Al-Qamar	The Moon	54
5	Al-Mursalat	Those Sent Forth	77
6	Al-Burooj	The Zodiacal Signs	85
7	Al-Tariq	The Night Visitant	86
8	Al-Shams	The Sun	91

Section VII Surahs Related to People

This section is concerned with people, nations, their attributes, and whatever is related to them. This group of Surahs are (17) Seventeen in number, they are the following:

No.	Name of Surah	English Meaning	Surah #
1	An-Nisaa''	The Women	4
2	Al-Kahf	The Cave	18
3	Al-Muminoon	The Believers	23
4	Ash-Shu'araa'	The Poets	26
5	Al-Room	The Romans	30
6	Al-Ahzaab	The Confederations	33
7	Saba	The City of Saba'	34
8	Al-Zumar	The Groups	39
9	Al-Shuraa	Consultation	42
10	Az-Zukhruf	Gold Adornments	43
11	Al-Jathiya	Bowing the Knee	45
12	Al-Munaafiqonn	The Hypocrites	63
13	Al-Jinn	The Jinn	72
14	Al-Insaan	Man	76
15	Quraysh	Tribe of Quraysh	106
16	Al-Kaafiroon	Those Who Reject Faith	109
17	An-Naas	Mankind	114

Section VIII Surahs Related to Behavior

This section represents the characters and social behaviors of people as well as their economic activities such as family values, disputes, divorce, cheating in business, hypocrisy, and etc. It is composed of (12) Twelve Surahs:

No.	Name of Surah	English Meaning	Surah #
1	Al-Anfaal	The Spoils of War	8
2	Al-Tawbah	Repentance	9
3	Al-Mujaadalah	The Woman who Pleads	58
4	Al-Mumtahanah	The Woman to be Examined	60
5	Assaff	Battle Array	61
6	Al-Talaq	Divorce	65
7	Al-Tahreem	Holding to be Forbidden	66
8	Abasa	He Frowned	80
9	Al-Mutaffifeen	Dealing in Fraud	83
10	Al-Takathur	Piling Up	102
11	Al-Humazah	Scandal – Monger	104
12	Al-Ikhlas	Purity of Faith	112

Section IX Surahs Related to Places

This list of Surahs are after names of places and locations in the history of mankind. Their number is (9) nine. They are the following:

No.	Name of Surah	English Meaning	Surah #
1	Al-A'raaf	The Heights	7
2	Al-Hijr	The Rocky Tract	15
3	Al-Israa'	The Night Travel	17
4	Al-Ahqaaf	Winding Sand-Tracts	46
5	Al-Hujurat	The Inner Apartments	49
6	Al-Toor	The Mount	52

No.	Name of Surah	English Meaning	Surah #
7	Al-Balad	The City	90
8	Al-Teen	The Fig	95
9	Al-Kawthar	Abundance	108

Section X Surahs Related to Days

The following list of Surahs are named after certain time in history, or section of a day or night or even a week. Their number is (8) eight. They are the following:

No.	Name of Surah	English Meaning	Surah #
1	Al-Hajj	Pilgrimage	22
2	Al-Jumu'ah	Friday	62
3	Al-Fajr	Dawn	89
4	Al-Layl	The Night	92
5	Al-Duha	The Glorious Morning Light	93
6	Al-Qadr	The Night of Power	97
7	Al-'Assr	Time through the Ages	103
8	Al- Falaq	The Dawn	113

Section XI Surahs Related to Animals

The following list of Surahs are named after animals, insects, flies, etc. Their total number is (8) Eight.

No.	Name of Surah	English Meaning	Surah #
1	Al-Baqarah	The Cow	2
2	Al-An'aam	The Cattles	6

No.	Name of Surah	English Meaning	Surah #
3	Al-Nahl	The Bees	16
4	Al-Naml	The Ants	27
5	Al-'Ankaboot	The Spider	29
6	Al-'Alaq	The Leech –like clot/Read	96
7	Al-A'adiyat	Those that Run	100
8	Al-Feel	The Elephant	105

Section XII   Surahs   Related to Matters

The following Surahs are named after inanimate matters. Their number is (5) five.

No.	Name of Surah	English Meaning	Surah #
1	Al-Maa'idah	Table-Spread	5
2	Al-Hadeed	Iron	57
3	Al-Qalam	The Pen	68
4	Al-Maa'oon	Neighborly Needs	107
5	Al-Masad	The Flame	111

C. Final Remarks

From the above   classification of the 114 Surahs, one can immediately recognize that the whole chapters of the Qur'an have been grouped into (12) twelve sections. By so doing we can understand and appreciate the Qur'an much better. The name of each Surah is being given and revealed by Allah, the source of Revelation. For each name there is a wisdom behind it. People have to read each Surah in depth, and they should try to understand its meaning, the historical occasion, the wisdom behind its title, its theme, and its topics that are discussed in each Surah.

On the other hand, one cannot understand any Surah without going back to the rest of all the Surahs in the Qur'an. For example: The story of any Prophet cannot be understood completely in one Surah, because the Qur'an is not a book of stories and narrations of stories. The whole mission of a particular prophet, the message that he received, the activities, the performance, the da'wah of inviting people to Allah, and other areas have to be found in a good number of Surahs. The wisdom is that each Surah has a theme, topics, explanations, and results. Accordingly, Allah with His Final Wisdom has revealed several Surahs, but He included certain prophets who had gone into difficulties in their lives. Whoever followed them were successful, and whoever rejected them were the losers. Therefore, one can realize the incident, the mission with such groups or nations, and the results of rejection or acceptance for each Prophet. Hence, by grouping them into different categories will help the reader to understand, and to appreciate the meaning of Qur'an.

Finally, One has to say again and again that the Qur'an is the Book from Allah (swt) revealed to Prophet Muhammad in a period of (23) years. It is considered as: The Summation, Culmination, and Purification of all the divine revealed books that Allah had revealed to all the previous Prophets and Messengers in the history of mankind. It has been preserved by Allah (swt), and it will continue to be preserved in totality till the Day of Judgement. Millions of people have memorized the Qur'an by heart even they are not Arabic speakers. This is one of the Miracles of Allah in the Qur'an. We pray to Allah to reward all those who love Allah and obey Him. Ameen.

XXIV. THE SUN AND THE MOON LETTERS

To read and recite Qur'an, one has to study a good number of Rules and Regulations. Among others, one has to know how to pronounce the letters, the words and the sentences. One has to know the verb, the subject, the predicate, object, preposition, phrases, adverb, adjective, etc. One has to know also the definite articles and how to pronounce those names that have definite articles.

In the Arabic language, there are (14) fourteen letters that are considered as Sun Letters, and another fourteen letters that are considered as Moon Letters. As far as the Sun Letters are concerned, one has to realize that, any time the definite article (The) is used for the Sun Letters, then the pronunciation of that word would be as follows: The definite article (The, Al-) is to be pronounced as if the "L" letter is not there. This means that the "L" letter is merged into the Sun Letter. The latter is to be pronounced as a double letter. An example of this discussion is as follows: If we take a word such as Rahman, the letter "R" is a Sun Letter. If we add the Definite Article for Rahman, then the way to be pronounced would be Ar-Rahman instead of Al-Rahman. The same thing would be applied to the word Sun. The addition of a definite article to it would make the word to be pronounced as Ash-Shams. The Sun Letters are as follows: Taa (ط), Ta (ت), Tha (ث), Saad (ص), Seen (س), Sheen (ش), Ra (ر), Daad (ض), Zaal (ذ), Noon (ن), Za (ظ), Zain (ز), Laam (ل), and Daal (د). The following is the List of the Sun Letters, where the Definite Article (The) is being added to them. The reader can recognize those words and how to pronounce them.

The Sun Letters
Ash-Shams
Al-Ahruf   Ash - Shamsiyah

حرف   حروف الإدغام في اللام الـاكنة :

المد	الإدغام	للثال		
١	ط الطاء	الطَّيِّبَات للطَّيِّبِين	1.	AT-TAYYIBAAT
٢	ث الثاء	نعم الثَّوَاب	2.	ATH - THAWAAB
٣	ص الصاد	وأقيموا الصَّلاة	3.	ASSALAAT
٤	ر الراء	الرَّحمن الرَّحيم	4.	AR - RAH.AAN
٥	ت التاء	التَّائبون	5.	AT - TAA - IBOONA
٦	ض الضاد	ولا الضَّالين	6.	AD-DAALLEEN
٧	ذ الذال	والذَّاكرين الله	7.	ATH - THAAKIREEN
٨	ن النون	ملك النَّاس	8.	AN - NAAS
٩	د الدال	ويكون الدَّين لله	9.	AD - DEEN
١٠	س الـسين	والسَّارق والسَّارقة	10.	ASSAARIQ
١١	ظ الظاء	الظَّاهر	11.	ATH - THAAHIRR
١٢	ز الزاي	الزَّكاة	12.	AZZAKAAT
١٣	ش الشين	والشَّمس	13.	ASH - SHAMS
١٤	ل اللام	واللَّيل	14.	ALLAYL

178

As far as the Moon-Letters are concerned, they are fourteen letters. They are: Hamza (ء), Ba (ب), Ghayn (غ), Ha (ح), Jeem (ج), Kaaf (ك), Wawe (و), Kha (خ), Fa (ف), 'Ain (ع), Qaf (ق), Ya (ي), Meem (م), and Ha (ه).

Any time the Definite article is being used to a word, then both the "L" letter is to be pronounced independent from the word. An example of this would be the following: Qamar (Moon). When the Definite article is being used, then the way to pronounce this word would be Al-Qamar. The same thing is to be said about the rest of the Moon Letters such as Hajj (Pilgrimage): Then the addition of the definite article would make it to be pronounced as: Al-Hajj.

The following is a List of the Moon Letters, whereby the Definite Article (The: Al) is being added to them. The reader can realize those words, and how to be pronounced.

The Moon letters
Al - Qamar
Al - Ahruf Al - Qamariyah

حروف الإظهار الأربعة عشر :

العدد	حرف الإظهار	المثال		
١	ء الهمزة	الأُول	1.	AL - AWWAL
٢	ب الباء	الباقي	2.	AL - BAAQEE
٣	غ الغين	الغني	3.	AL - GHANIYY
٤	ح الحاء	الحج	4.	AL - HAJJ

179

٥	ج الجيم	الْجنّة	5. AL - JANNAH
٦	ك الكاف	الْكريم	6. AL - KAREEM
٧	و الواو	الْودود	7. AL - WADOOD
٨	خ الخاء	الْخالق	8. AL - KHALIQ
٩	ف الفاء	الْفتاح	9. AL - FATTAH
١٠	ع العين	الْعليم	10. AL - 'ALEEM
١١	ق القاف	الْقمر	11. AL- QAMAR
١٢	ي الياء	الْيوم	12. AL - YAWM
١٣	م الميم	الْملك	13. AL - MULK
١٤	هـ الهاء	الْهدي	14. AL - HADIY

180

XXV. PREPOSITIONS

To study the Qur'an, a person has to have a teacher who is specialized in Qur'an. One has to study the alphabets, the verbs, subjects, objects, prepositions, phrases, pronunciation, noonation, elongation, assimilation, etc. Each and everyone of these is a course by itself so that a person may be able to read and recite the Qur'an with the rules of proper recitation: (Tarteel) and (Tajweed).

In as much as a person is to know the Sun and the Moon letters, he has to know the **prepositions** as well. Without these a person cannot even read and pronounce the words of the Qur'an. To punctuate a word with Aa, Oo, or Ee, one has to know among others, the prepositions. The presence of a preposition before a single subject will change the pronunciation of that subject from (oo) into (ee). To demonstrate an example of that would be the following:

Al-Masjid = Al-Masjidu

When a preposition comes before it, it will change its pronunciation from Al-Masjidu to Al-Masjidi. To give a sentence for this would be as follows:

أَنَا ذَهَبْتُ إِلَى الْمَسْجِدِ

I went to the Masjid
Anaa Zahabtu Ela (Ila) Al-Masjidi

When someone says:

الْمَسْجِدُ بَيْتُ اللّه

The Masjid is the House of Allah
Al-Masjidu Baitul Lah.

One cannot say *Al-Masjidu Baitil Lah,* but it should be pronounced as *Baitul.* However, if any preposition comes before such a word, the pronunciation of such a word will be *Baiti* but not *Baitu.*

In the Arabic language there are (14) words that are considered prepositions. One has to ask a teacher to give a good number of lessons as to the use of these prepositions with different sentences, and with different genders. One has to know also the influence of these prepositions on single words, double or multiple subjects or objects. Each and every one has its rules and regulations.

In this chapter, the reader has to recognize the importance of these prepositions in understanding the Qur'an. By knowing the rules and regulations of the presence of these Prepositions, the reader can read Qur'an easy. Then the reader does not need to look at each letter with its punctuation. He will read Qur'an properly and easy.

The following is the list of Prepositions in the Arabic Alphabets. No punctuation has been put on any letter. They are left blank. The reader has to go to a teacher of the Arabic language and learn more about them.

PREPOSITIONS

Transliteration	English	Arabic
Ila	to	الى
'Ala	On	على
'Ann	About	عن

Fee	In	في
Fawqa	Unto /above	فوق
Tahta	Under	تحت
'Inda	At	عند
Kaaf	As	كَ
Laam	To	ل
Ba	With/in	ب
Ma'a	with	مع
Bayn	between	بين
Hatta	Until	حتى
Min	From	من

183

XXVI. SIGNS OF STOPS AND ACCURACY OF PUNCTUATION

To read and recite Qur'an properly, one has to know when and where to stop. Otherwise the meaning of the Ayah is not achieved. Moreover, the meaning will be distorted or reversed. Therefore, the early Muslim scholars have put punctuation at every letter of each word in the Qur'an so that the reciter will be able to read properly. They also put different signs of stops to make sure that the readers will be able to read with proper meaning and proper understanding. Such types of signs will also help the ones who are listening to the Qur'an to realize the exact meaning of the Ayat of the Qur'an.

It should be stated here that not every stop is an obligatory stop. For example: We take the letters (م) Meem and (م) Meem. If it is found above a word, one has to stop completely, otherwise the meaning of the Ayah will be distorted. The second Meem is not a sign of stop, but it refers to conversion suppressed.

Another example for the Signs of stops would be: (صلى) Salaa, (قلى) Qalaa, and Jeem (ج). As for the letter (Salaa), one is allowed to stop at that particular word in an Ayah, but it is better to connect without stopping. As far as the letter Qalaa is concerned, it is preferable that one has to stop at that word which has the sign Qalaa on the Ayah. As far as the letter Jeem is concerned, one has the right to stop or not to stop whenever he sees this letter on the word.

In case one sees the letter (لا) Laa, he has no right to stop when he is reciting the Qur'an. If he stops at that word of the Ayah, the meaning will be distorted.

184

The rest of the Signs of Stops as well as the Signs of Accuracy of Punctuation are included here. It is recommended that the one who wishes to learn these Signs has to study with a teacher of the Qur'an. By so doing, then one will learn how to read Qur'an properly, and then he will understand what he is reading.

علامات الوقف وضبط علامات الضبط :

Signs of stops and Accuracy of Punctuation

Must stop	مـ تُفِيدُ لُزُومَ الوَقْفِ
Cannot stop	لا تُفِيدُ النَّهْيَ عَنِ الوَقْفِ
Allowed to stop but letter to connect	صلے تُفِيدُ بِأَنَّ الوَصْلَ أَوْلَى مَعَ جَوَازِ الوَقْفِ
Preferable to stop	قلے تُفِيدُ بِأَنَّ الوَقْفَ أَوْلَى
You may stop	ج تُفِيدُ جَوَازَ الوَقْفِ
You may stop at either sign but not at both place	∴ ∴ تُفِيدُ جَوَازَ الوَقْفِ بِأَحَدِ المَوْضِعَيْنِ وَلَيْسَ فِي كِلَيْهِمَا
The letter is extra, not to be pronounced	• الدِّلالَةُ عَلَى زِيَادَةِ الحَرْفِ وَعَدَمِ النُّطْقِ بِهِ
During the joining of 2 words the letter is silent	• الدِّلالَةُ عَلَى زِيَادَةِ وَ الحَرْفِ حِينَ الوَصْلِ
The letter is unvoweled	• الدِّلالَةُ عَلَى سُكُونِ الحَرْفِ

185

٢	Conversion suppressed	للدِّلَالَةِ عَلَى وُجُودِ الإِفَلَابِ
؏	Nunation	للدِّلَالَةِ عَلَى إِظْهَارِ التَّنْوِينِ
؏	Assimilation and pronunciation	للدِّلَالَةِ عَلَى الإِدغَامِ وَالإِخْفَاهِ
ء ه ن	To pronounce the deleted letters	ن للدِّلَالَةِ عَلَى وُجُوبِ النُّطْقِ بِأَحْرُفٍ المَترُوكَةِ
س	. If it is above a letter pronounce it soft (S.) . If it is underneath pronounce it strong (s)	للدِّلَا لَةِ عَلَى وُجُوبِ النُّطْقِ بِالسِّينِ بَدَلَ الصَّادِ وَاذَا وُضِعَتْ بِالأَسْفَلِ فَالنُّطْقُ بِالصَّادِ أَشْهَر
⁓	Longer beat is a must	للدِّلَالَةِ عَلَى لزُومِ المَدِّ الزَّائِـدِ
🕌	Place of prostration	للدِّلَالَةِ عَلَى مَوضِعِ السُّجُودِ ، أَمَّا كَلِمَة وُجُوبِ السُّجُودِ فَقَدْ وُضِعَ تَحْتَهَا خَط
✿	Starting of Juzu', Hibz, half of Hizb, quarter of Hibz	للدِّلَالَةِ عَلَى بِدَايَةِ الأَجْزَاءِ وَالأَحْـزَابِ وَأَنصَافِهَا وَأَرْبَاعِهَا
۝	End of Ayah and its number	۝ للدِّلَالَةِ عَلَى نِهَايَةِ الآيَةِ وَرَقِمِهَا

186

XXVII. TRANSLATIONS OF THE QUR'AN

The Qur'an was revealed to the Prophet in Arabic. It was preserved by Allah throughout the history till now. It will be preserved till the Day of Judgement. Its originality, its totality, its meaning, its purity, its message and its language (Arabic) will continue to be preserved and saved without any changes. Allah (swt) has assured its preservation. In the Qur'an Allah says in Surah Al-Hijr (The Rocky Tract) the following:

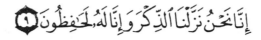

We have, without doubt, sent down the Message; and We will assuredly guard it from corruption. (15:9)

Muslims and non-Muslims tried to translate the Qur'an to different languages of the world. Some of them were honest and sincere people. Others were either orientalists or missionary personnel whose interests were to confuse the Muslims, or to stop the non-Muslims from accepting Islam. Those honest individuals have done their best and translated the Qur'an to different languages of the world. Not a single translation could be taken for granted. **The Qur'an is in the Arabic text. It cannot be translated to any language. It will lose its meaning, its beauty of language, its rhyme, its rhythm, its echo, its spirituality and its being a Revealed Book from Allah. Any other language is no more the Qur'an. It could be considered: The Meaning of the Qur'an.**

It should be stated here that no one can translate the Qur'an by any means. The Qur'an is the word of Allah. No one can comprehend the total meaning of the Qur'an. The Qur'an is the summation, culmination and purification of all the previous revealed books that Allah revealed to His Prophets and Messengers. The Qur'an is a comprehensive Book of Guidance to mankind. It includes spirituality, social and family values, history of previous nations, scientific facts including biology, zoology, pathology, histology, embryology, chemistry, physics, astronomy, inheritance, economics, politics, treaties, ethics, manners, unseen creatures (angels and jinns), life in the graves, life in Paradise, life in Hell, and so on. Therefore, no one personality will be able to translate the Qur'an by himself. It needs a team of Muslim scholars composed of at least fifty personalities with different specialties. They should be able to know at least two languages: Arabic and the other language that the Qur'an is to be translated to.

Unfortunately, up till now we see that almost all the translations of the Qur'an have been made by individuals. For that reason, no one translation is void of mistakes in meaning or language. Most of them are full of mistakes in one way or the other. Recently, some individuals in America have followed the footsteps of the early translators. They made more mistakes than others. Those individuals feels that they should compete with others, or they want to get the credit from people. They might be looking for fame and reputation. They should be humble enough to refrain from such a big job.

The burden therefore falls upon the Muslim Governments and the umbrella that they work together such as The League of Arab States whose headquarters is in Cairo, Egypt. The other umbrella is the Organization of Islamic Conference (OIC) that represents (58) Muslim sovereign countries. Their headquarters is in Jeddah, Saudi Arabia. These Muslim countries have Department of Islamic Affairs, as well as they have Muslim universities.

They teach Qur'an, Tafseer, Hadith, Seerah, Da'wah, 'Aqeedah, etc. They do have even Mufti or Grand Mufti, and they have a large member of Muslim scholars in many disciplines and specialties. They do have enough money to give grants to a good number of Muslim scholars to spend a minimum of one year or so to revise all the previous translations and come up with a new one that is approved by the whole Muslim world. Until then, Muslims are to be blamed for not assuming such a responsibility.

The following is a partial list of translated books about the Qur'an that are partially accepted and being circulated among the Muslims in English, French and Spanish. The Saudi Government has printed a good number of translations in a good number of languages. Attached is also a partial list of those books. We pray to Allah to guide the Muslim Ummah to do their obligation toward the Book of Allah, namely Al-Qur'an Al-Kareem. Ameen.

A.   Partial List of Translated Qur'an

1. The Holy Qur'an: Text, Translation & Commentary; A. Yusuf Ali.

2. The Holy Qur'an: Text, Translation & Commentary; M.M. Pickthal.

3. The Message of the Qur'an: Translation & Explained; Muhammad Asad.

4. The Qur'an: Translation & Commentary; T.B. Irving.

5. The Noble Qur'an: Interpretation of the Meaning; Md Taqi-ud-Din Al-Hilali & Md. Muhsin Khan.

6. The Message of the Qur'an: Presented in Perspective; Hashim Amir-Ali

189

7. Al-Qur'an – Rendered into English; Dr. Syed Abdul Latif.

8. Le Saint Coran (French); Dr. M. Hamidullah & M. Leturny.

9. El Cor'an (Spanish); Julio Cortes.

10. The Holy Qur'an – Translated from the original Arabic with Lexical, Grammatical, Historical, Geographical and Eschatological Comments; Abdul Majid.

11. Qur'an for Children; A. Rauf.

12. In the Shade of the Qur'an, volume (30); Sayyid Qutb.

XXVIII. READING THE ENTIRE QUR'AN
KHATMUL QUR'AN

A practicing Muslim is supposed to read from Qur'an on a daily basis. The best time is at Fajr. Allah (swt) says in Surah Al-Israa' (night Travel) the following:

أَقِمِ
ٱلصَّلَوٰةَ لِدُلُوكِ ٱلشَّمْسِ إِلَىٰ غَسَقِ ٱلَّيْلِ وَقُرْءَانَ ٱلْفَجْرِ إِنَّ
قُرْءَانَ ٱلْفَجْرِ كَانَ مَشْهُودًا ۞ وَمِنَ ٱلَّيْلِ فَتَهَجَّدْ بِهِ
نَافِلَةً لَّكَ عَسَىٰٓ أَن يَبْعَثَكَ رَبُّكَ مَقَامًا مَّحْمُودًا ۞

Establish regular prayers-at the sun's decline till the darkness of the night, and the recital of the Qur'an in morning prayer for the recital of dawn is witnessed. And as for the night keep awake a part of it as an additional prayer for you: soon will your Lord raise you to a station of Praise and Glory. (17: 78-79)

Muslims try their best to read Qur'an daily. The Qur'an is divided into (30) thirty volumes (Juzu') on a systematic basis . They try to read one volume daily so that they will be able to finish reading the whole Qur'an every lunar month. At the end of reading the whole Qur'an, it is recommended that a person makes Du'a' (supplication). That Du'a' is called Du'a' khatmul Qur'an. One may make a Du'a' of his own, and may request Allah (swt) to accept from him what he has read from the Qur'an. Many Muslims are encouraged to attend a place where the Qur'an is to be recited in full in a Jama'ah. After which they finish reading the whole Qur'an. Each person assumes reading one volume. The

191

whole Qur'an will read by the group of Muslims in a period of 1-2 hours. Then the group will make a Du'a' for reading the whole Qur'an. That Du'a' is also called Du'a' Khatmul Qur'an.

Muslims in different parts of the world have adopted different ways to finish reading the whole Qur'an. The climax of finishing the recitation of Qur'an is in the month of Ramadan, the month of fasting and the month of the revelation of the Qur'an. During Ramadan, Muslims do pray Salatul Taraweeh every night after 'Isha Salat. During salat they read one volume every night. They try to finish reciting Qur'an on the eve of Lailatul Qadr. The night is mainly on the eve of the 27th day whereby Muslims come to the Masjid and attend the recitation of the last volume so as to get the blessings of Khatmul Qur'an. In Makkah, Arabian peninsula, the Imam tries to finish the Qur'an the last night of Taraweeh Salat, i.e. the last night of Ramadan. After finishing the recitation of the Qur'an, the Imam make Du'a' of khatmul Qur'an.

There is no specific Du'a' that the Imam has to recite. There are many way of asking Allah (swt) to accept whatever has been recited. They ask Allah (swt) forgiveness, rewards, Du'a' Shifaa', guidance, mercy, unity, peace, happiness, tranquility, etc. The following is a selected one Du'a' of the khatmul Qur'an. The Arabic text is included in this chapter as well as the English meaning of it. We do pray that Allah (swt) will inspire all of us to read the Qur'an, and to listen to the Qur'an.

دُعَاءُ خَتْمِ الْقُرْآنِ

اللَّهُمَّ ارْحَمْنِي بِالْقُرْآنِ وَاجْعَلْهُ لِي إِمَامًا وَنُورًا وَهُدًى وَرَحْمَةً اللَّهُمَّ ذَكِّرْنِي مِنْهُ مَا نَسِيتُ وَعَلِّمْنِي مِنْهُ مَا جَهِلْتُ وَارْزُقْنِي تِلاوَتَهُ آنَاءَ اللَّيْلِ وَأَطْرَافَ النَّهَارِ وَاجْعَلْهُ لِي حُجَّةً يَا رَبَّ الْعَالَمِينَ ٭ اللَّهُمَّ أَصْلِحْ لِي دِينِي الَّذِي هُوَ عِصْمَةُ أَمْرِي وَأَصْلِحْ لِي دُنْيَايَ الَّتِي فِيهَا مَعَاشِي وَأَصْلِحْ لِي آخِرَتِي الَّتِي فِيهَا مَعَادِي وَاجْعَلِ الْحَيَاةَ زِيَادَةً لِي فِي كُلِّ خَيْرٍ وَاجْعَلِ الْمَوْتَ رَاحَةً لِي مِنْ كُلِّ شَرٍّ ٭ اللَّهُمَّ اجْعَلْ خَيْرَ عُمْرِي آخِرَهُ وَخَيْرَ عَمَلِي خَوَاتِمَهُ وَخَيْرَ أَيَّامِي يَوْمَ أَلْقَاكَ فِيهِ ٭ اللَّهُمَّ إِنِّي أَسْأَلُكَ عِيشَةً هَنِيَّةً وَمِيتَةً سَوِيَّةً وَمَرَدًّا غَيْرَ مُخْزٍ وَلا فَاضِحٍ ٭ اللَّهُمَّ إِنِّي أَسْأَلُكَ خَيْرَ الْمَسْأَلَةِ وَخَيْرَ الدُّعَاءِ وَخَيْرَ النَّجَاحِ وَخَيْرَ الْعِلْمِ وَخَيْرَ الْعَمَلِ وَخَيْرَ الثَّوَابِ وَخَيْرَ الْحَيَاةِ وَخَيْرَ الْمَمَاتِ وَثَبِّتْنِي وَثَقِّلْ مَوَازِينِي وَحَقِّقْ إِيمَانِي وَارْفَعْ دَرَجَتِي وَتَقَبَّلْ صَلاتِي وَاغْفِرْ خَطِيئَاتِي

193

وَأَسْأَلُكَ الْعُلَا مِنَ الْجَنَّةِ ۞ اللَّهُمَّ إِنِّي أَسْأَلُكَ مُوجِبَاتِ رَحْمَتِكَ
وَعَزَائِمَ مَغْفِرَتِكَ وَالسَّلَامَةَ مِنْ كُلِّ إِثْمٍ وَالْغَنِيمَةَ مِنْ كُلِّ بِرٍّ
وَالْفَوْزَ بِالْجَنَّةِ وَالنَّجَاةَ مِنَ النَّارِ ۞ اللَّهُمَّ أَحْسِنْ عَاقِبَتَنَا فِي
الْأُمُورِ كُلِّهَا وَأَجِرْنَا مِنْ خِزْيِ الدُّنْيَا وَعَذَابِ الْآخِرَةِ ۞
اللَّهُمَّ اقْسِمْ لَنَا مِنْ خَشْيَتِكَ مَا تَحُولُ بِهِ بَيْنَنَا وَبَيْنَ مَعْصِيَتِكَ وَمِنْ
طَاعَتِكَ مَا تُبَلِّغُنَا بِهَا جَنَّتَكَ وَمِنَ الْيَقِينِ مَا تُهَوِّنُ بِهِ عَلَيْنَا
مَصَائِبَ الدُّنْيَا وَمَتِّعْنَا بِأَسْمَاعِنَا وَأَبْصَارِنَا وَقُوَّتِنَا مَا أَحْيَيْتَنَا
وَاجْعَلْهُ الْوَارِثَ مِنَّا وَاجْعَلْ ثَأْرَنَا عَلَى مَنْ ظَلَمَنَا وَانْصُرْنَا عَلَى مَنْ
عَادَانَا وَلَا تَجْعَلْ مُصِيبَتَنَا فِي دِينِنَا وَلَا تَجْعَلِ الدُّنْيَا أَكْبَرَ هَمِّنَا
وَلَا مَبْلَغَ عِلْمِنَا وَلَا تُسَلِّطْ عَلَيْنَا مَنْ لَا يَرْحَمُنَا ۞ اللَّهُمَّ لَا تَدَعْ لَنَا
ذَنْبًا إِلَّا غَفَرْتَهُ وَلَا هَمًّا إِلَّا فَرَّجْتَهُ وَلَا دَيْنًا إِلَّا قَضَيْتَهُ وَلَا حَاجَةً
مِنْ حَوَائِجِ الدُّنْيَا وَالْآخِرَةِ إِلَّا قَضَيْتَهَا يَا أَرْحَمَ الرَّاحِمِينَ ۞ رَبَّنَا
آتِنَا فِي الدُّنْيَا حَسَنَةً وَفِي الْآخِرَةِ حَسَنَةً وَقِنَا عَذَابَ النَّارِ
وَصَلَّى اللهُ عَلَى نَبِيِّنَا مُحَمَّدٍ وَعَلَى آلِهِ وَأَصْحَابِهِ
الْأَخْيَارِ وَسَلَّمَ تَسْلِيمًا كَثِيرًا

SUPPLICATION FOR RECITATION OF
THE WHOLE QUR'AN

In The Name of Allah, Most Beneficent, Most Merciful

❖ Oh Allah! Have mercy on me, in the name of the Great Qur'an; make it an Imam and light for me, as well as guidance and mercy.

❖ Oh Allah! Make me remember what I have forgotten of, and make me recite it in the hours of the night and the day; make it an argument for me, You are the Sustainer of (all) the worlds.

❖ Oh Allah! Make my religion accurate for me, in which lies the infallibility of existence. Make good for me this world in which I shall spend my life in, and make good for me the hereafter to which I shall return. Make life an increase in every good thing for me. Make death a rest from every evil for me.

❖ Oh Allah! Make the best part of my life to be the latter portion of it, and the best of my deeds their finishing and the best of my days is the day I meet You in the Day of Judgement.

❖ Oh Allah! I ask You for a happy life, and an equitable death, a return with neither humiliating or disgraceful.

❖ Oh Allah! I ask for the best that one can ask You for, and the best of supplication, the best success, the best deeds, the best reward, the best life, the best death, and strengthen me and increase the weight in the measure in my favor. Make true my faith and raise my ranking, accept my prayers, forgive my mistakes and I ask You a high level in heaven.

❖ Oh Allah! I ask You for those which cause me to earn Your mercy and invite Your forgiveness, and the safety from every sin, the gain from every righteousness, the success of going to heaven, and of the salvation from the fire.

❖ Oh Allah! Make good our ending in all deeds, and prevent us from the humiliation of this world and the punishment of the hereafter.

❖ Oh Allah! Give us the amount of fearing You which is enough to be a barrier between us and disobeying You, and enough obedience to let us reach Your heaven, enough certainty to ease on us the calamities of this world. Make us enjoy our hearing, our vision, and our strength as long as we live. Make them all to be what will be inherited to us (or what remains in our account). Make possible our revenge against those who did injustice to us. Give us victory on those who chose to be our enemies. Do not let our main misfortune be in our religion nor let the world be our main concern and the goal of our knowledge nor empower against us those who do not show us mercy.

❖ Oh Allah! Do not let any of our sins without forgiving it, nor any stress without relieving it, nor a debt without paying it, nor any need of the needs of this world and the hereafter without being faithful. Oh, You are the Most Merciful among those who have mercy.

❖ Our Lord! Give us which is good in this world and which is good in the hereafter, and guard us from the doom of fire. May Allah's mercy be upon our Prophet Muhammad, his family, and his selected companions, and may He bless all of them with great blessings.

196

XXIX.   INQUIRIES ABOUT THE QUR'AN

In this section the author wishes to present some of the many questions that were posed to him either during his series of lectures in his classes on Islamic Shari'ah. Other questions were sent to him by mail. Moreso, there were questions which were asked on the phone. The author tried his best to answer some of the most pertinent questions that were asked so often. Some of these questions were presented by non-Muslims while others by Muslims. The following is a partial list of questions and their answers:

Q 1:   Why the Holy Book of Islam is called Qur'an?

A 1:   The name of the Holy Book is called Al-Qur'an. This name is given by the Creator namely Allah (swt) Who revealed it to Prophet Muhammad. The One God has the right to call it whatever He wants. Therefore, He called it Al-Qur'an. He gave it different adjectives and attributes such as Al-Qur'an Al-Kareem, Al-Qur'an Al-Hakeem, Al-Qur'an Al-Majeed, and so on.

Q 2:   Why therefore, the Qur'an is called Al-Qur'an. Does it have any meaning in the original Arabic language?

A 2:   Yes! The word Al-Qur'an came from the Arabic root word of Qara'a, Yaqra-oo, Qiraa-ah, Qur'aanan, and etc. This means that this Book is meant to be read with recitation, melody, rhyme, rhythm, and with rules and regulations.

The climax of reciting the Book with these adjectives is called Qur'an. Therefore it is a subject of the verb Qara'a: To read with recitation. Finally, the Qur'an is to be read, to be recited and to be utilized on a daily basis during the five daily prayers, as well as outside the prayers in the society.

Q 3:   Is it true that the Qur'an has its spiritual impact on the person by reading it or listening to its recitation?

A 3:   Yes indeed! This is one of the uniqueness of the Qur'an. It will definitely impact strongly on the person who recites it or the one who listens to it. As long as the Qur'an is being recited with its beauty of melody, it will unequivocally influence the reciter as well as the listener.

The Qur'anic recitation will penetrate the heart of both the reciter and the listener if they are honest, sincere, and are having good intention. By reading or listening with respect, the person will feel shivering, shaking, and trembling. The echo of the voice of the reciter hits the heart and hence penetrates it. Finally it molds the person to the right direction to be close to the Creator, Allah, the One God Who revealed that Qur'an.

Q 4:   Does the Qur'an have other names to be recognized with? If yes, what are those names?

A 4:   Yes! The Qur'an is recognized with other names. Those names are identified directly from the Qur'an itself. Other names of the Qur'an in the Qur'an are about 50 names. Some of the names are the following:

Figure I: **Some Names of the Qur'an**

Arabic Pronounciation	English Meaning
1. Al-Kitab	The Book
2. Al-Furqan	The Criterion
3. Al-Zikr	The Reminder

4.	Al-Tanzeel	The Revelation
5.	Ahsan Al-Hadeeth	The Best Message
6.	Al-Shifaa'	The Healer
7.	Al-Huda	The Guidance
8.	Al-Burhan	The Proof
9.	Al-Haqq	The Truth
10.	Al-Kareem	The Noble
11.	Al-Majeed	The Glorious

You may also read the Book: **"The Golden Book of Islamic Lists"** by the same author chapter (7) p. 25-30. You will definitely by pleased to know their meanings. Moreover, you will be excited to associate yourself with the beautiful description of each one. Then and only then will the Qur'an have a relationship with you.

Q 5: I heard that the Qur'an was written by Muhammad. Is this information true?

A 5:   This information is not true. The one who brought it to your attention is either biased, prejudiced or at least ignorant of the history and the historical documentation of Islam.

The Qur'an was revealed to the Prophet from Allah on a daily basis for a period of 23 years. Angel Gabriel used to come to him daily and revealed certain passages (Ayat, Verses) or certain chapters (Surahs).   Prophet Muhammad memorized it, lived it, explained it, and delivered it to all. His companions memorized it too, and delivered it to the new generations through memorization first. Nowadays, it is delivered through memory, printing, audio, video, C.D. ROM, Internet, and via satellites.

Q 6: **Since the Qur'an was revealed to Prophet Muhammad, so what was the role of Muhammad?**

A 6: The role of Prophet Muhammad was to receive the revelation, and to memorize it daily under the supervision of Angel Gabriel. The Prophet conveyed the Message to his Companions. They in turn, also memorized whatever was revealed to the Prophet. He lived the teachings perfectly, explained them properly, and requested his people to convey the Message to those who did not hear it yet.

Q 7: **Since Muhammad explained the Qur'an to his people, what is that document called?**

A 7: The document of the Sayings of the Prophet is called Hadith. It is the exact quotations of the Prophet. It has its transmitters (reporters) who are called Sanad. It has the exact text in verbatim for the sayings of the Prophet which is called Matn.

Those who collected the Hadith, scrutinized them, categorized them, and memorized them, are called the Collectors of the Hadith. The most important ones are Bukhari, Muslim, Ibn Dawood, Ibn Majah, Nasaa-ee, and Tarmazee.

Q 8: **It seems that the Qur'an is a huge Book. Was it revealed to the Prophet all at one time?**

A 8: No!...The Qur'an was not revealed at one time, but for a period of 23 years. If the Qur'an were revealed at one time, it would be difficult for the early Muslims to memorize it, to comprehend it, and to apply its teachings in their public and private life.

It was revealed at different places, at different times, and on different occasions. In this way it was taken seriously. The early Muslims appreciated the Revelation. It meant a lot for them, and they enjoyed the Message tremendously.

Q 9: Is it true that many Muslims have memorized the whole Qur'an by heart? It is a surprise for me because no one Holy Book has been memorized by heart!

A 9: Yes!...You are right. The Qur'an has been memorized by millions of Muslims throughout the world. Even a good number of non-Arabic speaking Muslims have memorized the whole Qur'an in Arabic by heart. I wish to add my voice to your observation. No one Holy Book other than the Qur'an has ever been memorized from cover to cover.

The Qur'an is really a miracle from Allah (swt). Whoever is honest, sincere, and is seeking the truth, Allah (swt) will definitely make him to read, understand, appreciate, memorize, and practice the Qur'an privately and publicly.

Q 10: The Qur'an was revealed in Arabic. We are non-Arabs. Can we translate the Qur'an to different languages and assume that the translated copies are also the True Revealed Qur'an?

A 10: You may translate the Qur'an to other languages. However, the translated copies are no more the Qur'an. Such translations could be considered as the meaning of the verses in the Qur'an. As you are aware, the Qur'an is the True Revealed words of Allah. Yes! It was revealed in Arabic. It will stay in Arabic...Early Muslims after they have accepted Islam learned the Arabic language. They understood it, and they studied the Qur'an from many different aspects. They also memorized it. Most of the

201

early Muslims were not Arabs. They accepted Islam and enjoyed the teachings of Allah in the Qur'an. Accordingly, they loved it, and they mastered the Arabic language. They made sure the language of the Qur'an should be the official language of the land. The Qur'anic language became also the language of science, technology, industry, business, arts, and international communication.

Q 11: We are non-Arabic speaking individuals. Can we read Qur'an through the process of Transliteration?!

A 11: Unfortunately No!...We cannot read any language through transliteration. One has to study and learn the language from within the language itself and from the tongue of its people. The same thing applied here to the language of the Qur'an.

The early people who accepted Islam never tried to transliterate the language of the Qur'an while studying it. They learned the Qur'anic language from the prophet and his companions. They memorized the Qur'an directly.

The method of transliteration cannot allow us to pronounce the Arabic letter properly. There is no difference in writing between Seen and Saad; Te and Taa; Ha and Haa; Daal and Daad; Zaal and Zaa; Alif and `Ain and so on.

Moreover, it is not easy to transliterate the rules of recitation of Tajweed and Tarteel of the Qur'an.

Therefore, let us make efforts to study the language of the Qur'an, the way it was revealed to Prophet Muhammad himself.

Q 12: I found out that the Qur'an has many scientific reflections. Does this means that the Qur'an is a scientific book.?

A 12: The Qur'an is not a scientific book. It is a book of Guidance to all of us. It is a revealed book from Allah (swt) through Prophet Muhammad to all generations and to all places till the Day of Judgment.

The Qur'an has information about many nations before us, as well as the ones around us. It has also information about the future and the life in the grave as well as the life in Day of Judgment.

It has encouraged us to look around and see how the Universe has been created. The Qur'an encouraged us to look around, to see things and to reflect. It talks about the sun and the moon; the mountains; the valleys; the rivers; the seas; and the oceans;...The creation of human being...the method of reproduction...the embryological synthesis of milk...; It talks about the collapse of the whole planet earth with all what is on it and, around it as well as the collapse of the other planets.

Finally, the Qur'an is meant to help us to live by its total teachings in our private and public life. It is also meant for the government to abide by its total teachings.

Q 13: I found out that the Qur'an is divided into volumes and sub-volumes. Can you inform me more about this approach?

A 13: For the sake of reading the Qur'an on a daily basis, and for the sake of finishing reading the whole Qur'an every month, it was divided into 30 volumes (Juzu'). In this way, it would be easy for a Muslim to read one volume on a daily basis.

Moreover, a Muslim may not be able to read one volume at one time. Therefore, each volume was subdivided into two sections (Hizb). In this way a Muslim may read one section in the morning and another section in the evening.

For those who would like to read a portion of a section after every Salat, it was made easy for them. Each section (Hizb) is subdivided into four quarters. In this way a Muslim may read early morning one section (Hizb) and then after every Salat he may read a quarter of Hizb. Therefore, a Muslim will enjoy reading a small portion of Qur'an after each Salat. Accordingly, he will be able to finish reading the whole Qur'an every lunar month.

Q 14: **I found out that there is a series of Sajdah (prostration) in the Qur'an. Would you like to inform me more about them?**

A 14: In the Qur'an there are 15 Sajdah in 14 surahs. This means that one Surah has two sajdah. It is called Surah Al-Hajj (The Pilgrimage), chapter 22. There is one surah in the Qur'an called Sajdah. It is chapter 32.

Any time, a person reads or hears the recitation of Qur'an where the Sajdah is, he should perform Sajdah to Allah (swt). It is only one Sajdah. If a person hears the recitation and he does not have ablution (wudoo') he should glorify Allah (swt) three times. He should say:

204

Subhan Allah...Wal Hamdu Lillah...Wa la Ilaha Illa Allah...Wallahu Akbar.

Glory be to Allah...Praise is to Allah...There is no one worthy of worship except Allah...and Allah is the Greatest.

Q 15: While reading Qur'an , I recognized that there is one Surah that does not have Bismillah Ar-Rahman Ar-Raheem. Can you tell me more about that?

A 15: Yes! You are right. There is one Surah in Qur'an that does not have Bismillah...It is Surah Tawbah (Repentance). It is Surah number nine.

The theme of that Surah deals with the hypocrites; those who breached their contracts with the Prophet and with Allah (swt) several times. They claimed excuses not to go to Jihad with the Prophet (pbuh). Some did not pay Zakat. Others played dirty tricks against the Prophet. Other joined hands-in hands with the non-believers against the Prophet.

Such groups of people don't deserve the Mercy of Allah (swt). As you are aware, the starting sentence of Bismillah Ar-Rahman, Ar-Raheem, reflects the Mercy of Allah. Those people did not deserve such a mercy. Therefore, the Surah starts without Bismillah.

Q 16: While trying my best to browse in the Qur'an, I recognized that some chapters start with symbolic letters such as A.L.M. What are these? And what do they signify?

A 16: You are smart!...It is true that there are some surahs in the Qur'an that start with symbolic letters such as A.L.M. Indeed there are 29 symbolic letters in 29 surahs. Some of them start with one letter, two letters, three letters, four letters, or five letters. You may read the book of this author entitled: **"The Golden Book of Islamic Lists."** In that book the author explained in detail about those letters. They are called Luminous Letters..

The Qur'an challenged all the poets and the literary people to reproduce a book similar to the Qur'an. No one was able to do so. Then the Qur'an challenged everyone to reproduce ten surahs similar to those of the Qur'an. They failed. The Qur'an went further with his challenges to all mankind by reproducing one Surah or ten ayat. Finally, the big shock came to all when Allah challenged every person by choosing symbolic letters.

The Arabs were experts in the Arabic language but failed to understand the meaning of the Single Letters. Therefore, no one is able to know their meanings. It is left up to Allah (swt) Who will explain their meaning in the Day of Judgment.

Q 17: Is it true that Muslims have to read and recite Qur'an in Arabic during their daily prayers? Can't they pray in other language other than Arabic?

A 17: Muslim have to pray (Salat) five time a day. They have to pray in the language of the Qur'an. We cannot use any other language during Salat. During Salt we read Al-Fatiha of Qur'an and other Surah or section of a Surah. All should be in the language of Revelation, i.e., Arabic. Each person who accepts to become a Muslim and makes a pledge of Islam, has to learn the language of Qur'an. The least of all is to make use of that language while praying. Allah (swt) created all languages of the world, and it was He Who selected the Arabic Language for prayers. To demonstrate our Allegiance and Obedience to Him, we should learn that language and make use of it not only in Salat, but in our daily life.

Q 18: **What is the most Miracle of the Qur'an?**

A 18: The most important miracle of the Qur'an is the Qur'an itself. There are many aspects through which we can appreciate the Qur'an as a Miracle from the Creator Himself, namely Allah (swt). Among his miracles are the following:

1. Linguistic, literary and poetic language.
2. Melodic and rhythmic pronunciations.
3. Information of past, present, future, and the hereafter.
4. Psychological, scientific, prophetic information of the future.
5. The challenges that the Qur'an presented to all those who wish to reproduce another book similar to it.
6. The degree of preservation of its authenticity, originality, and totality.
7. The degree of memorization by millions of Muslims in different parts of the world, including the non-Arabic speaking communities as well. No one book has been memorized by such a large number as much as the Qur'an.

Q 19: **It seems that the Qur'an is a huge book. If one wants to summarize the themes of the Qur'an, what are those themes in a nut shell?**

A 19: Yes! You are right! The Qur'an is some how a huge book consisting of 114 chapters, 6236 verses, 77437 words and 323,671 letters. The themes of the Qur'an can be summarized as to:

1. Creed or 'Aqeeda: Belief in Allah (swt); Angels; Jinns; Hereafter of Paradise and Hell; all the Previous Prophets sent by Allah, their books; and etc.
2. Religious practices such as Daily Salat (Prayers); Fasting; Zakat, Pilgrimage, and etc.
3. Business and society transactions including government itself with all the institutions needed to established a stable society based on justice to all.

XXX. QUR'ANIC QUESTIONS

In this section a series of questions are selected directly from Qur'an. They were asked by people during the life of Prophet Muhammad. The answers to these questions were revealed by Allah (swt) to Prophet Muhammad and documented in the Qur'an till the Day of Judgment. Some of the questions were related to this life while others are about the life after. Some questions had to deal with charity, alcohol, orphans, menses, Halal and Haram, booties, history of other nations and many more. Other questions had to deal with the soul, Day of Judgment, the Big Bang and others.

On the other hand there are questions raised by Allah (swt) through the tongue of Prophet Muhammad (pbuh). The answers were even given in a straight way with truth and full of evidence. The following is a short and concise number of questions divided into different categories.

Category (1) Ask

No one human being knows everything in every field of specialties. Therefore we should seek knowledge, and we should ask the knowledgeable, the wise and the righteous ones. In this regard Allah(swt) demanded us to ask so as to get the right answer. In Surah Al- Nahl (The Bees) Allah (swt) says the following:

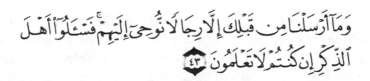

And before you We sent none but men, to whom We granted inspiration: if you realize this not, ask of those who possess the Message. (16:43)

Category (2) Do Not Ask

We are to ask the knowledgeable, the wise, the scholars and the 'Ulamaa'. Whatever they inform us could be true and right. However one has to go back to his own heart and find out what to do. If you are not satisfied, you may ask someone else. But we are not to ask so many people in order to find out the tricks and the loopholes to get out of responsibilities. We are not to ask too much, otherwise we will disturb ourselves and others. We are to do whatever our conscience dictates upon us.

In the Day of Judgment we will be asked independently without a defendant. Therefore we should not ask too much, otherwise we may end up being disturbed, annoyed and unhappy. In this regard Allah (swt) instructed us in Surah Al-Ma-idah (Table-Spread) not to ask too much. The Qur'an stipulates the following:

يَٰٓأَيُّهَا ٱلَّذِينَ ءَامَنُواْ لَا تَسْـَٔلُواْ

عَنْ أَشْيَآءَ إِن تُبْدَ لَكُمْ تَسُؤْكُمْ وَإِن تَسْـَٔلُواْ عَنْهَا حِينَ يُنَزَّلُ

ٱلْقُرْءَانُ تُبْدَ لَكُمْ عَفَا ٱللَّهُ عَنْهَا وَٱللَّهُ غَفُورٌ حَلِيمٌ ۝ قَدْ

سَأَلَهَا قَوْمٌ مِّن قَبْلِكُمْ ثُمَّ أَصْبَحُواْ بِهَا كَٰفِرِينَ ۝

O you who believe! Ask not questions about things which, if made plain to you may cause you trouble. But if you ask about things when the Qur'an is being revealed, they will be made plain to you , Allah will forgive those: For Allah is Oft-forgiving, Most Forbearing. Some people before you did ask such questions, and on that account lost their faith. (5:101-102)

210

Category - (3) Allah

Muslims in the city of Madinah were encouraged to pray Salat Haajah anytime they were facing a problem or a difficulty. During Salat they were to make Du 'a' (Supplication). During the Battle of Badr some Muslims started raising their voices tremendously while they were making Du 'a'. Their voices were very noisy and disturbing. The Prophet demanded from them to lower their voices. They thought that Allah was too far to hear them.

In Surah Al-Baqarah (The Cow) Allah (swt) informed us the following.

وَإِذَا سَأَلَكَ

عِبَادِى عَنِّى فَإِنِّى قَرِيبٌ أُجِيبُ دَعْوَةَ ٱلدَّاعِ إِذَا دَعَانِ فَلْيَسْتَجِيبُوا لِى وَلْيُؤْمِنُوا بِى لَعَلَّهُمْ يَرْشُدُونَ ١٨٦

When My servants ask you concerning Me, I am indeed close to them: I respond to the prayer of every suppliant when he calls on Me: Let them also, with a will, listen to My call, and believe in Me: That they may walk in the right way. (2:186)

This means that Allah will answer our Du 'a' if and only if we believe in Him and obey Him. He also tells us that He is very close to us. We do not need to raise our voices.

In another place in the Qur'an in Surah Al-Qaaf, Allah informs us that He is closer to us than our jugular veins.

211

وَلَقَدْ خَلَقْنَا ٱلْإِنسَـٰنَ وَنَعْلَمُ مَا تُوَسْوِسُ بِهِۦ نَفْسُهُۥ وَنَحْنُ أَقْرَبُ إِلَيْهِ
مِنْ حَبْلِ ٱلْوَرِيدِ ﴿١٦﴾

It was We Who created man, and We know what suggestions his soul makes to him: for We are nearer to him than his jugular vein. (50:16)

Category (4) Money Spending

In Surah Al-Baqarah (The Cow), the people of Madinah asked Prophet Muhammad what to spend and to whom the charity was to be given. The answer was given to them in Ayah (215) as follows:

يَسْـَٔلُونَكَ مَاذَا يُنفِقُونَ قُلْ
مَآ أَنفَقْتُم مِّنْ خَيْرٍ فَلِلْوَٰلِدَيْنِ وَٱلْأَقْرَبِينَ وَٱلْيَتَـٰمَىٰ وَٱلْمَسَـٰكِينِ
وَٱبْنِ ٱلسَّبِيلِ وَمَا تَفْعَلُوا۟ مِنْ خَيْرٍ فَإِنَّ ٱللَّهَ بِهِۦ عَلِيمٌ ﴿٢١٥﴾

They ask Me what they should spend in charity. Say: whatever wealth you spend that is good, is for parents and kindred and orphans and those in want and for wayfarers, and whatever you do that is good, Allah knows it well. (2:215)

Therefore, spending money should be from the good and Halal sources. It should be given to parents, relatives, orphans, needy and those who lost their money while traveling. For those who spend in the name of Allah are the winners in this life and in the hereafter. Allah knows; He hears; He listens, He sees; He records; and He give multiples of credits.

212

Category (5) Orphans

In Surah Al-Baqarah (The Cow), some people asked Prophet Muhammad about orphans: What should they do for them. Allah informed them that they should do good. They are to be treated as brethrens. The Qur'an states the following.

وَيَسۡـَٔلُونَكَ عَنِ ٱلۡيَتَـٰمَىٰ قُلۡ إِصۡلَاحٞ لَّهُمۡ خَيۡرٞ وَإِن تُخَالِطُوهُمۡ فَإِخۡوَٰنُكُمۡ وَٱللَّهُ يَعۡلَمُ ٱلۡمُفۡسِدَ مِنَ ٱلۡمُصۡلِحِ وَلَوۡ شَآءَ ٱللَّهُ لَأَعۡنَتَكُمۡ إِنَّ ٱللَّهَ عَزِيزٌ حَكِيمٞ ٢٢٠

They ask you concerning orphans, say: the best thing to do is what is for their good; if you mix their affairs with yours, they are your brethren; but Allah knows the man who means mischief from the man who means good. And if Allah had wished, He could have put you into difficulties: He is indeed Exalted in Power, Wise. (2:220)

Muslims should take care of them in every aspect of life. They should be fostered but not adopted. The Latter is prohibited in Islam, but the former is encouraged. There is plenty of information from Qur'an, Hadith and Sirah about this topic. As far as taking care of the orphans is concerned, the Prophet (pbuh) said:

Category (6) Menses

In Surah Al-Baqarah (The Cow) Muslims of Madinah asked the Prophet about menses, and whether husband and wife may have matrimonial relationship during that period. The answer came from Allah (swt) teaching Muslims to abstain from having intercourse. Otherwise they will be harmed physically, biologically or physiologically. If and when their wives are over from their periods, they have to clean themselves and take a shower before they have any relation. In this aspect the Qur'an states the following:

وَيَسْـَٔلُونَكَ
عَنِ ٱلْمَحِيضِ قُلْ هُوَ أَذًى فَٱعْتَزِلُواْ ٱلنِّسَآءَ فِى ٱلْمَحِيضِ
وَلَا تَقْرَبُوهُنَّ حَتَّىٰ يَطْهُرْنَ فَإِذَا تَطَهَّرْنَ فَأْتُوهُنَّ مِنْ حَيْثُ
أَمَرَكُمُ ٱللَّهُ إِنَّ ٱللَّهَ يُحِبُّ ٱلتَّوَّٰبِينَ وَيُحِبُّ ٱلْمُتَطَهِّرِينَ ﴿٢٢٢﴾
نِسَآؤُكُمْ حَرْثٌ لَّكُمْ فَأْتُواْ حَرْثَكُمْ أَنَّىٰ شِئْتُمْ وَقَدِّمُواْ لِأَنفُسِكُمْ
وَٱتَّقُواْ ٱللَّهَ وَٱعْلَمُوٓاْ أَنَّكُم مُّلَٰقُوهُ وَبَشِّرِ ٱلْمُؤْمِنِينَ ﴿٢٢٣﴾

They ask you concerning women's courses. Say: they are a hurt and a pollution so keep away from women in their courses, and do not approach them until they are clean. But when they have purified themselves, you may approach them as ordained for you by Allah, for Allah loves those who turn to Him constantly and He loves those who keep themselves pure and clean. Your wives are as a tilth to you so approach your tilth when or how you will; but do some good act for your souls beforehand; and fear Allah, and know that you are to meet Him in the hereafter, and give these good tidings to those who believe. (2:222-223)

214

Category (7) Alcohol

After the migration of the Prophet from Makkah to Madinah the teachings of Allah started educating the Muslims to improve themselves, their families and their society. They were advised step by step to shun away the pagan way of life. One of the vices was the drinking of alcohol. It was a social habit, and a serious business to drink and to sell alcohol. It was not easy to demand the Muslims in one time to stop drinking and to shun away. It took sometime to do so. The first step was to educate the Muslims about the benefits and the disadvantages that may result from drinking alcohol.

During their stay in Madinah, Allah taught the Muslims later to shun away from drinking before coming to perform salat. (Qur'an 4:43). Finally Muslims were instructed to shun away from dealing with any type of alcohol as well as from spirit at all times. The Qur'an states the following:

يَـٰٓأَيُّهَا ٱلَّذِينَ ءَامَنُوٓا۟ إِنَّمَا ٱلۡخَمۡرُ وَٱلۡمَيۡسِرُ وَٱلۡأَنصَابُ وَٱلۡأَزۡلَٰمُ رِجۡسٌ مِّنۡ عَمَلِ ٱلشَّيۡطَـٰنِ فَٱجۡتَنِبُوهُ لَعَلَّكُمۡ تُفۡلِحُونَ ۝ إِنَّمَا يُرِيـدُ ٱلشَّيۡطَـٰنُ أَن يُوقِعَ بَيۡنَكُمُ ٱلۡعَدَٰوَةَ وَٱلۡبَغۡضَآءَ فِى ٱلۡخَمۡرِ وَٱلۡمَيۡسِرِ وَيَصُدَّكُمۡ عَن ذِكۡرِ ٱللَّهِ وَعَنِ ٱلصَّلَوٰةِ فَهَلۡ أَنتُم مُّنتَهُونَ ۝

O you who believe! Intoxicants and gambling, sacrificing to stones, and divination by arrows, are an abomination, of Satan's handiwork: Eschew such abominations, that you may prosper. Satan's plan is but to excite enmity and hatred between you, with intoxicants and gambling, and hinder you from the remembrance of Allah, and from prayer: will you not then abstain? (5:90-91)

However, in Surah Al-Baqarah (The Cow) Allah (swt) is teaching us the first question about alcohol. The Qur'an states the following:

$$\text{۞ يَسْـَٔلُونَكَ عَنِ ٱلْخَمْرِ}$$

$$\text{وَٱلْمَيْسِرِ قُلْ فِيهِمَآ إِثْمٌ كَبِيرٌ وَمَنَـٰفِعُ لِلنَّاسِ وَإِثْمُهُمَآ}$$

$$\text{أَكْبَرُ مِن نَّفْعِهِمَا وَيَسْـَٔلُونَكَ مَاذَا يُنفِقُونَ قُلِ ٱلْعَفْوَ}$$

$$\text{كَذَٰلِكَ يُبَيِّنُ ٱللَّهُ لَكُمُ ٱلْءَايَـٰتِ لَعَلَّكُمْ تَتَفَكَّرُونَ ﴿٢١٩﴾}$$

They ask you concerning wine and gambling. Say: in them is great sin, and some profit, for men; but the sin is greater than the profit. They ask you how much they are to spend; Say: what is beyond your needs. Thus does Allah make clear to you His signs in order that you may consider. (2:219)

Category (8) Halal

In Surah Al-Ma-idah (Table Spread) the early Muslims asked Prophet Muhammad (pbuh) about the Halal foods, and other aspects of social life. The revelation stipulated that all food which is good for their health was Halal. Allah (swt) informed them also that animals cannot be eaten or slaughtered without mentioning the name of Allah.

Since this Surah was among the last revelation (two months before the Prophet died), Allah (swt) allowed the Muslims to eat from the foods of the People of the Book (Al Al-Kitab), as well as to marry from their daughters if and only if they are (Muhsanat) chase. There are other conditions concerning this point too. However, Muslim women are not allowed to marry non-Muslims at all. They are not Halal to non-Muslims for many reasons. The Qur'an states the following:

بَسْـَٔلُونَكَ مَاذَآ أُحِلَّ لَهُمْۖ قُلْ أُحِلَّ لَكُمُ الطَّيِّبَـٰتُ وَمَا عَلَّمْتُم
مِّنَ الْجَوَارِحِ مُكَلِّبِينَ تُعَلِّمُونَهُنَّ مِمَّا عَلَّمَكُمُ اللَّهُ فَكُلُوا مِمَّآ أَمْسَكْنَ
عَلَيْكُمْ وَاذْكُرُوا اسْمَ اللَّهِ عَلَيْهِ وَاتَّقُوا اللَّهَ إِنَّ اللَّهَ سَرِيعُ الْحِسَابِ
﴿٤﴾ الْيَوْمَ أُحِلَّ لَكُمُ الطَّيِّبَـٰتُ وَطَعَامُ الَّذِينَ أُوتُوا الْكِتَـٰبَ حِلٌّ
لَّكُمْ وَطَعَامُكُمْ حِلٌّ لَّهُمْۖ وَالْمُحْصَنَـٰتُ مِنَ الْمُؤْمِنَـٰتِ وَالْمُحْصَنَـٰتُ
مِنَ الَّذِينَ أُوتُوا الْكِتَـٰبَ مِن قَبْلِكُمْ إِذَآ ءَاتَيْتُمُوهُنَّ أُجُورَهُنَّ
مُحْصِنِينَ غَيْرَ مُسَـٰفِحِينَ وَلَا مُتَّخِذِىٓ أَخْدَانٍۗ وَمَن يَكْفُرْ
بِالْإِيمَـٰنِ فَقَدْ حَبِطَ عَمَلُهُۥ وَهُوَ فِى الْـَٔاخِرَةِ مِنَ الْخَـٰسِرِينَ ﴿٥﴾

They ask you what is lawful to them as food. Say:
lawful to you are all things good and pure and what you
have taught the beasts and birds of prey, training them
to hunt in the manner directed to you by Allah: eat what
they catch for you, but pronounce the name of Allah
over it: and fear Allah; for Allah is swift in taking
account. This day are all things good and pure made
lawful to you. The food of the People of the Book is
lawful unto you and yours is lawful to them. Lawful to
you in marriage are not only chaste women who are
believers, but chaste women among the People of the
Book, revealed before your time, when you give them
their due dowers, and desire chastity, not lewdness nor
taking them as lovers. If any one rejects faith, fruitless is
his work, and in the hereafter he will be in the ranks of
those who have lost all spiritual good. (5:4-5)

217

Category (9) New Moon

In Surah Al-Baqarah(The Cow) Allah (swt) informs us how the People asked the Prophet the question about the New Moon. It seems there were many superstitions those days about the new moon. The answer is that the New Moon is nothing more than a planet to be used for calculations and a measure of time, days, months and years. It is also to be used for the sake of performing pilgrimage. The Qur'an states the following question as well as the answer:

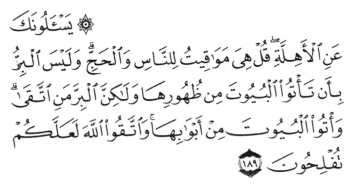

They ask you concerning the new moons. Say: they are but signs to mark fixed periods of time in the affairs of men. And for pilgrimage. It is no virtue if you enter your houses from the back; it is virtue if you fear Allah. Enter houses through the proper doors and fear Allah that you may prosper. (2:189)

Therefore, no one should associate the new moon with any superstitions. Muslims do use the new moon for the sake of fasting the month of Ramadan, for pilgrimage, for festivities, for traveling at night in deserts, and for other geophysical knowledge. It is associated sometimes with the tides of seas, rivers and oceans. Muslims of today should benefit from the creation of Allah in every aspect of life.

Category (10) The Spirit

In Surah Al-Israa' (Night Journey), the Qur'an tells us about the question raised during the life of Prophet Muhammad. People asked the Prophet about "Al-Rooh" The meaning of it could be "Angle Gabriel" himself or the spirit and the soul of each human being. When people asked the Prophet such a question, Allah (swt) revealed him to tell them that the spirit is from the Command of God. Angel Gabriel comes down only when Allah wants him to do so. He communicates with the prophets only. He is the Chief of all angels. The following is the Qur'anic information:

They ask you concerning the spirit say: the spirit is of the command of my Lord of knowledge it is only a little that is communicated to you, O men! If it were Our Will, We could take away that which We have sent you by inspiration: Then would you find none to plead your affair in that matter as against Us. (17:85-86)

Angel Gabriel is to come down from heaven in Lailatul Qadr to greet the most honorable individuals on behalf of Allah- In Surah Al-Qadr (the Night of Power), Allah says the following:

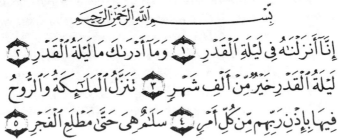

219

We have indeed revealed this Message in the Night of Power: and We will explain to you what the Night of Power is. The Night of Power is better than a thousand months. Therein come down the angels and the Spirit by Allah's permission on every errand: Peace!... This until the rise of Morn! (97:1-5)

Category (11) Day Judgment

The early people of Makkah asked Prophet Muhammad about the Day of Judgment. In two places one may read in Qur'an such a question. In Surah Al-A'raf (The Heights) Allah answered them that no one knows when it is going to happen except Allah (swt) Himself It has precursor signs, but Allah alone is the One Who decides when and how it is going to take place. In this Surah Allah (swt) says the followings:

يَسۡـَٔلُونَكَ عَنِ ٱلسَّاعَةِ أَيَّانَ مُرۡسَىٰهَا قُلۡ إِنَّمَا عِلۡمُهَا عِندَ رَبِّى لَا يُجَلِّيهَا لِوَقۡتِهَآ إِلَّا هُوَۚ ثَقُلَتۡ فِى ٱلسَّمَٰوَٰتِ وَٱلۡأَرۡضِۚ لَا تَأۡتِيكُمۡ إِلَّا بَغۡتَةٗۗ يَسۡـَٔلُونَكَ كَأَنَّكَ حَفِىٌّ عَنۡهَاۖ قُلۡ إِنَّمَا عِلۡمُهَا عِندَ ٱللَّهِ وَلَٰكِنَّ أَكۡثَرَ ٱلنَّاسِ لَا يَعۡلَمُونَ ﴿١٨٧﴾

They ask you about the final Hour- when will be its appointed time? Say: "The knowledge thereof is with my Lord alone: None but He can reveal as to when it will occur. Heavy were its burdens through the heavens and the earth. Only all of a sudden will it come to you." They ask you as if you were eager in search thereof: Say: "The knowledge thereof is with Allah alone, but most men know not." (7:187)

Similarly in Surah Al-Nazi-'aat (Those Who Tear-Out), Allah (swt) informed us that the early people of Makkah asked the Prophet again and again about the coming date of the Day of Judgment. The answer was that no one knows at all. The Prophet was to inform them that there is a Day of Judgment, His role was to warn them if they do not heed in Allah. it will be a shock to all when it is to take place. The Qur'an states the following:

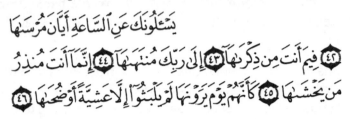

They ask you about the Hour, 'When will be its appointed time?" Wherein are you concerned with the declaration thereof? With my Lord is the final end of it. I am but a Warner for such as fear it. The Day they see it, it will be as if they had tarried but a single evening, or at most till the following morn! (79:42-46)

Category 12 Mountains

In Surah Taha, we are informed that people asked the Prophet about Mountains. What is going to happen to them in the Day of Judgment. The answer was given to them that they will be blown-up and demolished into pieces. One will never see a hill or a mountain- Everything will be as a plateau all over. The Qur'an is very clear about it. The question and answer in Surah Taha go as follows:

They ask you concerning the mountains: say, "My Lord will uproot them and scatter them as dust. (20:105-106)

Category (13) Non-Muslim questioning Prophet

Non-Muslims in the city of Madinah asked the prophet to bring a book from heaven. The Qur'an was revealed to the Prophet in a period of 23 years. Non-Muslims want the whole book at one time to be revealed so they will be able to see it, to look at it and to browse in it.

The answer came from Allah to the prophet that Bani Israel asked Prophet Moosa a bigger question. They wanted to see Allah in the daytime, where everyone can see Him, identify Him and talk to Him. However, they were penalized with a hurricane and an earthquake. In Surah An-Nisaa' (The Women) Allah says the following: يَسْئَلُكَ

أَهْلُ ٱلْكِتَٰبِ أَن تُنَزِّلَ عَلَيْهِمْ كِتَٰبًا مِّنَ ٱلسَّمَآءِ فَقَدْ سَأَلُواْ
مُوسَىٰٓ أَكْبَرَ مِن ذَٰلِكَ فَقَالُوٓاْ أَرِنَا ٱللَّهَ جَهْرَةً فَأَخَذَتْهُمُ
ٱلصَّٰعِقَةُ بِظُلْمِهِمْ ثُمَّ ٱتَّخَذُواْ ٱلْعِجْلَ مِنۢ بَعْدِ مَا جَآءَتْهُمُ
ٱلْبَيِّنَٰتُ فَعَفَوْنَا عَن ذَٰلِكَ وَءَاتَيْنَا مُوسَىٰ سُلْطَٰنًا مُّبِينًا ﴿١٥٣﴾

The People of the Book ask you to cause a book to descend to them from heaven: indeed they asked Moses for an even greater miracle, for they said: "Show us Allah in public," but they were seized for their presumption by thunder and lightning. Yet they worshipped the calf even after clear signs had come to them; even so We forgave them; and gave Moses manifest proofs of authority. (4:153)

Addendum A

STORY OF AL-IFK

I. Introduction

The incident of Al-Ifk is very important to all people of the world regardless of color, nationality, ethnic background, or creed. This incident took place in the days of Prophet Muhammad (pbuh) against his wife, Aisha. She was accused of having relationship with someone. Those who accused her had no proof at all. They spread the bad news in the city of Madina five or six years after Hijra, and also after the revelation of Hijab was prescribed.

The ones who accused her were among the hypocrites. They spread rumors for one whole month, while she was innocent of any relationship or even intimacy. She never knew that rumors were going around. During that period she was not feeling well, but when the rumors were brought to her attention, she started crying. She could not sleep. She was shocked to know that the people in the City of Madina were talking about such an incident.

It seems that Abdullah Ibn Sallool was the chief architect and the leader of the rumors. The other person was Mustah Ibn Athaatha. They went from store to store and from house to house spreading rumors, that Aisha (the wife of the Prophet and the daughter of Abu Bakr) had relationship with Safwan Ibn Al-Mu'tal Al-Salmi.

II. Historical Incidence

The Prophet had to go to a battlefield of Mu'tah. He selected Aisha to go with him. After the battle was over in the fifth year after Hijra, they made arrangements to come back to Madina. Aisha left for a short while to go take care of some personal issue, then she realized that she lost her necklace. She went back to look for it, and it took her time to find it. Meanwhile the caravan left without her; the companions of the Prophet did not recognize her absence, and they drove her camel with the howdah (carriage), assuming that Aisha was inside it – she was slim, and of very light weight, for that reason the companions did not feel her absence.

When she returned, she did not find her caravan. So she stayed in her place waiting for someone from the caravan to come back and pick her up. No one came. So she stayed in her place overnight. Safwan Al-Salmi was trying to look after the luggage that might have been left behind un-noticed by the Muslims who went with the prophet to the battlefield. He never talked to her, but took her on his camel, while he was walking back to Madina. They arrived during noon. She joined the Prophet and his group. From the moment Safwan brought her, she never exposed her face, and she never talked to him.

The hypocrites from the Muslim community were jealous of Aisha. They were waiting for an opportunity to play the game of trouble and commotion. That incident was enough for them to make Fitnah against the Prophet himself and the Muslims at large.

During one whole month, Aisha felt that the Prophet was not as usual with her. He was depressed, and he could not do anything till he received revelation from Allah. Instead of greeting her with smiling face, and instead of treating her as usual, he used to say, "Kaifa Teekum?" (How is that?), referring to Aisha.

Later a lady friend informed Aisha about the rumor! It was a shock to her. Accordingly, Aisha requested from the Prophet to visit her parents. He allowed her and she went. She asked her mother about the rumor. Her mother told her that the rumor had been going around for one whole month! However, her mother tried to pacify her because there were people who were jealous of her. Aisha could not sleep all night long. She became sicker than before.

The second day the Prophet called Ali and Usama Ibn Zaid, seeking their advice. Usama praised the Prophet and his family. He told the Prophet that his family members had been the best role models to all of them. However, Ali told the Prophet not to feel bad. You can marry any other lady! Then the Prophet asked Buraira, the servant, if she observed anything different about Aisha! She praised Aisha so much.

The second day, the Prophet went to the Masjid and called the people. He spoke to them by telling them, that he could not find any mistake about Aisha. The one who accused her had to be penalized. Sa'ad Ibn Mu'az from Ansar told the Prophet, "If that person is from our tribe Al-Aws, we will kill him. However, if he is from Al-Khazraj, then you give us the permission to kill him." Sa'ad Ibn 'Ubadah, who was the leader of Al-Khazraj, objected and insulted Sa'ad Ibn Mu'az. A third person by the name of Aseed Ibn Hudair (cousin of Sa'ad Ibn Mu'az), resented what Sa'ad Ibn 'Ubadah said and insulted him back. It became a big commotion inside the Masjid while the Prophet was still standing at the pulpit (Minbar). If the Prophet did not interfere several times to calm them down, a fight was going to start between Al-Aws and Al-Khazraj.

Aisha started weeping and crying. She was unable to sleep all night long. Her parents later visited her. One lady from Al-Ansar visited her also and started sharing the distress with her. She also started weeping and crying. While they were there, the Prophet came to the house and greeted them all. For one whole month he never stayed with Aisha. He never also received any revelation about that incident. He declared the Shahada. Then he said to Aisha whatever he heard about her. He told her, "If you are innocent, Allah will purify you. However, if you committed a mistake, you have to ask Allah forgiveness, and repent. If a person makes a mistake, he should admit, and then should repent, so that Allah will forgive that person."

Aisha was shocked with what she heard from the Prophet. She became more tense than before. She asked her father to answer the Prophet! He said, "I don't know what to say to the Prophet." Then she asked her mother to answer the Prophet, she said the same thing, "I don't know what to say!" Then Aisha said, "You have heard this story so many times till you reached a point of believing it. If I say to you I am innocent (and Allah knows that I am innocent), you are not going to believe me! If I admit that I committed a mistake, so that you will believe me, I will be lying. I will only say what the father of Yusuf said:

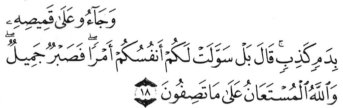

(For me) patience is most fitting; Against that which you assert, it is Allah (alone) whose help can be sought... (12: 18)

Then I threw myself on my bed. I fully knew that I was innocent; and I knew that Allah knows that I am innocent. I hoped at that time that the Prophet would see a dream of me being innocent. I never thought that Allah is going to reveal Qur'anic verses about me to defend me, and to tell the whole world that I am innocent. I do know that I am an insignificant person."

While sitting in the house, the Prophet's face changed. Sweat started coming from his face, as if he was in a state of absence from us for a few minutes. We knew that he was receiving some type of revelation. Later on, he came to his conscience and smiled. He looked at his wife Aisha and told her the good news already revealed to him. "Allah purified you O Aisha!" "My mother at that time told me to go to the Prophet and thank him." Aisha said, "I will not do that. It was Allah who defended me and purified me."

It should be mentioned here that Abu Bakr used to help his relative Mustah Ibn Athaatha. The latter person was poor. Abu Bakr was hurt when that person was among those who accused Aisha, and spread the rumors against her; therefore, Abu Bakr decided to stop his help to that person. Such was a human decision. However, when Allah revealed in Chapter 24 (An-Noor), Verse 22, he felt the impact of it. He wanted Allah to forgive him, and to reward him. Therefore, he continued his support. This Ayah goes as follows:

وَلَا يَأْتَلِ أُوْلُوا الْفَضْلِ مِنكُمْ
وَالسَّعَةِ أَن يُؤْتُوٓا أُوْلِي الْقُرْبَىٰ وَالْمَسَـٰكِينَ وَالْمُهَـٰجِرِينَ فِى
سَبِيلِ اللَّهِ وَلْيَعْفُوا وَلْيَصْفَحُوٓا أَلَا تُحِبُّونَ أَن يَغْفِرَ اللَّهُ لَكُمْ
وَاللَّهُ غَفُورٌ رَّحِيمٌ ﴿٢٢﴾

Let not those among you who are endued with grace and amplitude of means resolve by oath against helping their kinsmen, those in want, and those who have left their homes in Allah's cause. Let them forgive and overlook, do you not wish that Allah is Oft-Forgiving, Most Merciful. (24: 22)

227

III. Qur'anic Revelation

The Mercy of Allah came to the Prophet by defending and purifying Aisha after a whole month of rumor spreading. Surah An-Noor is an excellent chapter for manners, behaviors, conduct, and human relations based on justice and fairness. Ten Ayat were revealed concerning Aisha, the wife of the Prophet. The rest of the Ayat are rules and regulations for eliminating backbiting, and rumor spreading. Otherwise people should be penalized for that.

The following is the list of the ten Ayat that were revealed, purifying Aisha. Allah says the following:

وَلَوْلَا فَضْلُ اللَّهِ عَلَيْكُمْ وَرَحْمَتُهُ وَأَنَّ اللَّهَ تَوَّابٌ حَكِيمٌ ﴿١٠﴾ إِنَّ الَّذِينَ جَاءُو بِالْإِفْكِ عُصْبَةٌ مِّنكُمْ لَا تَحْسَبُوهُ شَرًّا لَّكُم بَلْ هُوَ خَيْرٌ لَّكُمْ لِكُلِّ امْرِئٍ مِّنْهُم مَّا اكْتَسَبَ مِنَ الْإِثْمِ وَالَّذِي تَوَلَّىٰ كِبْرَهُ مِنْهُمْ لَهُ عَذَابٌ عَظِيمٌ ﴿١١﴾ لَّوْلَا إِذْ سَمِعْتُمُوهُ ظَنَّ الْمُؤْمِنُونَ وَالْمُؤْمِنَاتُ بِأَنفُسِهِمْ خَيْرًا وَقَالُوا هَٰذَا إِفْكٌ مُّبِينٌ ﴿١٢﴾ لَّوْلَا جَاءُو عَلَيْهِ بِأَرْبَعَةِ شُهَدَاءَ فَإِذْ لَمْ يَأْتُوا بِالشُّهَدَاءِ فَأُولَٰئِكَ عِندَ اللَّهِ هُمُ الْكَاذِبُونَ ﴿١٣﴾ وَلَوْلَا فَضْلُ اللَّهِ عَلَيْكُمْ وَرَحْمَتُهُ فِي الدُّنْيَا وَالْآخِرَةِ لَمَسَّكُمْ فِي مَا أَفَضْتُمْ فِيهِ عَذَابٌ عَظِيمٌ ﴿١٤﴾ إِذْ تَلَقَّوْنَهُ بِأَلْسِنَتِكُمْ وَتَقُولُونَ بِأَفْوَاهِكُم مَّا لَيْسَ لَكُم بِهِ عِلْمٌ وَتَحْسَبُونَهُ هَيِّنًا وَهُوَ عِندَ اللَّهِ عَظِيمٌ ﴿١٥﴾

وَلَوْلَا إِذْ سَمِعْتُمُوهُ

قُلْتُم مَّا يَكُونُ لَنَا أَن نَّتَكَلَّمَ بِهَذَا سُبْحَنَكَ هَذَا بُهْتَنٌ عَظِيمٌ ﴿١٦﴾ يَعِظُكُمُ اللَّهُ أَن تَعُودُوا لِمِثْلِهِ أَبَدًا إِن كُنتُم مُّؤْمِنِينَ ﴿١٧﴾ وَيُبَيِّنُ اللَّهُ لَكُمُ الْآيَتِ وَاللَّهُ عَلِيمٌ حَكِيمٌ ﴿١٨﴾ إِنَّ الَّذِينَ يُحِبُّونَ أَن تَشِيعَ الْفَحِشَةُ فِي الَّذِينَ ءَامَنُوا لَهُمْ عَذَابٌ أَلِيمٌ فِي الدُّنْيَا وَالْآخِرَةِ وَاللَّهُ يَعْلَمُ وَأَنتُمْ لَا تَعْلَمُونَ ﴿١٩﴾ وَلَوْلَا فَضْلُ اللَّهِ عَلَيْكُمْ وَرَحْمَتُهُ وَأَنَّ اللَّهَ رَءُوفٌ رَّحِيمٌ ﴿٢٠﴾

If it were not for Allah's grace and mercy on you, and that Allah is Oft-Returning, full of Wisdom – (you would be ruined indeed). Those who brought forward the lie are a body among yourselves. Think it not to be an evil to you; on the contrary it is good for you. To every man among them (will come the punishment) of the sin that he earned, and to him who took on himself the lead among them, will be a penalty grievous. Why did not the believers – men and women – when you heard of the affair – put the best construction on it in their own minds and say, "This (charge) is an obvious lie"? Why did they not bring four witnesses to prove it? When they have not brought the witnesses, such men, in the sight of Allah (stand forth) themselves as liars! Were it not for the grace and mercy of Allah on you, in this world and the Hereafter, a grievous penalty would have seized you in that you rushed glibly into this affair. Behold, you received it on your tongues and said out of your mouth things of which you had no knowledge; and you thought it to be a light matter. While it was most serious in the sight of Allah. And why did you not when you heard it, say "It is not right of us to speak of this; Glory to You (our Lord) this is a most serious slander!" Allah doesn't admonish you, that you may never repeat such (conduct), if you are (true) believers. And Allah makes the signs plain to you, for Allah is full of knowledge and wisdom. Those who love (to see) scandal published broadcast among the believers, will have a grievous penalty in this life and in the Hereafter. Allah knows, and you know not. Were it not for the grace and mercy of Allah on you, and that Allah is full of kindness and mercy (you would be ruined indeed)? (24: 10-20)

IV Moral Aspects

This incident has many lessons to learn from:

1. In every society there are a group of hypocrites who wish to destroy the people; and especially in a faithful society.

2. Jealousy is most of the time a source of trouble among people. Those of us who are successful in society are going to be attacked by those who are failure in the community at large.

3. The more a person does favor to others, the more he should expect individuals to hurt him.

4. Anyone who accuses others for sex relations without proof of four witnesses, he should be penalized by beating him 80 times with a whip.

5. When a person is facing a problem, he should pray salatul Haajah, so that Allah will solve his problem in one way or the other.

6. One has to try his best not to suspect any person. Even if he sees something wrong, he should not come to a conclusion. He should not allow any person to inform him about others. Listening to a backbiter, means that the one who listens is as if he is involved in backbiting. No one should allow any person to spread rumors against others.

7. One should try his best to protect himself as much as possible from putting himself into areas of doubt.

8. No one is safe from being attacked, blamed or fall into a situation similar to Aisha.

9. A mistake cannot be corrected by another mistake. One should find the better solution in eradicating a mistake.

10. The Ummah of Islam should protect themselves and make a solid community. They should make sure that no infiltrator will be among them.

Finally, we hope and pray that we take a lesson from our history so that we will be able to live peacefully, Insha-Allah.

Addendum B

STORY OF AL-UKHDOOD

It was reported by Suhaib ® that the Prophet (pbuh) said:

The King, the Magician and the Boy:

*There was a king who had a magician. When the magician got old, he said to the king," I became old, and my end is coming soon. Therefore, send me a young person so that I may teach him magic." The king gave him a young boy who started learning magic from the old person.

The Pious person and the Boy:

*On the way between the palace of the king and the house of the magician, there was a house of a pious person. On his way, the boy passed by the pious man, and he heard him giving a speech. He was fascinated with his talk and he started listening to him. Therefore, he used to be late going to the magician, as well as to his house. The magician became mad, and he would beat the boy for being late! His family beat him as well when he was late going home.

*The boy complained to the pious man about his situation. He was advised to tell the magician that he was late because of his family's needs; and similarly he was to say to his family that the magician delayed him.

The Boy and the Animal:

*One day, while on his way, he saw a huge animal that prevented people from crossing the street. They young boy said to himself, " I will know who is more liked by Allah : The pious person or the magician"!! He took a piece of rock, and said to Allah, "O Allah! If the pious person is more liked to You than the magician, and if he is more pleasing to You, let this animal die with this piece of rock, allowing people to cross the street". He threw the rock at the animal, and indeed the animal died. Therefore, people were able to cross without being harmed.

*When the young boy reached the pious man, he told him what happened. The pious man told the boy that he is better than him, but he is going to be tested. At that time, don't tell anyone about me! The young boy was blessed by Allah; he used to cure different diseases, especially the blinds and the lepers as well as other diseases.

The Blind person:

*One of the assistants of the king became blind. He heard about the miracles of the young boy, and gave him plenty of gifts, requesting the boy to heal him. The boy told him, I am not the healer! It is Allah, Himself Who heals. If you believe in Him, I will make a special prayer so that Allah will heal you. The assistant of the king believed in Allah; and the boy made his Du'a' so that Allah will heal him. Allah gave Shifaa' to the man. Then he went back to the king to assist him. The king was surprised with happiness. He asked his assistant about the person who cured him. He said to the king: It is my God, Allah! The king asked him, "Is it me?!" The man said to the king, "No! It is not you!! It is my God, Who is also your God!"

233

The king was shocked with such an answer. He said to his assistant, " Do you have any god other than me?" He answered him, "Yes! It is my God, and your God, It is Allah"..

The king and his Assistant:

*The king started penalizing his assistant. The assistant could not tolerate the penalty. He told the king about the young boy! The king brought that young person, and told him, "Look here young boy! I was informed that through your magic you heal the blind, the lepers and other diseases!" The young boy said, "No! It is not me! I am not the healer! The Healer is Allah (swt)"! The king said, " I am god! Do you mean me?" the boy said, "No! You are not god!" The king said to the boy, "Do you have another god other than me?!" The boy said, "My God and your God is Allah". The king could not believe what he was hearing. He started punishing him and torturing him. Finally, the boy referred the king to the pious man.

The King and Pious person:

*The king brought the pious person and demanded from him to quit his religion, and to come back to the king. He should believe that the king is god, but the pious man refused. The king ordered his soldiers to kill the pious man by using a saw. They cut him into two pieces. They started cutting him from his head! This, of course, killed him. The two pieces fell onto the floor.

*Then, the king told his assistant to do the same, that is, to revert and to believe that the king is the only god. He refused! The soldiers killed him in the same way, that is, by using a saw. They cut him into two pieces, and of course he died. Finally, he said to the young boy, " You have to revert back and leave your religion." However, the boy refused.

The King and the Boy:

*The king sent the boy with his soldiers to be taken to a mountain. If he reverts back, they should leave him. Otherwise they should throw him from the top of the mountain into the valley so that he will die there. They did as they were instructed. When they reached the top of the mountain, he said, "O Allah! Take care of me, and prevent me from their penalty". Allah sent an earthquake to the mountain, and they died while the boy was saved by Allah.

*The boy went back to the king by himself. The king was surprised, and asked the boy about the soldiers. He said, "Allah took care of them, and He saved me". The king was shocked, and he got even angrier than before. He told his soldiers to take him to the sea. If he reverts, they should leave him; otherwise, they should throw him into the sea to die. They did as they were told. When they reached the sea, they asked him to revert or he would be thrown into the sea. He prayed to Allah, to save him from the soldiers. Allah made the soldiers drown in the sea, and saved the boy.

*The boy told the king, "You cannot kill me until you do what I tell you. If you do as I instruct you, then you will be able to kill me. Otherwise you will never be able to overcome me!" The king asked the boy, "What is that?" The boy said, "You bring people to one huge place, and you tie me to a tree. Then, take an arrow from my quiver. Then you say, "In the Name of Allah, the Lord of this boy". Then and only then you will be able to kill me.

People became Believers:

*The king did exactly what the boy said. People were gathered to see what is going to happen. While people watched, the king took the arrow, and said, "In the Name of Allah, the God of this boy", and shot the boy. The arrow hit the boy in his head and he died. People said, " We also believe in the same God of this boy."

Story of Al-Ukhdood:

*The king was told, "This is what you were afraid of happening. It seems people have already believed in Allah as their own God. They don't believe in you as their god!" He got mad and frustrated. He ordered to have trenches dug into the land. He then put fire into the ditches and the trenches. He gave orders to his soldiers, that whoever revert back to me, leave them, otherwise, dump them into the fire. It was mentioned that people were not afraid. They were dumped into the fire one after the other. None was reluctant, except one woman who was nursing her child. Her baby spoke the truth, and said to his mother, "My mom, have patience! You are on the right path. Go ahead!" Being encouraged by the words of her baby, she threw herself into the fire.

PS.: This story of Al-Ukhdood could be found in Qur'an in Surah Al-Burooj (Constellations), chapter 85. However, the detail of this story is translated from the Book of Tafseer Al-Qur'an from Ibn Katheer, regarding Surah Al-Burooj, volume IV, page 493.

WORKSHEET

FILL IN THE BLANKS:

1. The number of Surahs in the Qur'an is: _____
2. The total number of volumes (Juzu') in the Qur'an is:_____
3. Each Juzu' is composed of how many Hizb? _____
4. Each Hizb is composed of how many Quarters?_____
5. The first Surah in the Qur'an is: _____
6. The last Surah in the Qur'an is:_____
7. The longest Surah in the Qur'an is:_____
8. The longest Ayah in the Qur'an is:_____
9. The shortest Surah in the Qur'an is:_____
10. The shortest Ayah in the Qur'an is _____
11. The Qur'an was revealed in how many years?_____
12. Preservation of the Qur'an by Allah (swt) is through _____ and _____
13. Rules of reciting Qur'an are through _____ and _____
14. The Surah which does **Not** start with Bismillah is: _____
15. The Surah which has Bismillah twice in it is: _____
16. There are _____Sajdah in the Qur'an and they are found in _____Surahs. Name one of these Surahs:_____
17. The Qur'an is composed of 30 Juzu'. The middle of the Qur'an is found in which Surah: _____
18. There are how many Ayat in the Qur'an _____

PS: Answers on page 269-270

19. The letter denoting half of the Qur'an is found in Surah
_____. Surah no. _____ and Ayah
No._____

20. Name 5 Surahs with Prophets' names: (a)_____
(b)_____(c)_____
(d) _____ (e) _____

21. Name 3 Surahs named for animals: (a) _____
(b)_____   (c) _____

22. Name 3 Surahs named for planets and Stars.:
(a)_____   (b)_____
(c) _____

23. Which Surah is named after an insect: _____

24. Which Surah is named for a particular day:
_____

25. What other Surahs are named for a part of a day:
(a) _____   (b) _____

26. One Surah is named for one woman _____

27. Which Surah is named for a tribe:_____

28. Which Surah is named for a nation: _____

29. The first Surah revealed to the Prophet (saw) is: _____
_____

30. The last Surah revealed to the Prophet (saw) is: _____
_____

31. Which Surah in the Qur'an is considered to be 1/3 of the
Qur'an:_____

32. Which Ayah in the Qur'an is meant for protection: _____
_____

33. Which two Surahs in the Qur'an are for protection:
_____ and _____

34. Two Ayat in the Qur'an are equal to Tahajjud all night
long. They are found in Surah: _____
They are Ayah numbers: _____ and _____

PROPOSAL

AMERICAN SCHOOL OF QUR'AN

A. Introduction

Throughout history, Muslims have loved Qur'an so much that a good number have memorized it totally. A substantial number of those who memorized it are of non-Arabic speakers. Many Muslim professionals, are called Hafiz of Al-Qur'an along side with their profession.

Throughout the Muslim world one may find a great number of schools, colleges and universities which are designated for Hifz Al-Qur'an. Outside the academic professions one my find a number of efforts that have been made to encourage children and/or adults to memorize the Qur'an. Such efforts could be in the form of competitions held locally, nationally and internationally, with gifts presented to the best reciters of the Qur'an.

Many parents invite Hafiz to teach their children how to read the Qur'an and/or make them recite and memorize it. Others send their children away from home—out of town, out of the state and out of the country-for the sake of Hifz of Al-Qur'an, and they gladly pay a great amount of money to participate in such a project.

The love of the Qur'an by Muslims is ingrained deeply in their hearts and minds. Those who love Allah are attached to the Qur'an. The more the people love Allah, the more they try to read the Qur'an. They read it for spirituality, memorization, recitation, understanding, practicing its teachings, and delivering its message to others as well as helping others do the same. Others have spent their life-time in writing it with beautiful calligraphy of Arabesques.

As one may be aware of, there is no single book in the world that has been memorized by heart as the Qur'an. No other religious holy book has been memorized by millions of people of different language backgrounds as has the Qur'an. Those who are called Hafiz do memorize the Qur'an to the perfection of the sequence of chapters and verse. They know the subjects and their location in the Qur'an. An author of any book might not know about his book as does a Hafiz know about the Qur'an. It is truly miraculous how Muslims in different parts of the world make efforts to spread the Message of Qur'an in one way or another.

Muslims in America have been requesting Hafiz (Huffaz) to come to them during the month of Ramadan. Few Muslims countries have responded positively by sending various Huffaz to recite the Qur'an during the entire month of Ramadan. The number of Muslims in America has increased tremendously. This year, 2000, their number is about 10 million. Their local Masajid and Islamic Centers have increased to more 5,000. It is important that they build up their own academic and religious institutions by themselves.

B. Components of Institutions

To build any institutions, the following factors are essential:

1. Manpower
2. System
3. Community Support
4. Trust/ Endowment (waqf)
5. Certification and Accreditation
6. Parent-Teacher Association
7. Place
8. Management
9. Teachers
10. Finance
11. Publicity
12. Students

C. School Board

1. The Administration is composed of a group of Muslim brothers and sisters who will assume the responsibility of taking care of the school.
2. These members should reduce their activities with their local Islamic Centers to a minimum and increase their time, effort, knowledge, wisdom and services to this School of Qur'an.
3. Their total number should not exceed seven (7) members. Each has to assume certain responsibilities in maintaining and running the school properly.

Note:

1. Members of the Board are to lay down the rules and regulations of the school.
2. They select the school administrators.
3. They meet on a quarterly basis.
4. The principal of the school will be ex-officio.

5. The Board members' responsibility lies within the jurisprudence of the policy of the Islamic Center.

D. Responsibilities of the Board

1. Finance
2. Legality
3. Academic
4. Administration
5. Secretarial/Recording
6. Religious
7. Public Relations
8. School principal: Ex Officio

E. School Administration

The administrators of the school comprise the of individuals who are going to maintain and run the school professionally. They will be selected accordingly by the School Board. These individuals are:

1. Principal
2. Assistant principal
3. Secretary
4. Treasurer
5. Nurse

F. Curriculum

I. Academic Programs:

1. Math
2. English
3. Science
4. Computer
5. Bilingual Programs

II. Qur'anic Studies:

1. Study alphabets
2. Reading/Writing
3. Recitation, Tarteel and Tajweed
4. Memorization
5. Tafseer with understanding
6. Application in daily life
7. Teaching others
8. Pledges to practice Islam
9. Computer program of Qur'an
10. Video/audio program
11. Islamic games on computer
12. Books
13. Stories from Qur'an
14. Moral Values

G. The Program

The academic and religious programs are designed for four (4) academic years. The students are to commute between the school and their homes. Parents are responsible for their transportation.

Concerning the Qur'an memorization, the children are to make Hifz according to their schedules:

1. First Year: Students are to memorize 7 to 8 volumes of the Qur'an.
2. Second Year: Revision of previous volumes plus memorization of another 7 to 8 volumes.
3. Third Year: Revision of previous volumes plus memorization of another 8 volumes.

4. Fourth Year: Revision of previous   volumes plus memorization of the remainder of the Qur'an.

H. Teachers

1. Arabic Teacher
2. Urdu Teacher
3. Qur'an Teacher (1-2)
4. Academic Teacher
5. Physical Education Teacher
6. Islamic Studies Teacher

I. Final Remarks

The Islamic Education Center is planning with the help of Allah (swt) to start a new school called: American School of Qur'an. The school program should start in summer of 2001 on a daily basis from 9:00 a.m. to 4:30 p.m. This school is designed to accept commuting student at elementary and junior high school levels. The students will perform Zuhr and `Asr prayers at school. They will have  lunch and two  snacks  periods. They will have  the Islamic  teachings of Aadaab (plural), or  Adab (singular), Fada-`il, Shamaa-il and the moral teachings of Islam. Along with the Islamic classes, they will have the academic programs as well. For more information please call:

Islamic Education Center
659 Brea Canyon Road Suite #2
Phone: (909) 594-1310
Fax: (909) 444-0832
IRS ID #95-4363993

Proposed Financial Statement
American School of Qur'an

Staffing:

• Director of Program	$3,500/month
• Teacher/Hafiz (Full Time)	$2,500/month
• Administrative Asst (Part Time)	$1,500/month
• Teacher for Academic Education (Part Time)	$1,500/month
• Administrator (Part Time)	Volunteer
• Teacher's Aide	$1,000/month
• Fringe Benefits	$3,000/month

Sub-Total   **$13,000/month**

School Expenses

• Books and computer supplies	$500/month
• Food/Lunches/snack	$200/month
• Insurance/Medical	$300/month
(may be a Muslim doctor clinic)	

Sub-Total   **$1,000/month**

Sport, Indoor and Field Trips $500.00

Sub-Total   **$500/month**

Parent Participation (PTA)

• For lunch program and aide to the teacher $500/month

Sub-Total   **$500/month**

Operating Expenses

- Rent $1,000/month
- Utilities $400/month
- Telephone $100/month

Sub-Total **$1,500/month**

Grand Total **$16,500/month**

The Qur'an
Quiz #1

Choose the correct letter:

1. The Qur'an was revealed to Prophet Muhammad (pbuh) in the month of:
   (a) Shawwal   (c) Sha'ban
   (b) Zul-Hijjah   (d) Ramadan

2. The Qur'an was revealed to Prophet Muhammad (pbuh) first in:
   (a) Yathrib/Thawr Cave   (c) Hira' Cave
   (b) Makkah   (d) Jeddah

3. The Qur'an was revealed to Prophet Muhammad (pbuh) over a period of:
   (a) All at one time   (c) Thirteen years
   (b) 23 years   (d) Ten years

4. The first revelation to Prophet Muhammad (pbuh) was Surah:
   (a) Al-Fath   (c) Iqra'
   (b) Al-Muddathir   (d) Al-Muzzammil

5. The first Surah in Qur'an as it is sequentially now:
   (a) Al-Baqarah   (c) Al-'Alaq
   (b) Al-Muddathir   (d) Al-Fatiha

   PS: Answers on page 270

6. The total number of Surahs in the Qur'an is:
   (a) 112   (c) 113
   (b) 114   (d) 14

7. The Qur'an is categorized into how many Juzu'?
   (a) 60   (c) 120
   (b) 30   (d) 40

8. How many Sajdah (Prostrations) are there in the Qur'an?
   (a) 15   (c) 14
   (b) 10   (d) 8

9. How many Surahs in the Qur'an have luminous letters?
   (a) 29   (c) 20
   (b) 19   (d) 9

10. The Qur'an was revealed in what cities?
    (a) Makkah only   (c) Madeenah only
    (b) Makkah & Madeenah   (d) Hijra

11. Which Surah in the Qur'an does not have **Bismillah** at the beginning?
    (a) Al-Fatiha   (c) Al-Tawbah/Baraa-ah
    (b) Al-Munafiqoon   (d) Al-Baqarah

12. All Heavenly books were revealed to their prophets during the month of:
    (a) Rabee' Al-Awwal (c) Zul-hijjah
    (b) Ramadan   (d) Sha'ban

13. The total number of Surahs in the Qur'an revealed in Makkah are:
    (a) 28   (c) 90
    (b) 87   (d) 99

14. The total number of Surahs in the Qur'an revealed in Madeenah are:
    (a) 86   (c) 27
    (b) 20   (d) 30

15. Bismillah is found twice in one Surah of the Qur'an:
    (a) Al-Fatiha   (c) Al-Baqarah
    (b) Al-'Ankaboot   (d) Al-Naml
16. In which Surah does Allah (swt) demand that believers, men and women, cast down their sight when looking at the opposite gender:
    (a) An-Nisaa''   (c) Al-Tawbah
    (b) Al-Ahzab   (d) Al-Noor
17. In which Surah does Allah (swt) prescribe the Hijab and that the Hijab should cover the chest as well:
    (a) An-Nisaa''   (c) Al-Noor
    (b) Al-Baqarah   (d) Al-Ahzab
18. In which Surah are women instructed to extend their dresses down the ankles:
    (a) Al-Noor   (c) An-Nisaa'
    (b) Al-Hujurat   (d) Al-Ahzab
19. In which Surah are women instructed not to show their beauty and ornament to outsiders:
    (a) Al-Mumtahanah   (c) Al-Ahzab
    (b) Al-Noor   (d) An-Nisaa'
20. In which Surah does Allah (swt) demand from women not to strike their shoes hard, so as not to attract the attention of men.
    (a) An-Nisaa'   (c) Al-Talaaq
    (b) Al-Tahreem   (d) Al-Noor

The Qur'an
Quiz #2

Choose the Right Answer:

1. Two ladies mentioned in the Qur'an were accused of committing zina; Allah (swt) purified them by defending them:
   (a) Wives of Pharoah & Loot (c) Aiysha & Fatimah
   (b) Wives of Nooh & Al-Aziz (d) Aiysha & Mariam
2. Which Surah in the Qur'an is to be read for those who are dying?
   (a) Al-Fatiha   (c) Yaseen
   (b) Al-Mulk   (d) Taha
3. Which Surah in the Qur'an is to be read before sleeping so that you will not be poor or needy?
   (a) Ayat Al-Kursi   (c) Al-Waqi'ah
   (b) Al-Dukhan   (d) Al-Mu'awazatain
4. Which Surah in the Qur'an, if read before sleeping, will prevent the person from penalty in the grave?
   (a) Al-Fatiha   (c) Yaseen
   (b) Al-Rahman   (d) Al-Mulk
5. Which two (2) Surahs in the Qur'an, when read before sleeping, protect you from Shaitan?
   (a) Yaseen & Al-Dukhan   (c) Mu'awazatain
   (b) Yaseen & Al-Mulk   (d) Al-Fatiha & Al-Ikhlass

PS: Answers on page 271

250

6. The revelation of Qur'an during the month of Ramadan is mentioned in the Qur'an in which three Surahs?
   (a) Fatiha/Baqarah/Qadr   (c) Baqarah/Najm/Qadr
   (b) Baqarah/Israa'/Najm   (d) Baqarah/Dukhan/Qadr

7. In which Surah of the Qur'an does a wise father advise his son to be good, to pray, and to be obedient to Allah (swt)?
   (a) Ibrahim   (c) Yacoob
   (b) Nooah   (d) Luqman

8. Which three types of Quakes are mentioned in the Qur'an?
   (a) Earth, Heart, Spirit   (c) Earth, heart, Hereafter
   (b) Earth, Volcanoes, Heart (d)Earth, Volcanoes, Hereafter

9. Which person, in his youth, advised his father to worship Allah (swt) and to quit worshipping idols?
   (a) Yahya   (c) Ya'coob-Ibrahim
   (b) Ismail-   (d) Ibrahim-Azar

10. Which Surah in the Qur'an tells, in detail, about manners among Muslims; not to spy, not to backbite, and not to think wrongly of others?
    (a) Al-Noor   (c) Al-Ahzab
    (b) An-Nisaa'   (d) Al-Hujurat

11. In which two Surahs does the Qur'an speak, in details, about Al-Jinns?
    (a) Al-Ahqaf & Al-Jinn   (c) Al-Jinn & Al-Baqarah
    (b) Al-Jinn & Al-Rahman   (d) Al-Jinn & Al-Zariyat

12. Ayatul Kursi is found in which Surah:
    (a) Al-Tawbah   (c) Al-Baqarah
    (b) Al-A'raf   (d) An-Nisaa''

13. Which Surah was the key factor in Umar's acceptance of Islam?
    (a) Yaseen   (c) Al-Fatiha
    (b) Taha   (d) Al-Rahman

14. which Surah of the Qur'an is the equivalent of 1/3 of the Qur'an?
    (a) Al-Baqarah   (c) Al-Mu'awazatain
    (b) Al-Ikhlas   (d) Ayatul Kursi
15. Which of the following grandfather, father, and son were all Prophets and lived at the same time?
    (a) Ibrahim, Ishaaq, Yusuf   (c) Ibrahim, Ismail, Ishaaq
    (b)Ibrahim, Ishaaq, Ya'coob (d) Ibrahim, Yacoob, Yusuf
16. In which Surah is fasting (sawm) mentioned?
    (a) Al-Qadr   (c) Al-Hajj
    (b) Al-Baqarah   (d) Al-Siyam
17. In which Surah are we told that children are asked to knock at bedroom doors three times a day?
    (a) An-Nisaa''   (c) Al-Hujurat
    (b) Al-Ahzab   (d) Al-Noor
18. Which wives of two prophets were disobedient and non-believers?
    (a) Ibrahim & Ismail   (c) Nooh & Yusuf
    (b) Nooh & Loot   (d) Muhammad (pbuh) & 'Issa
19. According to Qur'an, who are the Ahl Al-Bayt?
    (a) Fatima & Offspring   (c) Offspring of Hussain
    (b) Ali, Fatima & Offspring (d) Muhammad & His Wives
20. Allah (swt) tells us in Qur'an about the birth of five (5) prophets who were named before they were born. They are:
    (a) Ibrahim-Ismail-Ishaaq-Yacoob-Yusuf
    (b) Muhammad –Ishaaq-Ya'coob-'Issa-Yahya
    (c) 'Issa-Mariam-Muhammad –Moosa-Ibrahim
    (d) Ibrahim-Muhammad –'Issa-Moosa-Nooh

The Qur'an
Quiz #3

Fill in the blanks:

1. There are ten (10) Surahs in the Qur'an whose titles reflect
    the meaning of the Day of Judgement. Mention some.
    (a) _____ (c) _____
    (b) _____ (d) _____

2. In which two Surahs of Qur'an is the story of Israa' and
    Mi'raaj mentioned?
    (a) _____ (b) _____

3. There are five (5) Surahs in the Qur'an that start with
    "Alhamdu Lillah". List their names:
    (a) _____ (d) _____
    (b) _____ (e) _____
    (c) _____

4. In which Surah is the name "Al-Rahman" mentioned 12
    (twelve) times?
    (a) _____

5. In which Surah of the Qur'an does Prophet Ibrahim tell his
    son, Ismail, that he saw himself in a dream, slaughtering
    Ismail? _____

6. How many Surah are there in Juzu' (para) 'Amma (vol 30)
    (a) _____

PS: Answers on page 272

7. All Surahs of Juzu' `Amma are Makkan Surah, except three
   (3) Surahs. Which are they?
   (a) _____ (c) _____
   (b) _____
8. There were five (5) idols that the people of Nooh were
   worshipping. What are their names?
   (a) _____ (d) _____
   (b) _____ (e) _____
   (c) _____
9. There were three (3) main idols that the people of Quraish
   were worshipping. What are their names?
   (a) _____ (c) _____
   (b) _____
10. There are fourteen (14) Surahs in the Qur'an with fifteen
    (15) Sajdah. Write the names of these Surah and the Ayah
    number (s).
    (a) _____ (h) _____
    (b) _____ (i) _____
    (c) _____ (j) _____
    (d) _____ (k) _____
    (e) _____ (l) _____
    (f) _____ (m) _____
    (g) _____ (n) _____
11. What is the name of the Surah wherein sixteen (16) names
    of Prophets were mentioned personally?
    (a) _____
12. Name the seven (7) Makkan Surah in the Qur'an that begin
    with the luminous letters of "Haa, Meem"
    (a) _____ (e) _____
    (b) _____ (f) _____
    (c) _____ (g) _____
    (d) _____

13. What prophet was sent to jail, through no fault of his own, because of his message? In which Surah is this found?
(a) _____ (b) _____
14. Give the names of two (2) brothers who were Prophets:
(a) _____ (b) _____
15. Give the names of two Prophets where one is the father-in-law and the other the son-in-law:
(a) _____ (b) _____
16. What is the name of the Sahabi who was given the title of "Munafiq" until the Day of Judgement?
(a) _____
17. After Ramadan, Muslims are to fast a Fard. Complete the following partial list as to why or when:
(a) One (1) day _____
(b) Thre (3) days _____
(c) Ten (10) consecutive days _____
(d) Sixty (60) consecutive days because of:
(1) _____
(2) _____
(3) _____

The Glorious Qur'an establishes man's dignity and honour in unequivocal terms.

REFERENCES

1. Abdul Baqi, M.F. **Al-Mu'jam Al-Mufahrass** (Arabic) Al-Sha'ab Pub., Cairo, Egypt (1945)
2. Abdul Baqi, M.F. **Al-Mu'jam Al-Mufahrass** (Arabic) Al-Andalus, Gibraltar (1945)
3. Abdul Majid **Holy Qur'an** Vol 1-2 Arabic Text with translation and commentary in English Enayatullah, Managing Agent, Taj Co. Ltd., Lahore, Pakistan (1957)
4. Amir Ali, H. **The Message of the Qur'an** The Charles E. Tuttle Co., Tokyo, Japan (1974)
5. Ali, A. Y. **The Glorious Qur'an** Translations & Commentary The MSA of U.S. & Canada Indianapolis, IN (1975)
6. Ali, A. Y. **The Glorious Qur'an; Text, Translation & Commentary;** McGregor & Werner, Inc. U.S.A. (1946)
7. Ali, Abdullah Yusuf **The Holy Qur'an** Text, Transliteration and Commentary New Edition, Amana Corp,. Brentwood MD (1989)
8. Ali, Ahmed **Al-Qur'an , A Contemporary Translation** Akrash Pub., Karachi, Pakistan (1986)
9. Al-Kateeb, A.K. **I'jazul Qur'an** (Arabic) Daar Al-Ma'rifah, Beirut, Lebanon (1975)
10. Al-Salih , Subhi **Mabahith Fi "Uloom Al-Qur'an** (Arabic) Dar Al-"Ilm Lill-Malayeen, Beirut, Lebanon (1983)
11. Al-Suyouty, J. **Al-Itqan Fi 'Uloom Al-Qur'an** vol 1-2 (Arabic) Dal Al-Fikr Pub., Beirut, Lebanon
12. Asad, Muhammad **The Message of the Qur'an** Mouton and Co. The Haque , Netherlands (1964)
13. Asad, Muhammad **The Message of the Qur'an** Dar Al-Andalus, Gibraltar (1980 & 1984)
14. Asad, Muhammad **The Message of the Qur'an** The Muslim World League Mecca, Saudi Arabia (1964)
15. Husaini, S.K. **Easy Tajwid** MCC Chicago, Il (1982)

16. Ibn Katheer, Ismail **Tafseer Al-Qur'an** vol 1-4 (Arabic) Dal Al-Ma'rifah, Beirut, Lebanon (1969)
17. Irving, T.B. **The Qur'an** Amana Books, Brattleboro, Vermont (1985)
18. Irving, T.B. **Al-Qur'an , Selection from the Noble Reading** Unity Publishing Co., Cedar Rapids, Iowa (1968)
19. Ismail, Shaaban M. **Ma'al Qur'an Al-Kareem** (Arabic) General Libraries, Cairo, Egypt (1978)
20. Kari, Mazhar **A Glimpse into the Glorious Qur'an** American Trust Publication Indianapolis, IN (1986)
21. Khateeb, A.K. **I'Jaazul Qur'an** Second Ed (Arabic) Dar Al-Ma'rifa, Beirut, Lebanon (1975)
22. Maududi, S. A.A. **The Meaning of the Qur'an** Board of Islamic Publ., Delhi, India (1973)
23. Maududi, S. A.A. **Towards Understanding of the Qur'an** The Islamic Fund, United Kingdom (1989)
24. Muhajir, Ali M.R. **Lessons From the stories of the Qur'an** Ashraf Pub., Lahore, Pakistan (1981)
25. Mir, Mustansir **Coherencies in the Qur'an** American Trust Pub., Indianapolis, In (1986)
26. Nabi, Malik Ben **The Qur'anic Phenomenon** American Trust Pub., Indianapolis, IN (1983)
27. Nadvi, Syed M. **A Geographical History of the Qur'an** Ashraf Pub., Lahore, Pakistan (1981)
28. Nadwi, Dr. A. Abbas **Vocabulary of the Qur'an** Iqra' Int'l Chicago, IL (1986)
29. Nisabioori, Ali Ibn Ahmad Al-Wahidy **Assbaab-un –Nuzool** (Arabic) Dar Al-Kitab Al-Ilmiyah, Beirut, Lebanon (1975)
30. Pickthall, M.M. **The Glorious Qur'an** Text and Explanatory Translations., The Muslim World League, New York, N.Y. (1977)

31. Pickthall, M.M.   **The Meaning** of the Glorious Qur'an New American Library, Inc. 1301 Avenue of the Americans New York, NY (1977)
32. Pickthall, M.M.   **The Meaning** of the Glorious Text and Explanatory Translations, Taj Co., Ltd., Karachi, Pakistan
33. Pickthall, M. F.M. Jaladdhri, and Nusrat A. Nasri **Qur'anic Advice** Arabic Text with Translation Kitab Bhavan, New Delhi, India (1984)
34. Prizadah, S. **Dawatul Qur'an /Surah Al-Fatihah and Al-Baqarah** Idara Dawatul Qur'an, Bombay, India (1981)
35. Qutb, Sayid **Fi Zilal Al-Qur'an** (Arabic) 4th Edition Vol 8 (28-30 Juzu') pp 196-208 Dar Al-Arabiyah, Beirut Lebanon
36. Qutb, Sayid **In the Shade of the Qur'an** (V 30) Taj Printers, New Delhi, India (1985)
37. Rahman, Afzalur **Qur'anic Sciences** Muslims School Trust, London England (1981)
38. Rahman. Afzalur **Subject Index of Qur'an** Islamic Pub., Ltd., Lahore, Pakistan (1988)
39. Sha'ban, Muhammad Saeed **Ma'al Qur'an** **Al-Kareem** (Arabic) General Libraries, Cairo, Egypt (1978)
40. Zakariya, Maaulan M. **The Blessings of the Holy Qur'an** Malik Brothers, Karshana Bazar, Lyallpur, Pakistan (1970)

FOUNDATION FOR ISLAMIC KNOWLEDGE

KNOWLEDGE

Islam emphasizes the importance of knowledge to all mankind. It is only through true knowledge that one can appreciate the Creator of the Universe namely Allah (swt). Muslims are ordained to seek knowledge from cradle to grave and as far as a person can to obtain it.

In as much as seeking knowledge is a must on every Muslim, dissemination of knowledge is also incumbent on Muslims to the members of the society. The methods of disseminating the information should be lawful, as well as the truth is to be released to everyone. Hiding or keeping the true knowledge away from those who seek it, is considered a sin.

The best investment for every human being is through: perpetual charity (Sadaqa Jariya), useful knowledge that people shall benefit or, and a loving child who shall make special prayers for his/her parents.

LEGALITY

The Foundation has been established and registered with the Secretary of the State of Illinois since January 8,1987 as a non-profit, charitable, educational, religious and /or scientific society within the meaning of section 501 (c) (3) of the Internal Revenue Code.

The Foundation has a tax-exempt status with the IRS, and donations are considered tax-deductible.

FINANCES

The finances of the FOUNDATION are mainly from donations and contributions in the form of cash, assets and wills.

INUMERENT OF INCOME

No part of the net earnings of the Corporation shall inure to the benefit of, or be distributed to, its members, directors, officers or other private persons except that the Corporation shall be authorized and empowered to pay reasonable compensation for services rendered.

PURPOSES

The purposes of the FOUNDATION are summarized as follows:

1. To promote Islamic Knowledge through education.

2. To create a better understanding of Islam among Muslims

   and non-Muslims through education and communication.

3. To publish books and other literature about Islam and its teachings

4. To disseminate Islamic Knowledge and education through TV, Radio, Video, and other means of mass communications.

5. To establish ecumenical among the religious people of America so that a better understanding will be created.

ACTIVITIES

The activities of the FOUNDATION shall include, but not be limited to the following:

1. Publishing literature pertaining to Islam.
2. Producing audio cassettes and audio-visual tapes on certain topics of Islam.
3. Giving lectures related to Islam as a religion, culture and civilization.
4. Cooperation with other societies, foundations and organizations whose aims and objectives are similar to the FOUNDATION.

KNOWLEDGE IN THE QUR'AN

The word knowledge ('ILM) is mentioned in the Qur'an more than 700 times in 87 different forms. Some of the pertinent Ayat are listed below.

1. The first Ayat revealed to Prophet Muhammad (pbuh) at Cave Hira' are in Surah Al-Alaq (The Clot) (96:1-5). They are related to knowledge of embryology through scientific investigation.

2. Allah honors all those who are knowledgeable. These

people cannot be compared with the ignorant ones. See Surah Al-Zumar (The Troops) (35:28)

3. Only the knowledgeable people are those who do appreciate the creations of Allah (swt) . They are the ones who respect Him and worship Him with knowledge and humility. Please read Surah Fatir (The Creator) (35:28)

4. Knowledge is in the Hands of Allah and it is at His disposal. People are to seek the true knowledge from its source namely Allah. Read Surah Al-Mulk (The Sovereignty) (67:26).

5. People are to seek knowledge from Allah (swt) are to request Him to enrich them daily with 'ILM. Read Surah Taha (20:114).

KNOWLEDGE IN THE HADITH

Prophet Muhammad (pbuh) emphasized 'ILM tremendously and encouraged Muslims to seek knowledge in any part of the world. The following is a summary:

1. In one Hadith the Prophet says: "The Knowledgeable people ('Ulama) are the inheritors to the Prophets."

2. In another Hadith He encouraged Muslims to seek knowledge, saying: "Seeking knowledge is a must on every Muslim."

3. In another place, He demanded that knowledge is to be sought throughout lifetime, saying: "Seek knowledge from cradle to grave."

4. Knowledge is to be disseminated to all, and the best knowledge is that of the Qur'an, saying: "The best amongst you are the ones who learn Qur'an and teach it to others."

5. Knowledge is to be taught and to be carried on even after death. In His Hadith the Prophet said: "When a person dies, his deeds are over, except from three things; perpetual charity, a useful knowledge, or a good child who makes supplications for him."

The FOUNDATION will continue, with the help of Almighty God (Allah), to publish more useful literature.

With the generous help of the friends, The Foundation will be able to achieve its purposes, Inshaallah.

For More Information, Please Write To:

Foundation For Islamic Knowledge
P.O. Box 665 Lombard, Illinois 60148 U.S.A.
Phone: (630) 495-4817   Fax (630) 627-8894

PUBLICATIONS

BY

AHMAD H. SAKR, Ph. D.

I.   BOOKS ON HEALTH, FOOD AND NUTRITION:

1. Dietary Regulations & Food Habits of Muslims
2. Overeating and Behavior
3. Islam on Alcohol
4. Alcohol in Beverages, Drugs, Foods and Vitamins
5. Cheese
6. AFTO and FAO
* 7. Fasting in Islam
8. Food and Overpopulation
9. Honey: Food and a Medicine
10. Gelatin
11. Shortening in Foods
12. A Manual on Food Shortenings
* 13. Pork: Possible Reasons for its Prohibition
14. Food Supplementation
15. World Health Organization for Muslim Nations
* 16. A Muslim Guide to Food Ingredients
17. Natural Therapeutics of Medicine in Islam
    (co-authored)
18. Islamic Dietary Laws & Practices (co-authored)
19. Food and Nutrition Manual (co-authored)
20. A Handbook of Muslim Foods
* 21. Understanding Halal Foods: Fallacies and Facts

II.   BOOKS ABOUT FRIDAY KHUTAB:

* 1.   Book of Al-Khutab
* 2.   Islamic Orations
* 3.   Orations from the Pulpit
* 4.   Chronicle of Khutab
* 5.   Friday Khutab
* 6.   A Manual of Friday Khutab
* 7.   Khutab Al-Masjid
* 8.   Khutab From Mihrab

III.   GENERAL SUBJECTS:

* 1.   Islamic Fundamentalism (co-authored)
  2.   Du 'a' After Completing the Recitation of Qur'an
* 3.   Introducing Islam to non-Muslims (co-authored)
* 4.   Prostration – Sujood (new edition)
  5.   Guidelines of Employment by Muslim
        Communities (co-authored)
* 6.   Farewell Khutbah of the Prophet – Its Universal
        Values
  7.   Understanding Islam and Muslims
* 8.   Muslims and non-Muslims: Face to Face
* 9.   Matrimonial Education in Islam (New Edition)
* 10.   Life, Death and the Life After
* 11.   The Golden Book of Islamic Lists
* 12.   Al-Jinn
* 13.   Islam and Muslims: Myth or Reality
* 14.   Islamic Awareness
* 15.   Death and Dying
* 16.   Family Values in Islam
* 17.   Book of Inquiries
* 18.   The Adolescent Life
* 19.   Social Services and Counseling
* 20.   A Course on Islamic Shari'ah
* 21.   Da'wah Through Dialogue
* 22.   Understanding the Qur'an

These publications are available from:

Foundation for Islamic Knowledge
P.O. Box 665
Lombard, IL 60148
Phone: (630) 495-4817 / Fax: (630) 627-8894

NEWSLETTER

The Foundation has a newsletter called Perspectives, it is published bi-monthly, and distributed free. If you wish to have a copy of the newsletter, please write to the address below.

Virginia Office
(Newsletter/Perspectives)
P. O. Box 65250
Hampton, VA 23665

BOOKS TO BE PUBLISHED

1. Islamic Perspectives
2. Islamic Understanding
3. Islam vs. Muslims
4. The Book of Healing
5. Speakers Bureau Guide Book
6. Health, Hygiene and Nutrition
7. Halal – Haram book of Khutab
8. Reflections From A Flying Falcon
9. Book of Du 'a'
10. The Book of Targheeb
11. Scientific Reflections from the Qur'an
12. Biological Terms in the Qur'an
13. Educational Institutions in Islam
14. Writing an Islamic Will
15. Qur'an Commentary in Summary
16. Book of Knowledge
17. Book of Wisdom
18. Welcome to the World of Islam
19. A Lifetime Journey
20. Arafa of the Hereafter
21. Al-Insaan: The Human Being

These and other books will not be published unless someone like you comes forward and extend a hand of help. You may sponsor any of the above books, or any number of copies of a particular book.

Your help in any capacity is greatly needed even to pay the previous debts to the printers.

The foundation is tax-exempt from the IRS and your donations are tax-deductible. The employer I.D. number with the I.R.S. is 36-352-8916.

For more information, or to send your donation, please contact:

Foundation for Islamic Knowledge

P.O. Box 665, Lombard, IL 60148,USA

Phone: (630) 495-4817 / Fax: (630) 627-8894

In the name of Allah, Most Gracious, Most Merciful.
Read! In the name of your Lord and Cherisher who created,
Created man out of a clot.
Read! And your Lord is Most Bountiful,
He who taught the use of the pen,
Taught man that which he knew not.

Answers to Worksheet

1. 114
2. 30
3. 2
4. 4
5. Al-Fatiha
6. Al-Naas
7. Al-Baqarah
8. 2:281
9. Al-Nasr/Al-Kawthar/Al-Asr
10. Ha. Meem
11. 23 years
12. Memorization/Writing
13. Tarteel/Tajweed
14. Chapter 9 Al-Tawbah
15. Al-Naml Chapter 27
16. 15/14 chapters/Al-Sajdah or anyone
17. Al-Kahf
18. 6236
19. Al-Kalf (18) Ayah 19.
20. a. Nooh, b. Ibrahim, c. Loot, e.Yusuf f. Muhammad
21. a. Al-Nahl b. Al-Ankaboot, c.Al-Feel d.Al-Baqarah and f. Al-Naml
22. a. Al-Shams b. Al-Qamar c. Al-Najm
23. Al-Naml, and Al-Nahl
24. Al-Jumuah (62)
25. Al-Duha b. Al-Fajr or Al-Lail
26. Mariam (19)
27. Quraish (106)
28. Al-Room (30)
29. Iqrah (96)
30. Al-Maidah (5)

31. Al-Ikhlas (112)
32. Ayah Kursi: Chapter 2 verse (255)
33. Al-Falaaq (113); and Al –Nass (114)
34. Al-Baraqah 285, 286

Answers to Quizzes.

Quiz # 1

1. D. Ramadan
2. C. Cave Hira
3. B. 23 years
4. C. Iqra'
5. D. Al-Fatiha
6. B. 114
7. B. 30
8. A. 15
9. A. 29
10. B Makkah & Madinah
11. C. Tawbah
12. B. Ramadan
13. B. 87
14. C. 27
15. D. Al-Naml
16. D. Al-Noor
17. C. Noor
18. D. Al-Ahzab
19. B. Al-Noor
20. D. Al-Noor

Answers to Quiz # 2

1. D. Aiysha & Mariam
2. C. Yaseen
3. C. Al- Waqi'ah
4. D. Al-Mulk
5. C. Mu'awazatain
6. C. Baqarah/Najm/Qadr
7. D. Luqman
8. C. Earth, Heart & Hereafter
9. D. Ibrahim-Azar
10. D. Al-Hujurat
11. A. Al-Ahqaf & Al- Jinn
12. C. Al-Baqarah
13. B. Taha
14. B. Al-Ikhlas
15. B. Ibrahim, Ishaaq & Ya'coob
16. B. Al-Baqarah
17. D. Al-Noor
18. B. Nooh & Loot
19. Muhammad & His Wives
20. Muhammad-Ishaaq-Ya'coob-"Issa-Yahya

Answers to Quiz # 3

1. Al-Waqiah (56),   Al-Hashr (59),   Al-Taghabun (64)
   Al-Haqah (69),   Al-Qiyamah (75) Al-Naba' (78),
   Al-Takweer (81),   Al-Infitar (82),   Al-Inshiqaq (84),
   Al-Ghashiya (88).
2. (a) Israa' (17)   (b) Al-Najm (53)
3. (a) Al-An'am (6), (b) Al-Kahf (18),   (c) Saba (34),
   (d) Fatir (35), (e) Al-Fatiha (1),
4. a. Mariam
5. Al-Saaffat (37)
6. 37 Surahs
7. (a) Al-Baiynah(98), (b) Al-Zalzalah (99,)
   (c) Al-Nasr (110), Al-Falaq (113) or Al-Nash (114)
8. a. Waddan b. Siwaa'an c. Yaghootha d. Nasraa
   e. Ya'ooga
9. a. Al-Laat b. Al-'Uzza c Manat
10. a. Al-A'raaf   (7:206)   b. Al-Ra'ad   (13:15)
    c. Al-Nahl   (16:49)   d. Al-Israa'   (17:07)
    e. Maryam   (19:58)   f. Al-Hajj   (22:18)
    g. Al-Hajj   (22:77)   h. Al-Furqan   (25:60)
    i. Al-Naml   (27:25)   j. Al-Sajdah   (32:15)
    k. Saad   (38:24)   l. Fussilat   (41:38)
    m. Al-Najm   (53:62)   n. Al-Inshiqaaq (84:21)
    Or Al-'Alaq   (96:19)
11. Al-An-aam (6: 83-86)
12. a. Ghafir (40)   b. Fussilat (41)   c. Ash-shura (42)
    d. Al-Zukhruf (43) e. Al-Dukhan (44)
    f. Al- Jathiya   g. Al Ahqaf (46)

13. a. Prophet Yusuf   b. Surah Yusuf (12)
14. a. Haroon- Moosa   b. Ismail-Ishaq
15. a. Shu'aib   b. Moosa
16. a. Tha'laba
17. a. Breaking one day in Ramadan
    b. Breaking Oath
    c. During & after Hajj
    1. Killing a person by mistake
    2. Marital Relations during fasting Ramadan
    3. Zihaar: A man saying to his: she is like his mother.
    He has no relationship with her.

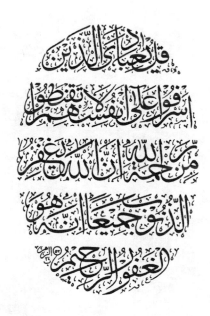

Books Available From the Foundation for Islamic Knowledge

AL-KHUTAB
Volume I
(ISLAMIC RELIGIOUS ADDRESSES)

Ahmad H. Sakr

Chronicle of Khutab
Volume IV

AHMAD HUSSEIN SAKR

Friday Khutab

Ahmad H. Sakr

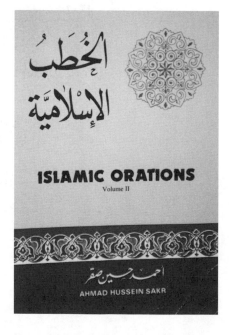

ISLAMIC ORATIONS
Volume II

AHMAD HUSSEIN SAKR

Books Available From the Foundation for Islamic Knowledge

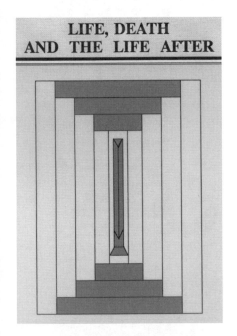

LIFE, DEATH AND THE LIFE AFTER

الخِنْزِير ..

PORK

POSSIBLE REASONS

FOR ITS PROHIBITION

by

Ahmad H. Sakr
Professor of Biochemistry and Nutrition

MATRIMONIAL EDUCATION IN ISLAM

And among His Signs
Is this, that He created
For you mates from among
Yourselves, that ye may
Dwell in tranquility with them,
And He has put love
And mercy between your (hearts):
Verily in that are Signs
For those who reflect.
Qur'an (30:21)

Ahmad H. Sakr, Ph.D.

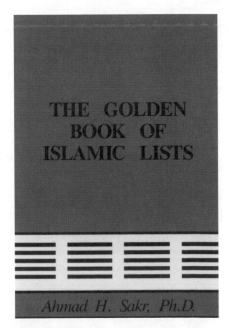

THE GOLDEN BOOK OF ISLAMIC LISTS

Ahmad H. Sakr, Ph.D.

Books Available From the Foundation for Islamic Knowledge

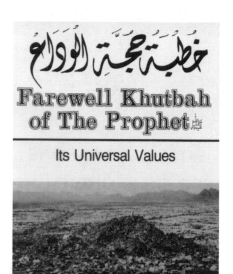

Books Available From the
Foundation for Islamic Knowledge

ISLAMIC
FUNDAMENTALISM

KARM B. AKHTAR, Ph.D.
AHMAD H. SAKR, Ph.D.

العلاج الطبي
الطبيعي
في الأسلام

NATURAL
THERAPEUTICS
OF MEDICINE
IN ISLAM

By
ZEYD A. ALI, M.D.
SADIQ H. HUSSAIN, D.N.
AHMAD H. SAKR, Ph.D.

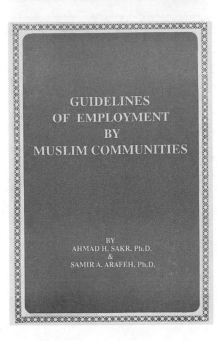

GUIDELINES
OF EMPLOYMENT
BY
MUSLIM COMMUNITIES

BY
AHMAD H. SAKR, Ph.D.
&
SAMIR A. ARAFEH, Ph.D.

FASTING
Regulations and Practices

Ahmad H. Sakr, Ph.D.

Books Available From the Foundation for Islamic Knowledge

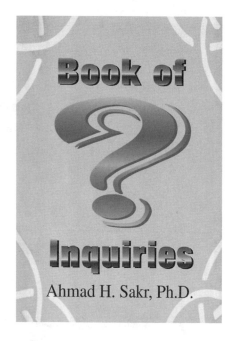

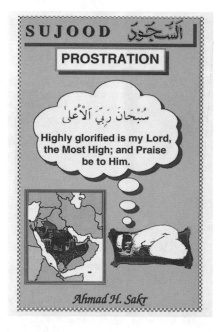

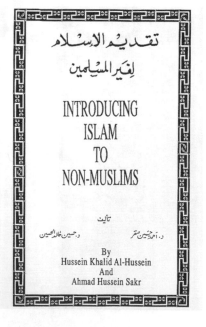

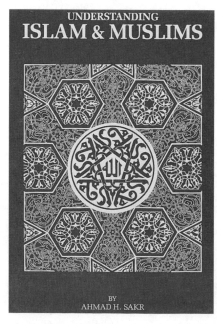

Books Available From the Foundation for Islamic Knowledge

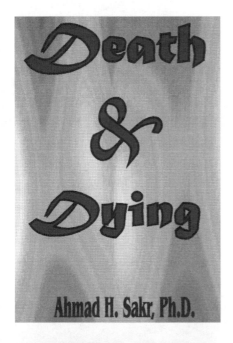

Books Available From the
Foundation for Islamic Knowledge

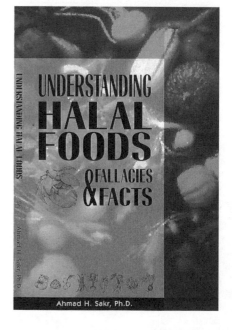

Books Available From the Foundation for Islamic Knowledge

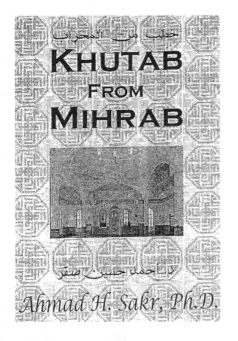

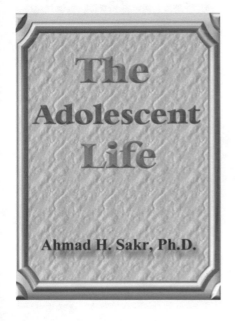

Books Available From the Foundation for Islamic Knowledge

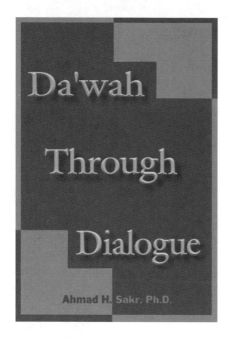

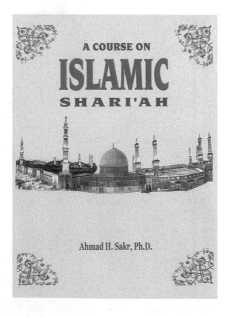